European integration: trade and industry

Confindustria

Confindustria, the Confederazione dell'Industria Italiana, is the association of privately-owned industrial enterprises representing over 100,000 companies, from very large (such as Fiat, Montedison, Olivetti, Pirelli) to very small, operating in all sectors of the economy.

The basic conviction which inspires the work of the organisation is that free enterprise and the free conduct of business contribute to the development and progress of the entire community.

Confindustria aims to collaborate with political institutions and economic, cultural and social organisations, both at national and international level, to contribute to the economic growth and social progress of the country.

Confindustria represents the needs and proposals of the industrial system – in its economic and productive development – in dealing with political and administrative institutions, trade unions, and all other social organisations and forces.

Officers

President	Sergio Pininfarina
Executive Vice Presidents	Luigi Abete, Ernesto Gismondi, Carlo Patrucco
Vice Presidents	Carlo De Benedetti, Pietro Marzotto
Director General	Innocenzo Cipolletta

STEP

STEP (Centro Interuniversitario di Studi Teorici per la Politica Economica) is a joint research centre of the Economics Departments of the Universities of Bologna and Venezia and the Institute of Economics of Bocconi University, Milan. The Centre promotes research in the area of economic policy and, through its collaboration with the Centre for Economic Policy Research, provides another STEP in furthering the Italian contribution to European economics.

Directors

Giorgio Basevi, Mario Monti, Gianni Toniolo

Scientific Advisory Board

Fiorella Padoa Schioppa, Richard Portes, Luigi Spaventa

30 September 1990

Centre for Economic Policy Research

The Centre for Economic Policy Research is a network of over 140 Research Fellows, based primarily in European universities. The Centre coordinates its Fellows' research activities and communicates their results to the public and private sectors. CEPR is an entrepreneur, developing research initiatives with the producers, consumers and sponsors of research. Established in 1983, CEPR is already a European economics research organisation with uniquely wide-ranging scope and activities.

CEPR is a registered educational charity. Grants from the Leverhulme Trust, the Esmée Fairbairn Charitable Trust, the Baring Foundation, the Bank of England and Citibank provide institutional finance. The ESRC supports the Centre's dissemination programme and, with the Nuffield Foundation, its programme of research workshops. None of these organisations gives prior review to the Centre's publications nor necessarily endorses the views expressed therein.

The Centre is pluralist and non-partisan, bringing economic research to bear on the analysis of medium- and long-run policy questions. CEPR research may include views on policy, but the Executive Committee of the Centre does not give prior review to its publication and the Centre itself takes no institutional policy positions. The opinions expressed in this volume are those of the authors and not those of the Centre for Economic Policy Research.

European integration: trade and industry

Edited by

L. ALAN WINTERS

and

ANTHONY J. VENABLES

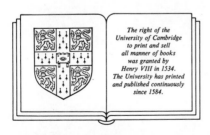

The right of the
University of Cambridge
to print and sell
all manner of books
was granted by
Henry VIII in 1534.
The University has printed
and published continuously
since 1584.

CAMBRIDGE UNIVERSITY PRESS

Cambridge   New York   Port Chester
Melbourne   Sydney

Published by the Press Syndicate of the University of Cambridge
The Pitt Building, Trumpington Street, Cambridge CB2 1RP
40 West 20th Street, New York, NY 10011-4211, USA
10 Stamford Road, Oakleigh, Melbourne 3166, Australia

First published 1991

Printed in Great Britain at the University Press, Cambridge

British Library cataloguing in publication data

European integration: trade and industry – (Centre for Economic Policy Research)
1. European Community countries. Economic integration
I. Winters. L. Alan   II. Venables, Anthony J.   III. Series
337.142

Library of Congress cataloguing in publication data applied for

ISBN 0 521 40528 9   hardback

Contents

Figures

Tables

Preface

This volume contains the proceedings of the conference 'The Impact of 1992 on European Trade and Industry', which was organised by the Centre for Economic Policy Research, the Centro Interuniversitario di Studi Teorici per la Politica Economica and Confindustria in Urbino on 15–16 March 1990. The programme committee comprised Stefano Micossi, Anthony J. Venables and L. Alan Winters. Much of the work reported forms part of the Centre for Economic Policy Research's programme 'The Consequences of "1992" for International Trade', supported by the UK Department of Trade and Industry and the Foreign and Commonwealth Office. This research is also funded by the Commission of the European Communities under the SPES programme.

We are grateful to Cillian Ryan who acted as Rapporteur for the conference, to Sarah Wellburn, Ann Shearlock and David Guthrie of the CEPR for logistical help with the conference and the volume, and to Barbara Docherty, who served as Production Editor. We are also grateful to Richard Portes, Director of the CEPR, for his support and encouragement for the conference and programme of research in general. Ente Nazionale Idrocarburi provided excellent conference facilities, and the German Marshall Fund of the United States contributed to the travel costs entailed. Finally we should express our gratitude to the participants at the conference, whose contributions to the debate and stimulating comments helped to make the conference and volume so successful. The contributions to this volume represent a small step towards the complete analysis of 1992 and, indeed, some of the institutional details discussed may change as the process of integration and the Uruguay Round run to completion. Nevertheless, if the analysis here promotes and informs further research, it will have achieved its goal.

L. Alan Winters and Anthony J. Venables
30 September 1990

Acknowledgements

The editors and publishers wish to thank the following for permission to reproduce copyright material.

Ministry of Finance, Tokyo, for data in Figure 10.1 and Table 10.1.
Jetro, for data in Figure 10.2 and Table 10.4, from *Current management situation of Japanese manufacturing enterprises in Europe, 5th survey report* (1989), and for data in Table 10.1, from *Japan's changing overseas direct investment* (1988).
European Economic Review, for data in Tables 7.1 and 7.2, from A. Smith and A.J. Venables, 'Completing the internal market in the European Community' (1988).
Centre for Applied Research, Bergen, for data in Tables 7.1, 7.2 and 7.7, from V. Norman and L. Orvedal, 'Stordriftsfordeler, konkurranse og markedsintegrasjon' (1990).
OECD, for data in Table 7.3, from *Competition in Banking* (1989).
University of Chicago Press, for data in Table 7.5, from V. Norman and S.P. Strandenes, 'Deregulating Scandinavian airlines: a case study of the Oslo–Stockholm route', in P. Krugman and A. Smith (eds), *Empirical Studies of Strategic Trade Policy* (forthcoming).
DATAR, for data in Table 10.2, from 'Les Investissements de Production Japonais dans 17 Pays d'Europe' (1989).

List of conference participants

Giorgio Basevi *Università degli Studi di Bologna, and CEPR*
Carlo Andrea Bollino *Ente Nazionale Idrocarburi, Roma*
Paul Brenton *University of Wales, Bangor*
Jean-Marc Burniaux *OECD*
Giuliano Conti *Università di Ancona*
Riccardo Faini *Johns Hopkins University, Bologna*
Harry Flam *Institute for International Economic Studies, Stockholm*
Konstantine Gatsios *Fitzwilliam College, Cambridge, and CEPR*
Stephen Green *UK Department of Trade and Industry*
Jan Haaland *Norwegian School of Economics and Business Administration, Bergen*
Carl Hamilton *Institute for International Economic Studies, Stockholm, and CEPR*
Alberto Heimler *Confindustria*
Arye Hillman *Bar-Ilan University*
Peter Holmes *University of Sussex*
Larry Karp *University of Southampton, and CEPR*
Michael Keen *University of Essex*
Gernot Klepper *Institut für Weltwirtschaft, Kiel, and CEPR*
Richard Lyons *Columbia University*
Stefano Micossi *Confindustria*
Willem Molle *Netherlands Economic Institute*
Sergio de Nardis *Confindustria*
Damien Neven *Institut Européen d'Administration d'Affaires, and CEPR*
Victor Norman *Norwegian School of Economics and Business Administration, Bergen, and CEPR*
Joaquim Olivcira-Martins *Centre d'Etudes Prospectives et d'Informations Internationales*
Morten Jung Olsen *Commission of the European Communities*
Fabrizio Onida *Università L. Bocconi, Milano*

Pier Carlo Padoan *Università Urbino*
Roberta Placidi *Ente Nazionale Idrocarburi, Roma*
Lars-Hendrik Röller *Institut Européen d'Administration des Affaires*
Manuela Rondoni *Ente Nazionale Idrocarburi, Roma*
Cillian Ryan *University of Wales, Bangor*
André Sapir *Université Libre de Bruxelles, and CEPR*
Alasdair Smith *University of Sussex, and CEPR*
David Ulph *University of Bristol, and CEPR*
Anthony Venables *University of Southampton, and CEPR*
Gianfranco Viesti *Università L. Bocconi, Milano*
John Whalley *University of Western Ontario*
L. Alan Winters *University of Wales, Bangor, and CEPR*
Ian Wooton *University of Western Ontario*
Hideki Yamawaki *Wissenschaftszentrum Berlin für Sozialforschung*
Stephen Yeo *CEPR*

1 European integration: trade and industry

L. ALAN WINTERS and
ANTHONY J. VENABLES

The completion of the internal market in the European Community (EC) has now been the subject of much research. The likely direct effects of '1992' have been catalogued and quantified, and the possible implications of these changes for trade and industry have been estimated. Emerson *et al.* (1988) provides the best overview of this work, and it is fair to say that something of a consensus has developed around it. '1992' is expected to increase competition, encourage some rationalisation of industry and thereby generate efficiency gains, possibly yielding net benefits amounting to several per cent of EC income.

Comforting though the consensus is, it is built on relatively shaky foundations. Emerson *et al.* (1988) represents a high point of applied economics, combining the results of several different modes of analysis in an original and innovative fashion. The study did not, however, have the time, or the intention, to explore the mutual consistency of such approaches, nor to elucidate the precise mechanisms involved in some of the economic relationships assumed. Nor, of course, did it examine the full range of consequences and alternative approaches to predicting the effects of '1992'. These tasks have fallen to academic researchers. While there has been a huge volume of comment and casual analysis of the completion of the market, the detailed work required to analyse these issues is only just beginning to appear.

The studies in this volume comprise a number of explorations going beyond the Emerson consensus. They do not offer a comprehensive reappraisal of '1992', but rather seek to examine particular issues in greater detail. As such, they underpin (rather than undermine) the analysis of Emerson *et al.*, and provide a base-line from which further predictive work, and eventually hypothesis-testing, may be undertaken. The explorations focus around three sets of issues: the mechanisms through which '1992' may change the real income of the EC; '1992' and factor markets; and '1992' and the external economic relations of the EC.

1

Most analyses of the effects of '1992' on the real income of the EC have concentrated on the interaction between the degree of competition and the scale and efficiency of firms. However, it is clear that the '1992' package may be transmitted into changes in income through other routes. For example, Baldwin (1989) has investigated the effect of '1992' on saving, and hence on economic growth. Chapters in this volume investigate the implications of EC policy towards research and development (R & D), and hence for the rate of technical innovation, and explore the possibility that external economies may magnify income gains due to '1992'.

Formal economic analysis of R & D is the subject of Chapter 8 by David Ulph. Three questions are posed by Ulph: What are the likely consequences of encouraging research joint ventures between European firms? Can such a policy enable Europe to gain technological leadership? Could this lead to higher income? There are certainly potential gains from joint ventures which can coordinate research and save research costs, but market failures mean that we cannot be sure that these potential benefits will be achieved. Ulph shows, for example, that it is quite possible for the market to lead to either too much or too little cooperation, as firms forming joint ventures ignore the implications of their actions on other firms in the economy. Ulph concludes that while encouragement of research joint ventures may be a route through which the integration process may raise income, it is not assured of success. A better policy would be to identify the particular market failures associated with R & D, and target policies directly at these failures.

A further possible way in which integration may increase income is if there are external economies of scale between firms. In Chapter 3 Riccardo Caballero and Richard Lyons estimate the potential benefits of '1992' accruing through this route. In previous work on the US economy and on individual European economies, they found that external economies of scale existed. In addition to any gains from internal economies of scale that firms may realise as a result of market integration, there may thus be beneficial external effects that will increase output in the larger market. Chapter 3 extends this previous work to examine the existence of external returns to scale in an EC dimension, and attempts to measure international industry-specific external effects in addition to the national external effects detected in previous studies. Caballero and Lyons' results suggest that such international effects may well exist, but that the data cannot distinguish them incontrovertibly from intra-country cross-industry externalities. Their best estimate is that a 1% increase in the level of economic activity in the EC as a whole would yield an additional dividend of 0.1–0.2% of industrial output as a result of these external effects. This seems like good news, especially since these external effects are logically additional to those used by Emerson *et al.* (1988), for the latter were derived by Pratten (1987), largely from engineering data, and hence are wholly internal in nature. On the other hand, Caballero and Lyons' own estimates of internal returns to scale, based on industry data, are lower than Pratten's so that their overall growth predictions are, if anything, below the Commission's.

Chapters 8 and 3 suggest that there is potentially more to the economic stimulus from '1992' than Emerson's pro-competitive shocks and sliding down the average cost curve. They both caution, however, that there is also considerably more uncertainty about the overall outcome than the consensus typically recognises. Important policy issues remain – such as ensuring that R & D cooperation is not anti-competitive and that regulation in particular sectors does not inhibit the flow of external stimuli from one sector to another. The remaining intellectual tasks include determining the crucial parameters affecting R & D effort in joint ventures, and identifying the channels of causation for external effects.

The second set of issues explored in the volume concerns the implications of '1992' for factor markets. The importance of this issue stems from the fact that the spatial implications of '1992' – how the costs and benefits are likely to be distributed across the EC – cannot be fully addressed without consideration of factor markets. Which countries are abundantly endowed with the factors intensively used in expanding industries? Which countries are likely to be beneficiaries of new investment? Some of these issues are addressed in the chapters by Michael Gasiorek, Alasdair Smith and Anthony Venables (Chapter 2) and by Michael Keen (Chapter 9). Gasiorek, Smith and Venables concentrate on labour markets, and use a computable general equilibrium model to investigate possible changes in factor demands and factor prices stemming from economic integration. They consider five EC 'countries', plus the 'rest of the world', where each country is endowed with capital and three types of labour. Each economy has a perfectly competitive sector and thirteen manufacturing industries, assumed to exhibit increasing returns to scale and to operate in an imperfectly competitive environment. The results suggest that integration is likely to increase the demand for skilled relative to unskilled labour. For example, the model predicts that in France, West Germany and the United Kingdom 'professional and scientific' labour will experience the largest relative increase in demand, while in Italy and the 'rest of the EC', 'other non-manual' workers will experience the largest increase. If wages adjust to hold employment of each type of labour constant, then real wages of 'professional and scientific' workers in France, West Germany and the

United Kingdom could rise by up to 1%, while there may be small real wage cuts for lower-skilled groups.

Chapter 9 looks at the capital market, and the important issue of corporate taxation, and the extent to which this will have incentives concerning the location of production. Keen argues that corporation tax has no place as a means of extracting revenue from foreign nationals in an integrated Community, and should therefore be neutral to both the import and the export of capital (in order to ensure that investment decisions are not affected by considerations of differential tax rates, or of double tax relief), even if autonomous national tax rates are to be retained. Keen presents a detailed taxonomy of corporate taxation methods for both domestic and foreign firms and evaluates the extent to which different tax systems achieve the goals of capital export and capital import neutrality.

Chapters 3 and 9 make a start on areas in which much more extensive research is now needed. Factor market outcomes are important not only for their efficiency and direct distributive effects, but also for the incentives they set up for inter-member migration. Completing the internal market strictly entails totally free labour mobility, but this is one of the most sensitive issues on the agenda.

The third set of studies deals with different aspects of the external economic relations of the EC. In Chapter 5 Alexis Jacquemin and André Sapir consider the effects of imports from outside the EC on competition within it. They show that external imports (actual and potential) serve to reduce EC firms' market power, and thus provide a pro-competitive force similar to internal competition policy. Jacquemin and Sapir compare the relative trade discipline of intra-EC and extra-EC imports on European industry, pooling data for over 100 industries in each of the 'Big Four' EC countries. They relate industry price–cost margins to intra-EC import penetration, extra-EC import penetration and a set of variables characterising industry structure. The major result of the study is that only extra-EC imports exert a significant disciplinary effect on price–cost margins: intra-EC imports seem to exert no disciplinary effect at all. They do find, however, that barriers to intra-EC trade are associated with higher EC price–cost margins. This may arise because the barriers at internal borders affect goods from all origins as they move within the EC, or because internal barriers are matched by barriers against third countries on external borders. In the former case the removal of the internal barriers would imply a greater opening of the EC market to extra-EC imports, but in the latter case the outcome would depend on whether the related external barriers were reduced at the same time. Jacquemin and Sapir conclude that the EC ought to avail itself of the opportunity of the

Uruguay Round to strive towards freer world trade. However, it is recognised that if a small number of foreign firms dominate EC sales, then external trade liberalisation could have a perverse effect, and thus that a strong competition policy would still be necessary.

The relationship between external trade and the performance of EC industry is also the theme of Chapter 4 by Riccardo Faini and Alberto Heimler. They address a very specific question: what is the effect of protection on the quality of goods produced by the EC textile and clothing (T & C) industry? T & C imports are tightly controlled by quantitative restrictions of the Multi-Fibre Arrangement, which discriminates against industrial countries' imports from developing countries, with the result that those industrial countries such as Italy which have the least comparative disadvantage in T & C are able to increase their exports. If quality is endogenous, it seems likely that it will change relative to free trade as this trade diversion occurs. Previous research on quality responses resulting from quantitative barriers to trade has focused on the quality of the imported good, and has generally suggested that it would rise. The implication has usually been that domestic quality would fall, although only rarely is this explicitly addressed. Faini and Heimler show that in general it is possible to generate any combination of quality increase or decrease for domestic and foreign supplies, depending on the assumptions that one makes about the cross-effects of quantity and quality on costs and demand. Of special interest to Faini and Heimler is the case where longer production runs (as a result of the protected market) lead to higher domestic quality. This could arise, for example, if there were significant sunk costs in higher-quality development. Which outcome we would actually observe in any industry is a matter for empirical analysis.

In order to estimate the differences in product quality of different suppliers to the EC, Faini and Heimler exploit recent developments in the theory of index numbers. They estimate the quality of T & C imports from seventeen countries to the four major EC markets for the period 1982–7. They find that within each market quality differences exist: around half of the differences in the crude unit values of imports from different supplying countries can be explained by quality differentials, with suppliers from more affluent countries supplying better goods. After allowing for quality, Faini and Heimler derive a more precise indicator of price than the usual unit value. Examining this, they show that there are still substantial price differentials for similar products across Europe, and that the degree of difference varies with the tightness of the quota on EC imports. They speculate that these differences will be squeezed by the completion of the internal market as the separate member quotas under the Multi Arrangement are replaced by an EC-wide quota.

Foreign firms affect EC industrial performance not only by trade pressures, but also through foreign direct investment. Japanese investment in the EC is the subject of the chapter by Stefano Micossi and Gianfranco Viesti (Chapter 10). They find that Japanese investment in EC manufacturing is still relatively small, and primarily based on the organisational superiority of Japanese producers in particular sectors (notably scale-intensive, mass-production, assembly industries) and on technological superiority in electronics; however, this investment is growing rapidly in scope as well as in magnitude. Their analysis of the consequences of this investment shows that the expected gains to the EC from such investment are likely to be concentrated in the localities in which it occurs, to the possible disadvantage of other countries. Micossi and Viesti conclude from this that an EC-wide policy on foreign direct investment should be a priority both during the run-up to 1992, and after it.

The studies in Chapters 5, 4 and 10 serve as a salutary reminder of the importance of external trade and trade policy. '1992' may bring trade creation but, if external trade barriers are significant, it will also bring trade diversion. It may increase competition between EC firms, but this may be less important than competition from outside the Community: many of the benefits of completing the market will be lost if the disciplines of a liberal external trade policy are eroded. Similarly if the benefits of Japanese investments – such as technology, management and design – are rejected, the EC will fail to reap the maximum benefit of '1992'.

The official study – Emerson *et al.* (1988) – understandably ignored issues of intra-EC distribution and was very light on detail about the effects of '1992' on third countries. But in the European and international debates about the process, such matters figure large. The remaining two studies in the volume point the way to analysing such effects: by means of two important case studies. Chapter 7 by Victor Norman deals with EC trade with EFTA, and Chapter 6 by Damien Neven and Lars-Hendrik Röller deals with EC integration with Eastern Europe.

Norman analyses the dilemma faced by the small open EFTA countries in their negotiations with the EC about mutual trade arrangements or full membership. Their smallness suggests a potential for significant gains from unrestricted access to an integrated market, while their existing openness and reliance on comparative advantage suggest a possibility that most of the gains that might be expected from integration may have already been achieved. Focusing particularly on Norway and Sweden, Norman reports a number of empirical estimates of the scale economies and competitive gains to EFTA from the integrated market, the extent of unexploited comparative advantage between EFTA and the EC, and the losses to EFTA from a more protectionist external policy. Norman's results suggest that modest scale economies and competitive gains are to be expected in manufacturing, and much larger potential gains in services. As regards comparative advantage, wage differentials between EC and EFTA countries are so small that '1992' should have little effect on the broad pattern of inter-industry specialisation, although there may be substantial gains at the level of individual industries. He also finds that while a more protectionist external trade policy could significantly dampen the gains to EFTA from integration, it would not reverse them.

The changes in Eastern Europe and the new trading arrangements with the West that emerge are likely to have a significant effect on the European economy. They are of particular concern to the southern Community members as there is a common perception that the comparative advantage of Eastern Europe is similar to that of the southern European economies (low-skilled, labour-intensive and agricultural goods). If Eastern Europe is granted significant trading concessions, the southern economies' gains from '1992' might thus be diminished. If, on the other hand, this characterisation of Eastern Europe's comparative advantage is incorrect, and East-West trade is of an intra-industry nature, then it should lead to further pro-competitive gains of the type already expected to be generated by '1992'. Neven and Röller explore the basis for the common perception of the Eastern countries, and attempt to analyse the economic rationale underlying existing East-West trade.

Neven and Röller offer a descriptive analysis of the trade flows between COMECON countries and a sample of Western countries (including EC and EFTA countries, Japan and the United States) in terms of size, direction and commodity content; they also conduct an econometric study of trade between the 'Big Four' European countries and COMECON. The latter examines net trade between COMECON and the 'Big Four' EC members for 29 manufacturing industries over the period 1975–87, the explanatory variables including variables representing both inter-industry and intra-industry trade barriers. From both parts of the analysis Neven and Röller conclude that there is little evidence that trade based upon traditional comparative advantage factors is significant, but that there is strong evidence of intra-industry trade in the capital- and human capital-intensive sectors. The Southern European economies, for whom the comparative advantage gains from '1992' might be significant, have thus apparently little to fear from increased East–North integration.

Neven and Röller emphasise that their results are predicated on the hypothesis that despite having been managed by the central authorities, current East–West manufactured trade reveals a pattern of comparative advantage between East and West, and that this is not greatly distorted by trade in non-manufactured products which account for a high proportion of the total flow. Clearly, the next step is to investigate the validity of such hypotheses.

'1992' presents a great challenge and opportunity for Europe traders and industrialists; so also it does for economists. The studies in this volume represent the early fruits of academic endeavour to analyse the process of European integration. They shed light on several substantive issues and, just as important, they illustrate the breadth of the remaining research agenda and the depth of the analysis required. We are as far as ever from closing the book on the economics of '1992'.

REFERENCES

Baldwin, R. (1989) 'The growth effects of 1992', *Economic Policy*, **9**, 247–81.
Emerson, M. *et al.* (1988) *The Economics of 1992*, Oxford: Oxford University Press.
Pratten, C. (1987) 'A Survey of Economics of Scale', in *Research on the Costs of non-Europe, Basic Findings*, vol. 2, Brussels: Commission of the European Communities.

2 Completing the internal market in the EC: factor demands and comparative advantage

MICHAEL GASIOREK, ALASDAIR SMITH
and ANTHONY J. VENABLES

1 Introduction

The aim of this study is to set partial equilibrium models of the effects of completion of the internal market on particular industries into a wider general equilibrium framework. The contribution of industry-level partial equilibrium models is to capture the effects of 1992 on intra-industry trade, on competition, and hence on prices, output and welfare. As was demonstrated in Smith and Venables (1988), a pro-competitive policy change, such as completion of the internal market, can lead to substantial increases in firm scale, bringing welfare gains from lower prices and, with increasing returns to scale, lower average costs.

Partial equilibrium studies alone can for two reasons provide an incomplete, and possibly misleading, picture of the effects of completion of the internal market. First, it is assumed that resources drawn into the industry under study are available at a price equal to their marginal social opportunity cost. If one imperfectly competitive industry's expansion is – because of overall resource constraints – another's contraction, then this assumption is invalid. Employing this assumption may cause us to misestimate the welfare change associated with a policy. Second, the partial equilibrium studies assume that resources are available to the industry at a constant price, so input supply curves are horizontal. If input supply curves to each industry are in fact upward sloping, partial equilibrium studies will overestimate the quantity effects of the policy. Input supply considerations affect not only inputs of primary factors, but also inputs of intermediates, which may themselves be produced by imperfectly competitive industries, so generating 'linkages' between industries.

In this study we do not address the welfare implications of completion of the internal market, so leave aside the first of the problems outlined in the previous paragraph. We concentrate on modelling inputs to each industry and, by permitting input prices to change, obtaining improved estimates of the quantity effects of completion of the internal market. To do this we construct a general equilibrium model in which production uses intermediate goods and four primary factors of production. The model contains a perfectly competitive composite sector, and a number of imperfectly competitive industries. These industries operate under increasing returns to scale, and support an equilibrium with intra-industry trade. The policy experiments we consider are a reduction in intra-EC trade costs for these industries, and a change in market behaviour, from a 'segmented' market quantity equilibrium to an 'integrated' market quantity equilibrium. We first evaluate the effects of these experiments on factor demand in each country, at constant factor prices; we then assume factor market clearing, and find the consequent changes in input prices.

The study is organised as follows. Section 2 sets out a brief sketch of the model. Section 3 discusses data issues and the calibration of the model to the base data set. Section 4 reports and discusses the effects of a reduction in trade costs. Section 5 discusses the effects of a reduction in trade costs combined with a move from segmented to integrated markets. A concluding section 6 is devoted primarily to discussing further development of research.

2   The model

Section 2 sketches out the structure of the model. We work with 6 countries, 5 representing the EC (France, Germany, Italy, the United Kingdom, and a 'rest of the EC' aggregate) and a sixth which is a rather crude representation of the rest of the world. The model has a commodity structure consisting of 13 manufacturing industries (listed in Table 1.1, in section 3) which are assumed to be imperfectly competitive, and which are modelled in some detail. The remainder of each economy is aggregated into a single perfectly competitive composite, which we take as the numéraire.

Each industry contains a number of firms, and n_i^k denotes the number of firms in industry k located in country i. For a particular industry k and country i, all n_i^k firms are symmetric. Each of these firms produces a number of varieties of differentiated product, which we denote m_i^k.

The output of each industry is used both in final demand, and as an intermediate. Consider first final demand. p_{ij}^k and x_{ij}^k denote the price and quantity of a single product variety of industry k produced in country i and used (as a final demand) in country j. (There are $n_i^k m_i^k$ such varieties and, because of symmetry, we do not need to introduce a notation for individual varieties.) Consumer preferences are such that the following aggregation procedure is possible. First, varieties within an industry and a country of sale are aggregated into a quantity index X_j^k with associated price index P_j^k. The constant elasticity of substitution aggregator has elasticity of substitution denoted ϵ^k; the functional form is given in the Appendix. It is important to note that at this level we aggregate over products from all sources of production; we do not adopt the Armington assumption which implies separate nesting of products by geographical source. Second, the quantity and price indices are aggregated into utility and expenditure functions. There is a single representative consumer with homothetic preferences in each country. If u_j is utility, E_j is the unit expenditure function, and M_j is income, then the budget constraint is

$$M_j = u_j E_j \tag{1}$$

E_j is defined over the P_j^k and is assumed to be Cobb–Douglas; its form is given in the Appendix. Consumer demands both for the aggregate quantity indices and for individual varieties are derived by partial differentiation of the expenditure function.

The price and quantity of a single product variety of industry k produced in i and used as an intermediate good in j are denoted q_{ij}^k and y_{ij}^k respectively. Notice that intermediate and final markets are segmented, in the sense that different prices may be charged for the same good. Technology is such that the following aggregation procedure is possible. First, varieties within an industry and country of sale are aggregated into a quantity index Y_j^k with associated price index Q_j^k. (Again, they are not separately nested by geographical source.) Second, the quantity and price indices are aggregated into a composite intermediate commodity; whose price index in country j is F_j (see Figure 2.1 and the Appendix.) Notice that this is a single composite intermediate commodity, so the proportions in which each industry uses the products of other industries are the same.

The costs of a firm in industry k of country i are given by a cost function:

$$c_i^k = m_i^k [h^k(z_i^k) G_i^k(F_i, w_i^1, w_i^2, w_i^3, w_i^4)] \tag{2}$$

where

$$z_i^k = \sum \{x_{ij}^k + y_{ij}^y\} \tag{3}$$

z_i^k is the total output per variety of a country i firm in industry k. The function h^k describes the returns to scale in industry k; and increasing returns to scale means that $h^k(z_i^k)/z_i^k$ is decreasing in z_i^k. Notice that this function is not country-specific. Furthermore, there are no economies of scope, since c_i^k is linear in m_i^k, and returns to scale are associated with output per variety, z_i^k. The function G_i^k aggregates input prices into cost per unit h. Its arguments are the intermediate price index, F_i, and the prices of four primary factors of production. There are Hicks-neutral

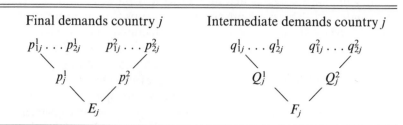

Final demands country j Intermediate demands country j

Figure 2.1 Aggregation of final and intermediate products

technical differences between countries, so that although the function G_i^k is country-specific, it differs across countries only by a scalar. Input demands are partial derivatives of these cost functions so we have, for example,

$$v_i^1 = \sum_k n_i^k m_i^k h^k(z_i^k) \frac{\partial G_i^k(F_i, w_i^1, w_i^2, w_i^3, w_i^4)}{\partial w^1} \tag{4}$$

The profits of firms are given by

$$\pi_i^k = m_i^k \sum_j \{p_{ij}^k x_{ij}^k + q_{ij}^k y_{ij}^k\}\{1 - t_{ij}^k\} - c_i^k \tag{5}$$

where t_{ij}^k is the *ad valorem* cost of shipping a unit of industry k output from economy i to economy j.

Firms have to choose sales both of final goods and of intermediates.

Two alternative equilibrium concepts are used to describe how firms take supply decisions on final sales quantities. The first is to assume that firms act as Cournot competitors in segmented markets. Each firm in industry k and country i then chooses sales in each market, x_{ij}^k, taking as constant the sales of all its rivals in each market. Optimisation requires the equating of marginal revenue and marginal cost in each market, where the slope of each firm's perceived demand curve depends on the extent of product differentiation, and on the share of the firm in that market. This will be referred to as the segmented market hypothesis. An explicit equation for the equality of marginal revenue to marginal cost is given in the Appendix.

The second equilibrium concept we employ is to assume that firms choose a total quantity for sale in the 5 EC markets combined, taking as constant total EC sales of rival firms; the distribution of these aggregate quantities between markets in the EC is then determined by arbitrage, and equates the producer prices of the product: making $p_{ij}^k(1 - t_{ij}^k) = p_{il}^k(1 - t_{il}^k)$

for all countries j, l, in the EC. This second hypothesis will be referred to as the integrated market hypothesis. Its force is that the slope of firms' perceived demand curves now depends on product differentiation, and on the firm's share in the EC as a whole, rather than in each separate market. Of course, alternative behavioural hypotheses are possible, some of which are discussed in Venables (1990).

Firms' choice of intermediate sales quantities, y_{ij}^k, is less straightforward, for two reasons. First, it is possible that purchasers of inputs have some monopsony power, to confront the monopoly power of sellers. Second – and perhaps more importantly – even if purchasers of intermediates are input price takers, the demand for intermediates is a derived demand, and establishing the elasticity of the derived demand curve is not straightforward. For these reasons we employ a rather *ad hoc* pricing rule for intermediate goods – namely, that their prices, q_{ij}^k, are set at average cost. Alternative pricing rules will be investigated in later stages of this research.

As has been noted above, each firm produces a number of varieties of product, m_i^k. It is assumed throughout this study that these numbers are constant. Furthermore, it is assumed that, at the base, output per variety, z_i^k, is the same for all firms. m_i^k should therefore be thought of as a scaling device, with different firm sizes in the base data set being attributed to differences in the number of varieties firms produce, not differences in output per variety. The force of this assumption is to ensure that all firms have the same degree of unexploited economies of scale.

All that remains to complete the description of the model is the determination of income. Each economy is endowed with quantities of four factors of production: capital, v_i^1; professional, scientific and managerial labour, v_i^2; other non-manual labour, v_i^3; and manual labour, v_i^4. National income is factor income accruing to these factors, plus the profits of firms:

$$M_i = v_i^1 w_i^1 + v_i^2 w_i^2 + v_i^3 w_i^3 + v_i^4 w_i^4 + \sum_k n_i^k \pi_i^k. \tag{6}$$

3   Data and calibration

The modelling exercise requires calibrating the model to a particular data set. The principal data requirements are trade and domestic sales data broken by industry and by country and a range of industry-specific parameters. Numerical specification of the model is then completed by calculating the values of remaining parameters and endogenous variables so that the base year observations are supported as an equilibrium of the model. Literature reviews were undertaken for a number of the industry-specific parameters required. (References are given below for key items only, but a complete list of sources is available on request.)

The overall structure of the model is one of 6 economic areas or 'countries': Germany, France, Italy, United Kingdom, the rest of the EEC, and the rest of the world, 13 imperfectly competitive industries (as listed in Table 2.1), and one perfectly competitive sector which comprises the rest of the economy. The industrial structure is based on the R25 subdivision of the European Community NACE–CLIO classification scheme. The R25 subdivision distinguishes between 13 manufacturing and 12 non-manufacturing sectors. Here we aggregate the non-manufacturing sectors into one perfectly competitive sector, and the manufacturing sector is divided into the 13 manufacturing industries. The base year for the calibration is 1985, the latest year for which an almost complete set of trade and production data was available. (Where the data was incomplete it was supplemented from other published EUROSTAT data and adjusted as appropriate.)

3.1   Trade and production

The trade data comes from the EC's VOLIMEX data base, and the production data from the EC's BDS data base. These data bases derive from the same source as published EUROSTAT data, but with adjustments which seek to improve the degree of compatibility both between different country returns and between the two data bases themselves. The reconciliation of trade and production data achieved in the data bases is, however, still imperfect.

Production statistics for 1985 for Ireland, Portugal, Greece and the Netherlands were not available on the BDS data base. For Ireland, Portugal and the Netherlands comparable data was obtained from EUROSTAT *Structure and Activity of Industry, 1985, Main Results* (SAI), and scaled as appropriate. For Greece, the latest available figures from SAI were for 1983, and these were rescaled to account for Greek growth between 1983 and 1985.

3.2   Industrial data

The industry-specific data required includes the share of value-added in production; the share of each factor in value-added; the elasticity of substitution between different factors of production; the share of final demand in the output of each industry; the degree of returns to scale in each industry; a measure of the number of symmetric firms competing in each industry and each country, this based on the numbers of firms in

Table 2.1. *Industry data*

Industry	Factor shares in VA				Cn	IRS	ϵ
	K	L1	L2	L3			
13 Metalliferous products	0.438	0.069	0.093	0.400	H	6	20.39
15 Non-metallic mineral products	0.280	0.090	0.173	0.457	M	8	10.55
17 Chemical products	0.330	0.139	0.207	0.324	M	15	7.13
19 Metal products	0.188	0.092	0.140	0.580	L	7	14.68
21 Agric. & ind. machinery	0.167	0.146	0.155	0.533	L	7	12.06
23 Office machinery & precision inst.	0.162	0.193	0.188	0.456	H	15	7.84
25 Electrical goods	0.153	0.253	0.166	0.428	M	10	8.74
28 Transport	0.227	0.121	0.128	0.523	H	7	22.69
36 Food products	0.294	0.080	0.165	0.462	L	4	22.72
42 Textiles, clothing & leather	0.191	0.077	0.203	0.529	L	3	28.03
47 Paper & printing products	0.240	0.148	0.178	0.434	L	13	6.64
48 Timber & other n.e.s.	0.234	0.102	0.310	0.354	L	5	18.78
49 Rubber & plastic products	0.167	0.078	0.321	0.435	M	5	16.79
perf. comp. sector	0.425	0.085	0.256	0.233			

K Capital share; L1 professional and related labour share; L2 other non-manual labour share; L3 manual labour share; Cn concentration; IRS return to scale; ϵ variety demand elasticity.

each of the aggregate industries, and the number of subindustries represented by each of these industries. Some of the key features of this data are presented in Table 2.1.

The model distinguishes between four factors of production – capital and three types of labour, professional and related non-manual workers ($L1$), managerial, clerical and other non-manual workers ($L2$), and manual workers ($L3$). Capital is treated as being internationally mobile, whereas labour is mobile only between firms and industries within each country. Both the share of value-added in production, and the share of capital in value-added were calculated from the BDS data base, whereas the share of consumption in final use was obtained from EUROSTAT, *National Accounts, Input–Output Tables, 1985*. The functional form of the cost function is nested CES (the function G_i^k) multiplied by a term which captures the degree of returns to scale in each industry (h^k). Given this functional form, the elasticity of substitution between capital and labour and between the different labour types needs to be specified. The capital–labour elasticity of substitution is derived from a review of the available literature and is largely based on the estimates in Piggott and Whalley (1985). In the version of the model presented in this study the same measure of elasticity is then also assumed between the different types of labour. The shares of the three different types of labour were calculated on the basis of UK earnings data, and the UK Census of Production. UK shares were taken to apply to all countries.

The factor shares in value-added are listed in Table 2.1. From Table 2.1 it is clear that the most capital-intensive sectors are metalliferous products and chemical products, and the most labour-intensive are electrical goods, office machinery and precision instruments, agricultural and industrial machinery, and rubber and plastic products. The industries most intensive in professional and highly skilled workers are the electrical goods industry and office machinery and precision instruments. The most manual labour-intensive industries are the metal products, agricultural and industrial machinery, transport products and textile industries.

Central to the model is the interaction between the degree of returns to scale and the extent of concentration in each industry. For the UK data on concentration was obtained from the UK Census of Production, and for France, Italy, Netherlands and Belgium the data was obtained from EUROSTAT. Unfortunately, primarily for reasons of statistical confidentiality, the largest size class for which data was available was rarely greater than 5,000 employees, and frequently only 1,000 employees. However, where one is interested in establishing the degree of market power firms may have, it is precisely in the largest size classes that the most important interactions take place. In order to capture the dispersion of firms in the top size class it was assumed that the size of firms in this class followed a Pareto distribution. A Herfindahl index for each industry and country was then computed on the basis of firms in size classes other than the top class all being of average size for their class, and the size of firms in the top size class following a Pareto distribution. The inverse of this Herfindahl index then gives the number of equal sized firms into which the industry is assumed to be divided.

For countries for which there was inadequate data, numbers of firms were estimated on the basis of firm size in other countries and total output, coupled with judgements made on the basis of secondary sources, in particular various European Commission reports on concentration and competition in selected industries – Hannah and Kay (1977), Phlips (1971), and the UK Monopolies and Mergers Commission (1978).

Table 2.1 lists the overall degree of concentration by industry, by differentiating between high, medium and low levels of concentration, indicated in the column headed Cn in Table 2.1. (The classification was done on the basis of the unweighted average Herfindahl index, adjusted to include import competition, for each industry across the four large EC countries.) From Table 2.1 it can be seen that there are three industries characterised by a high degree of concentration: metalliferous products, transport equipment, and the production of office machinery and precision instruments. Four industries are characterised by a medium degree of concentration and six by a low level of concentration.

Table 2.1 also lists the degree of assumed returns to scale. In each case, the percentage figure listed under IRS refers to the increase in costs as a result of a 50% reduction in output. These estimates are engineering estimates for which the primary source was Pratten (1988), supplemented by an extensive literature review.

3.3   Demand and calibration

The price elasticity of demand for the industry aggregates, X_j^k and Y_j^k, with respect to the associated price indices, are unity, by the Cobb–Douglas assumption. The price elasticities of demand for individual varieties depend on the elasticities of substitution in the CES aggregators. For intermediate products we assume that this elasticity of substitution is the same for all industries, and equal to 10. For final products we adopt the following approach. We assume that the base data set represents a long-run equilibrium in which profits are zero. Technology and firm scale imply a relationship between average cost and marginal cost and, with the assumption of long-run equilibrium, this also gives a relationship between price and marginal cost. This price–cost margin is supported in equilibrium by market power, deriving first from product differentiation and secondly from the degree of concentration in the industry and the form of inter-action between firms. We assume that the base case is a segmented market Cournot equilibrium. The price–cost margin then implies a measure of product differentiation, from which we obtain a value of the elasticity of substitution, ϵ^k. Calibrated values of ϵ^k are reported in the final column of Table 2.1. They are to be interpreted as the price elasticity of demand for an individual product variety, holding prices of other varieties and the overall industry price index, P_j^k, constant. These elasticities are very high (products are only slightly differentiated) in textiles and clothing, in food, in transport equipment, and in metalliferous products; the elasticities are decreasing through industries including timber, rubber, and are relatively low (so products are quite highly differentiated) in industries such as office machinery, and chemicals. This method of calibration does of course depend on the form of the base equilibrium. Sensitivity analysis over equilibrium concepts is undertaken in Venables (1990).

The final stage of calibration involves positioning demand curves (i.e., finding parameters of a_{ij}^k, of the aggregators given in the Appendix) such that consumption of products in each country is consistent with the matrix of production and consumption.

4   Reduced trade barriers

In section 4 we model the move towards completion of the internal market as a reduction in the cost of intra-EC trade. We assume that this trade liberalisation takes the form of an equiproportionate reduction in all the implicit barriers to trade between EC countries. The size of the reductions is chosen, as in Smith and Venables (1988), so that the direct cost saving achieved by the policy is equal to 2.5% of the value of base level intra-EC trade.

Table 2.2 reports the effect of this experiment on our 13 industries, under the assumption that the number of firms in each industry is held constant, and factor prices in each country are also constant. (These are not simply a set of partial equilibrium results because the policy changes income – and, more importantly, changes the prices of the intermediate, and hence cost, levels.) The pattern of output changes in Table 2.2 is essentially generated as a consequence of increased intra-EC trade volumes. For example in industry class 42 (textiles, clothing, leather goods and foot-wear), we see substantial increases in each country's imports and exports; Italy is a significant net exporter of these products to the rest of the EC, and the net effect of increased trade is to raise estimated Italian output by 7%. To take another example, UK production of Nace 23 (office and data

Table 2.2. *% change in total output and factor demands; markets segmented, firm numbers fixed, factor prices fixed*

Nace	Industry	F	G	I	UK	R of EC
% change in output						
13	Metalliferous products	5.12	1.14	− 2.49	− 4.29	2.76
15	Non-metallic mineral products	− 0.97	− 0.89	1.26	− 0.69	− 2.29
17	Chemical products	11.40	15.46	0.15	6.92	45.14
19	Metal products	− 1.38	0.05	0.83	− 0.98	− 2.75
21	Agric. & ind. machinery	1.14	4.31	− 0.19	− 0.41	0.39
23	Office machinery & precision inst.	− 0.74	6.14	− 1.08	8.28	6.49
25	Electrical goods	− 0.23	4.07	− 1.37	1.47	2.06
28	Transport	0.34	9.68	− 5.87	− 3.20	3.88
36	Food products	− 0.97	− 0.17	− 4.72	− 1.88	3.63
42	Textiles, clothing & leather	− 3.03	1.42	7.09	− 6.57	3.65
47	Paper & printing products	− 0.37	0.30	− 0.36	− 0.21	− 4.22
48	Timber & other n.e.s.	− 3.49	− 0.25	4.06	− 0.44	9.52
49	Rubber & plastic products	− 1.18	0.20	0.35	− 0.92	− 2.21
% Change in factor demands						
	Capital	1.68*	3.82	− 0.43	− 0.47	8.48*
	Non-manual 1	1.21	4.43*	− 0.18	0.33*	8.52*
	Non-manual 2	0.76	3.81	0.67*	− 0.14	8.45
	Manual	0.50	3.42	0.25	− 0.78	5.93

* Denotes maximal column element.

processing machinery, precision and optical instruments) increases by 8.3%, this again being the outcome of increases in both exports and imports.

The lower part of Table 2.2 reports the implications of these output changes for factor demands. Notice that demand for all factors increases in France, Germany and the rest of the EC, while some factor demands decrease in Italy and the United Kingdom. Once again, this is a reflection of the relatively strong net intra-EC trade position of France, Germany and the rest of the EC, as compared to Italy and the UK. Within each economy the factor experiencing the largest increase in demand is capital in France and in the rest of the EC; non-manual labour 1 in Germany and the United Kingdom; non-manual labour 2 in Italy. In no country does manual labour experience an increase in demand relative to all other factors.

The changes reported in Table 2.2 are associated with significant changes in the profitability of firms. These changes are essentially the product of two forces: first, because the effect of increased trade volumes is pro-competitive, there is generally a reduction in prices and loss of profits; second, where output expansions occur, the fact that price exceeds marginal cost and that there are increasing returns means an increase in profits. The experiment reported in Table 2.3 permits changes in the number of firms to occur until profits of firms in each industry and in each country are restored to their base levels. On average, the first effect dominates, so that overall there is a reduction in the number of active firms, due to exit or merger. However, in some cases where Table 2.2 suggests significant output increases, there is entry of firms. We do not report changes in the number of firms in Table 2.3, but merely the ensuing output changes. Exit of firms, of course, leads to increased concentration, and whereas in the experiment reported in Table 2.2 increased trade led to modest reductions in market power (with Herfindahl indices falling by around 8% on average), in this experiment there are some industries where the exit of firms leads to increased market power. As in Table 2.2, the experiment of Table 2.3 holds factor prices constant.

Inspection of Table 2.3 indicates that there is generally a magnification of the larger output changes reported in Table 2.2. For example, Italian production of Nace 42 (textiles, clothing, leather goods and footwear) now increases by 12% rather than 7%. This size expansion in one country's output is associated with exit of firms and significant contraction of output in other countries, particularly France and the United Kingdom. Similarly, for Nace 23 (office and data processing machinery, precision and optical instruments) the UK output increase of Table 2.2 is now magnified, while other countries experience exit and output contraction.

Table 2.3. *% change in output and factor demands; markets segmented, firm numbers flexible, factor prices fixed*

Nace	Industry	F	G	I	UK	R of EC
	% change in output					
13	Metalliferous products	5.75	1.12	− 3.50	− 6.21	1.19
15	Non-metallic mineral products	0.31	− 1.41	1.67	0.39	− 3.35
17	Chemical products	7.89	11.93	1.42	7.11	50.02
19	Metal products	− 0.85	− 0.14	1.36	− 0.29	− 4.48
21	Agric. & ind. machinery	0.62	8.61	− 1.88	− 2.31	− 7.33
23	Office machinery & precision inst.	− 24.77	10.50	− 20.37	42.52	8.92
25	Electrical goods	− 0.11	4.42	− 1.51	1.99	0.68
28	Transport	− 5.31	23.49	− 26.67	− 14.61	3.32
36	Food products	− 0.98	− 0.30	− 5.82	− 2.26	4.39
42	Textiles, clothing & leather	− 12.89	− 0.59	12.43	− 14.54	10.84
47	Paper & printing products	0.53	− 0.57	0.12	0.69	− 3.75
48	Timber & other n.e.s.	− 9.30	− 7.00	4.64	− 16.41	58.22
49	Rubber & plastic products	− 1.53	0.40	1.07	0.22	− 4.57
	% Change in factor demands					
	Capital	− 0.47*	4.83	− 1.51	− 1.91	11.33
	Non-manual 1	− 1.61	6.24*	− 1.86	0.04*	11.48
	Non-manual 2	− 2.25	4.63	0.27*	− 1.74	13.60*
	Manual	− 2.39	5.23	− 0.88	− 2.49	8.72

* Denotes maximal column element.

In terms of factor demands, there is once again increased demand for all factors in Germany and the rest of the EC, and reduced demand for most factors in Italy, the United Kingdom, and now also France. Only in France does capital experience the largest demand increase (or smallest decrease); elsewhere the largest demand increase occurs for one or the other of the types of non-manual labour.

Some of the output changes reported in Table 2.3 are large. One reason for this is that factor supply curves have so far been assumed to be horizontal. We now turn to the case where factor endowments are assumed to be constant, and factor prices adjust to equate supply and demand. The 13 industries analysed in preceding tables cover only around one-third of each economy, so the effects of a comparative advantage experiments are going to depend crucially on the rest of the economy, and in particular on its factor intensity. The 'rest of the economy' includes agriculture, energy, market services and nonmarket services. At the present stage of our research these are aggregated into a single perfectly competitive sector, which we assume not to be directly affected by completion of the internal market. This is unsatisfactory, as some parts of this sector – for example, financial services – are neither perfectly competitive nor unaffected by 1992. Furthermore, including these sectors in 'the rest of the economy' has a major effect on this sector's factor intensity, making it by far the least intensive user of manual labour.

Table 2.4 reports output changes and factor price changes. Capital is assumed to be internationally mobile, so has its price held constant, but the prices of the three types of labour in each country are now endogenous. Comparison of Table 2.4 with Table 2.3 indicates that some – though not all – of the larger output changes are damped by this endogeneity of factor prices. Of course, this model has 14 sectors and we are permitting the prices of only three factors to change. There are therefore some sectors in which output changes are greater when factor prices are flexible than when wages are held constant, and these include the two cases discussed in the previous example: the Italian output increase of 13% in Nace 42 rises to 15%, and the UK increase of 43% in Nace 23 rises to 65%.

The factor price changes are recorded in the bottom section of Table 2.4. The price of non-manual labour 1 increases, relative to the numéraire, and relative to the price of all other factors in three countries, France, Germany and the United Kingdom. It decreases in Italy where it is non-manual labour 2 which experiences a price increase relative to all other factor prices. Notice that all the changes in relative factor prices, especially in the price of manual labour, are quite small.

Table 2.4. *% change in output and factor prices; markets segmented, firm numbers flexible, factor prices flexible*

Nace	Industry	F	G	I	UK	R of EC
% change in output						
13	Metalliferous products	7.05	1.41	− 3.42	− 5.64	0.78
15	Non-metallic mineral products	− 0.27	− 0.38	1.41	− 0.35	− 2.32
17	Chemical products	8.13	12.27	1.85	6.34	50.88
19	Metal products	− 1.04	0.32	1.25	− 0.54	− 4.10
21	Agric. & ind. machinery	11.78	3.65	1.14	2.81	− 17.45
23	Office machinery & precision inst.	− 20.48	7.08	− 17.62	64.95	− 15.60
25	Electrical goods	0.75	2.70	0.24	1.49	− 1.35
28	Transport	3.97	14.66	− 20.76	− 6.10	− 4.06
36	Food products	− 0.19	− 0.72	− 5.19	− 1.64	3.34
42	Textiles, clothing & leather	− 9.83	− 9.89	14.86	− 10.32	6.16
47	Paper & printing products	− 0.08	0.37	− 0.11	− 0.29	− 2.60
48	Timber & other n.e.s.	− 9.02	− 5.88	4.41	− 13.65	52.49
49	Rubber & plastic products	− 2.32	2.00	0.61	− 0.77	− 3.12
% Change in factor demands						
	Capital	0	0	0	0	0
	Non-manual 1	0.27*	0.89*	− 0.49	0.93*	0.59
	Non-manual 2	− 0.12	− 1.02	0.11*	− 0.07	− 0.83
	Manual	0.03	0.80	0.06	− 0.26	0.70*

* Denotes maximal column element.

5   Reduced trade barriers and market integration

The second policy experiment we consider is one in which, in addition to a reduction in trade barriers, completion of the internal market forces firms to switch from segmented market to integrated market behaviour. This means that firms can no longer price discriminate between markets, but simply compete on an EC-wide basis, setting the same producer price in all markets. For this experiment we simulate the same three cases as in section 4.

Table 2.5 reports output changes when factor prices and the number of firms in each economy are held constant. These changes are now the product of two forces. As before, the reduction in trade barriers tends to magnify net trade patterns within the EC, so moving output in the same direction as for Table 2.2. In addition, the switch to integrated markets is very pro-competitive: firms no longer price on the basis of shares in national markets, but on the basis of shares in the EC market as a whole. This means that there are significant price reductions in countries and industries which, in the base, are highly concentrated; significant price reductions are associated with quantity increases. To illustrate this, consider Nace 23 (office and data processing machinery, precision and optical instruments). In the base data set this industry appears most concentrated in France and Italy; it is these countries in which market integration has the largest effect on price, and which now experience the largest increases in output (in section 4, the largest increase in output was recorded by the United Kingdom). Of course, the loss of market power is costly in terms of profits. Letting numbers of firms adjust (Table 2.6), we see that the largest output increase is once again recorded by the United Kingdom.

The implications of market integration for factor demands are recorded in the bottom sections of Tables 2.5 and 2.6. In France, Germany and the United Kingdom the largest increase in demands occur for non-manual labour 1. In Italy, manual labour has the largest increase in Table 2.5 and non-manual labour 2 the largest in Table 2.6, and in the rest of the EC the largest demand increases are for non-manual labour.

Table 2.7 reports how these changes in factor demands translate into factor price changes. Letting wages be flexible dampens some – but by no means all – of the larger quantity effects. The wage of non-manual labour 1 rises in France, Germany and the United Kingdom, relative both to the numéraire and to other wages. In Italy and the rest of the EC it is manual labour which experiences the wage increase.

6   Concluding comments

This study extends the methodology developed in Smith and Venables (1988) in two directions. First, we now have a wider coverage of the EC

Table 2.5. *% change in total output and factor demands; markets integrated, firm numbers fixed, factor prices fixed*

Nace	Industry	F	G	I	UK	R of EC
	% change in output					
13	Metalliferous products	4.67	1.49	− 2.09	− 2.35	2.88
15	Non-metallic mineral products	− 0.98	− 0.22	0.51	− 1.34	− 2.12
17	Chemical products	10.29	16.99	− 0.14	7.01	44.63
19	Metal products	− 1.42	0.32	0.36	− 1.38	− 2.57
21	Agric. & ind. machinery	1.21	4.35	− 0.19	− 0.37	0.15
23	Office machinery & precision inst.	9.10	4.68	8.84	5.13	4.62
25	Electrical goods	0.86	3.76	− 1.73	3.60	3.05
28	Transport	10.48	− 3.41	19.51	21.92	7.35
36	Food products	− 0.87	− 0.28	− 3.26	− 0.54	2.94
42	Textiles, clothing & leather	− 2.58	1.43	6.66	− 6.50	3.59
47	Paper & printing products	− 0.92	1.05	− 1.05	− 1.29	− 3.96
48	Timber & other n.e.s.	− 3.36	− 0.00	3.69	− 0.56	9.30
49	Rubber & plastic products	− 0.43	0.37	− 0.13	− 1.41	− 1.90
	% Change in factor demands					
	Capital	2.57	2.99	1.06	1.56	8.40
	Non-manual 1	2.63*	3.30*	1.55	2.46*	8.58*
	Non-manual 2	1.70	3.08	1.77	1.40	8.36
	Manual	1.88	2.07	1.98*	1.60	5.94

* Denotes maximal column element.

Table 2.6. *% change in output and factor demands; markets integrated, firm numbers flexible, factor prices fixed*

Nace	Industry	F	G	I	UK	R of EC
% change in output						
13	Metalliferous products	− 3.38	4.62	− 14.22	− 5.53	− 1.49
15	Non-metallic mineral products	1.40	0.16	1.84	1.18	− 2.36
17	Chemical products	7.69	14.41	1.87	8.74	47.02
19	Metal products	− 0.89	0.59	1.24	− 0.62	− 4.31
21	Agric. & ind. machinery	0.69	9.15	− 2.52	− 3.03	− 6.08
23	Office machinery & precision inst.	− 7.69	10.33	− 8.75	31.54	2.06
25	Electrical goods	0.83	4.98	− 1.24	3.03	2.03
28	Transport	7.43	− 0.65	13.06	17.56	10.83
36	Food products	− 0.57	1.02	− 6.00	− 2.58	4.47
42	Textiles, clothing & leather	− 14.97	1.37	12.39	− 15.90	11.78
47	Paper & printing products	0.79	0.25	1.10	1.27	− 2.62
48	Timber & other n.e.s.	− 9.85	− 6.63	4.42	− 18.44	61.48
49	Rubber & plastic products	− 5.50	3.79	0.61	− 0.08	− 5.40
% Change in factor demands						
	Capital	− 1.09	3.79	− 1.39	− 0.80	10.40
	Non-manual 1	− 0.60*	4.47*	− 0.05	1.40*	11.03
	Non-manual 2	− 2.08	3.74	1.16*	− 1.10	13.20*
	Manual	− 1.87	3.10	0.59	− 0.95	8.51

* Denotes maximal column element.

Table 2.7. % change in output and factor prices; markets integrated, firm numbers flexible, factor prices flexible

Nace	Industry	F	G	I	UK	R of EC
	% change in output					
13	Metalliferous products	−1.12	4.63	−14.26	−5.26	−3.56
15	Non-metallic mineral products	0.09	0.54	1.86	0.81	−1.31
17	Chemical products	7.96	14.47	2.39	8.34	47.69
19	Metal products	−0.98	0.74	1.25	−0.73	−3.95
21	Agric. & ind. machinery	10.49	7.05	−1.18	−0.17	−18.07
23	Office machinery & precision inst.	−4.87	9.24	−7.23	45.57	−15.85
25	Electrical goods	1.39	3.88	0.01	2.21	−0.29
28	Transport	10.62	−2.94	14.00	19.61	6.43
36	Food products	0.32	0.94	−5.70	−2.14	3.39
42	Textiles, clothing & leather	−10.76	−0.77	12.93	−12.58	4.28
47	Paper & printing products	0.29	0.55	1.20	0.72	−1.46
48	Timber & other n.e.s.	−9.32	−5.62	4.32	−15.38	54.76
49	Rubber & plastic products	−6.16	4.47	0.61	−0.58	−3.71
	% Change in factor demands					
	Capital	0	0	0	0	0
	Non-manual 1	0.42*	0.78*	−0.24	0.94*	0.59
	Non-manual 2	−0.13	−0.71	−0.12	−0.26	−0.81
	Manual	0.00	0.50	0.22*	−0.66	0.68*

* Denotes maximal column element.

economy, by working with 13 relatively highly aggregated industries covering the entire manufacturing sector of each economy. Second, the factor intensity of industries is now modelled, which enables us both to compute estimates of changes in factor demands associated with completion of the internal market and to calculate estimates of factor price changes. These in turn modify and improve estimates of the effects of 1992 on the relative size of different industries in different countries.

The most important and robust conclusion that we derive from our experiments concerns the differential effect of completion of the market on demand for different types of labour. For both our characterisations of the 1992 experiment we see that demand for skilled labour increases relative to demand for unskilled labour. In France, Germany and the United Kingdom it is the category of professional and scientific labour (non-manual 1) which experiences the relatively largest increase in demand; in Italy and the rest of the EC there are some differences between experiments but the increase in demand non-manual workers (2) is generally the largest increase. These demand differences translate into factor price changes in which the relative wage of professional and scientific labour rises in France, Germany and the United Kingdom.

Factor price changes occur as the 13 manufacturing sectors complete for factors with the large 'rest of the economy'. In future research, the rest of the economy has to be disaggregated, both so that we can model the effect of 1992 on some parts of this sector (such as financial services) and in order to separate out other important components (like government and agriculture) so that we can form a better view about the proportions in which this sector will release factors of production.

Appendix

Consumers in country j, $j = 1 \ldots J$, consume products which are produced in each country, so the number of product types available for consumption is $\sum_{i=1}^{J} n_i m_i$. Demands in each country are derived from a Dixit and Stiglitz (1977)-type welfare function – i.e., there is a CES aggregator of the form,

$$X_j^k = \left[\sum_{i=1}^{J} n_i^k m_i^k a_{ij}^{k(1/\epsilon^k)} x_{ij}^{k(\epsilon^k - 1)/\epsilon^k} \right]^{\epsilon^k/(\epsilon^k - 1)} \qquad j = 1 \ldots J \qquad (A1)$$

where a_{ij}^k are demand parameters describing the preferences for of a consumer in country j for product produced in country i. X_j^k can be regarded as a quantity index of aggregate consumption of the industry output.

Dual to the quantity index is a price index, P_j^k, taking the form,

$$P_j^k = \left[\sum_{i=1}^{I} n_i^k m_i^k a_{ij}^k p_{ij}^{k(1-\epsilon^k)} \right]^{1/(1-\epsilon^k)} \qquad j = 1 \ldots J \qquad (A2)$$

and representing the price of the aggregate product, where p_{ij}^k are the prices of the individual varieties. The unit expenditure function is Cobb–Douglas, so

$$E_j = \prod_k (P_j^k) \beta_j^k \qquad j = 1 \ldots J \qquad (A3)$$

where β_j^k give the share of industry k in country j expenditure.

Construction of the intermediate aggregators, Y_j^k, Q_j^k and F_j is exactly analogous. They have different parameters ϵ^k, a_{ij}^k and β_j^k.

Under the segmented market hypothesis, firms choose the quantity they supply to each market, given sales of other firms in that market. The first-order condition for profit maximisation takes the form,

$$p_{ij}^k (1 - t_{ij}^k) \left(1 - \frac{1}{e_{ij}^k} \right) = \frac{1}{m_i^k} \frac{\partial c_i^k}{\partial z_i^k} \qquad i, j = 1 \ldots J \qquad (A4)$$

where e_{ij} is the perceived elasticity of demand and is given by

$$\frac{1}{e_{ij}^k} = \frac{1}{\epsilon^k} + \left(1 + \frac{1}{\epsilon^k} \right) s_{ij}^k, \qquad i, j = 1 \ldots J \qquad (A5)$$

s_{ij}^k is the share of a single firm from country i in the country j market for industry k.

Under the integrated market hypothesis, firms choose total sales to the 5 EC markets, given total sales of their rivals. In this optimisation problem they anticipate that the allocation of all firms' sales between all markets will be such as to equate producer prices of a particular product in all markets – i.e., to satisfy the following equation,

$$p_{ij}^k (1 - t_{ij}^k) = p_{il}^k (1 - t_{il}^k), \qquad i, j, l = 1 \ldots J \qquad (A6)$$

NOTE

This research is supported by UK ESRC grant no. R000231763.

REFERENCES

Department of Employment (1985) *New Earnings Survey*, London: DoE.
Dixit, A. and J.E. Stiglitz (1977) 'Monopolistic Competition and Optimum Product Diversity', *American Economic Review*, **67**, pp. 297–308.

European Commission (198–) *Reports on Concentration and Competition*, Brussels: EUROSTAT.

EUROSTAT (1986) *National Accounts ESA, Input–Output Tables 1980*, Brussels: EUROSTAT.

EUROSTAT (1989) *Structure and Activity of Industry, Annual Inquiry 1985, Main Results 1984/85*, Brussels: EUROSTAT.

EUROSTAT (1989) *Structure and Activity of Industry, Annual Inquiry, Data by size of Enterprise, 1984*, Brussels: EUROSTAT.

Hannah, L. and J.A. Kay (1977) *Concentration in Modern Industry*, London: Macmillan.

Monopolies and Mergers Commission (1978) *A Review of Monopolies and Mergers Policy: A Consultative Document*, Cmnd. 7198, London: HMSO.

Office of Population and Census Surveys (1984) *Census 1981, Economic Activity, Great Britain*, London: Office of Population and Census Surveys.

Phlips, L. (1971) *Effects of Industrial Concentration*, Amsterdam: North-Holland.

Piggott, J. and J. Whalley (1985) *UK Tax Policy and Applied General Equilibrium Analysis*, Cambridge: Cambridge University Press.

Pratten, C. (1988) *A Survey of the Economies of Scale*, in 'Research on the "Costs of Non-Europe", Basic Findings', Vol. 2, Brussels: Commission of the European Communities.

Smith, A. and A.J. Venables (1988) 'Completing the Internal Market in the European Community: Some industry simulations', *European Economic Review*, **32**, pp. 1501–25.

Venables, A.J. (1990) 'International capacity choice and national market games', *Journal of International Economics*, **29**, pp. 23–42.

Discussion

PAUL BRENTON

This study describes the integration of a computable model of production and trade under conditions of increasing returns to scale and product differentiation into a general equilibrium framework. Traditional computable general equilibrium (CGE) models are specified on the basis of 'textbook comparative advantage'; they thus permit inter-industry trade only, or allow for *ad hoc* product differentiation and hence intra-industry trade by assuming that products are distinguished by country of production. Norman (1990), using a simple three-sector–two-region example, suggests that the inclusion of imperfect competition has a significant effect upon the quantitative effects of changes in trade policy in CGE models.

The basic model applied here is very similar to that usefully employed by two of the authors in a partial equilibrium context (Smith and Venables, 1988), excepting that in this case there is no allowance for economies of scope and hence the number of varieties of a product produced is fixed. In this study the links between the individual industries are provided via the explicit modelling of intermediate demand and the specification of factor demand equations and overall resource constraints.

The principal result presented in this study is that market integration within the EC will have differing effects on various types of labour. The predicted changes in factor prices suggest that the United Kingdom, for example, has an unexploited comparative advantage in high-skilled labour-intensive products, whilst after 1992 the rest of the EC will further exploit its advantage in unskilled labour-intensive products. This tends to confirm the analysis of Neven (1990) based upon differences in average wages between EC countries. Surprisingly, this model predicts that in Italy the price of manual labour will rise, suggesting a comparative advantage in products using such labour intensively. The robustness of this result to disaggregation of the perfectly competitive sector and the rest of the EC remains to be seen.

A feature of the factor price changes predicted under the scenario of integrated markets is the decline in wages across all countries for managerial, clerical and other non-manual workers. All these results thus highlight the important distributional consequences of market liberalisation within Europe, and suggest that with unemployment in Europe still close to 10% significant adjustment costs may be incurred. This is an issue which has received very little attention, although models such as that developed here should be able to make an important contribution to the debate.

The nature of models solved using calibration techniques is such that one cannot derive statistical measures of the accuracy (and therefore reliability) of the model and its predictions. A body of results from similar models employing slightly different specifications and applied to differing data sets is thus required before we can identify which results and policy implications are relatively robust. For traditional (perfectly competitive – constant returns to scale) computable general equilibrium models and partial equilibrium models of imperfect competition this has, to an extent, been done (see, for example, Shoven and Whalley, 1984 and Helpman and Krugman, 1989, respectively). Previous attempts to include industrial organisation features into a CGE model are few – Harris (1986) and Norman (1990). Nonetheless, a brief comparison of these models and their main results may be useful in highlighting the principal forces driving their outcomes and suggesting ways in which the current model could be developed.

Previous experience suggests that the predicted effects of trade liberalisation are sensitive to the way in which imperfect competition is modelled. In the Harris study, prices are set as the average of the tariff-inclusive world price and a price determined by the perceived demand curve. More conventionally, Norman and Smith and Venables impose Cournot competition. No information is provided here on the effects of alternative assumptions about the nature of competition. Harris models 'an almost small country' – Canada – and the rest of the world, Norman considers 'small' EFTA and 'large' EC, whilst in this study a richer country breakdown is employed with the four 'large' EC countries, the rest of the EC and the rest of the world (for which results are not reported). Additionally, Smith and Venables are able to separate labour into three types of according to skill levels, although they are forced to impose the share of each type in the United Kingdom across all countries.

The general result of the Harris and Norman studies is that, relative to traditional CGE models, the gains from trade liberalisation tend to be larger once imperfect competition, returns to scale and product differentiation are incorporated. The principal effect is that the increased competition induced by lower prices stimulates demand and output, but reduces profitability, so that firms exit the industry. The survivors increase the length of their production runs and so further exploit economies of scale, thus reducing average costs. Results presented by Harris show that a unilateral tariff cut by Canada would lead to substantial quantity changes and welfare gains, much greater than those predicted by the conventional models. However, Shoven and Whalley (1984) suggest that this result emanates as much from the asymmetries in the size of the countries as from returns to scale.

In this study the results suggest large quantity changes for many industries following a relatively small reduction in costs (2.5% of the base level of intra-EC trade). The country breakdown is such that small country effects will not be important – the value of output of the rest of the EC is of a similar magnitude to that of Italy and the UK. Yet in general the largest percentage changes in output and factor demands are recorded for the rest of the EC group. Further disaggregation of this group, preferably along 'North–South' lines and separately identifying 'a small country', should thus be informative.

Returns to scale were identified by Harris (1986) as providing a significant contribution to the overall effects of trade liberalisation, whilst Smith and Venables (1988) similarly found the ratio of the change in welfare to the change in the value of trade to be correlated with the degree of returns to scale. The results presented here also tend to reflect this feature – the two industries with the highest returns to scale (chemicals and office machinery) experience some of the largest changes in output following liberalisation. Given the current controversy over the extent of unexploited economies of scale within Europe, caution should be applied when interpreting results predicated on assumptions about returns to scale. Further, the view that benefits from trade barrier removal may accrue more from increases in the variety of products than from cheaper standardised products (Geroski, 1989), suggests that the model should be extended to allow for economies of scope and changes in the number of product types.

Developing the basic model in ways suggested by the authors and as I have outlined above would provide greater insights into the relative reliability of the study's main features – that trade liberalisation has differential effects on different types of labour and that (as in the Harris study) the inclusion of imperfect competition and returns to scale appear to have a significant influence upon the predicted effects of trade liberalisation in computable general equilibrium models.

REFERENCES

Geroski, P.A. (1989) 'The Choice Between Diversity and Scale', in *1992: Myths and Realities*, London: Centre for Business Strategy, London Business School.

Harris, R.G. (1986) 'Market Structure and Trade Liberalisation: A General Equilibrium Assessment', in T.N. Srinivasan and J. Whalley (eds), *General Equilibrium Trade Policy Modelling*, Cambridge, Mass: MIT Press.

Helpman, E. and P.R. Krugman (1989) *Trade Policy and Market Structure*, Cambridge, Mass: MIT Press.

Neven, D.J. (1990) 'EEC Integration towards 1992: Some Distributional Aspects', *Economic Policy*, **10**, pp. 14–62.

Norman, V. (1990) 'Assessing Trade and Welfare Effects of Trade Liberalisation: A Comparison of Alternative Approaches to CGE Modelling with Imperfect Competition', *European Economic Review*, **34**, pp. 725–51.

Shoven, J.B. and J. Whalley (1984) 'Applied General-Equilibrium Models of Taxation and International Trade: An Introduction and Survey', *Journal of Economic Literature*, **22**, pp. 1007–51.

Smith, A. and A.J. Venables (1988) 'Completing the Internal Market in the European Community', *European Economic Review*, **32**, pp. 1501–25.

3 External effects and Europe's integration

RICCARDO J. CABALLERO and RICHARD
K. LYONS

1 Introduction

The objective of this study is to bring greater relevance *vis-à-vis* the issue of European economic integration to our previous work on external economies (Caballero and Lyons, 1989, 1990a, 1990b, hereafter C & L). There we find strong evidence of external economies in both the United States and Europe. The type of external effect we pick up in those studies is a country-specific, inter-industry external effect: an industry is able to generate more real output for given level of inputs when other industries within that country are at higher production levels. Yet external effects come in a number of different varieties, the most popular in the international trade literature being intra-industry effects, and here we consider at greater depth whether there is any clear evidence on the presence of the latter. The European context is particularly appealing for such an investigation, given both the high degree of current integration of these economies and the further integration to come, and the issue is potentially even more important in properly evaluating the gains from 1992. To the extent that positive external effects are at work internationally, this channel could be expected to contribute to the 'energising' of Europe.

To set the stage for the evidence we present, it is helpful first to consider some of the theoretical work on external economies, which is both quite extensive and spans a number of different areas. Marshall (1920) is generally credited for having first made the distinction between internal and external economies. The fundamental importance of this distinction derives from the very different implications of internal versus external economies for firm behaviour, and this point figures prominently in the literature. Much of the subsequent work on external economies focuses on economies external to the firm but internal to the industry, so-called industry-specific external effects (for early examples see Ohlin, 1933 and Stigler, 1951). The most often cited sources for the external effects include

34

conglomeration, indivisibilities, within-industry specialisation, the incomplete appropriability of knowledge, and public intermediate inputs such as roads. Recent work in this area of inter-industry external effects includes Manning and Macmillan (1979), Chang (1981), and Herberg, Kemp and Tawada (1983). The central concern of these studies is the impact of this type of externality on the fundamental theorems of international trade.

In addition to the works noted above, the areas of macroeconomics and growth are increasingly making use of externalities.[1] When (positive) external effects are present business cycle fluctuations are likely to be more pronounced, as co-movements generate important reinforcing cross effects. Additionally, it is now widely recognised that external effects with positive feedback provide fertile ground for multiple equilibria (see Diamond, 1982; Diamond and Fudenberg, 1989; and Cooper and John, 1988). In the growth context, externalities are typically of a longer-term nature than those that our procedure is likely to pick up. A common specification here includes knowledge as an input to production, which can lead to increasing returns. In this context, spillovers of knowledge between firms are externalities because protection of proprietary information is incomplete (see, for example, Arrow, 1962 and Romer, 1986).[2]

We should make it clear at this point that in this study we do not attempt to isolate the underlying source of the external effects: indeed, the theoretical literature is anything but conclusive on this matter. Although the issue surely deserves future investigation, our task here is less ambitious than this. We limit our objective to evaluating evidence concerning the different varieties of the external economies and implications for evaluating further integration in Europe. Of course, some of the sources of external effects that appear in the studies cited above are more likely to be picked up by our procedure than by others. Yet, at the current level of resolving power, it remains premature to address the question of source directly. Additionally, we are well aware that there exist competing explanations of our results that do not rely on external effects. In our previous studies, we effected a number of tests of the robustness of our model and its interpretation against the principal alternatives (e.g., excess capacity or measurment error). In the end, we found that the alternatives to the presence of external economies were considerably less compelling. We shall return to the issue of robustness below in the context of our overview of previous results.

We turn now to a brief review of some of the more directly related empirical evidence. The earlier literature here is less than conclusive. Research on the presence of externalities resulting from R & D spillovers has not yet uncovered any strong evidence, though some evidence does exist (see, for example, Griliches and Lichtenberg, 1984). This has been the primary channel thus far investigated at the micro level through which external effects might be propagated. At the more aggregated level, C & L (1989) provided evidence of widespread external effects. The approach for that work is related to the approach pioneered by Hall (1988b). Hall's work aimed at measuring indexes of internal returns to scale; our innovation was the development of a method for the joint estimation of an index of internal returns to scale and an index of external economies. We found strong evidence of country-specific, inter-industry external economies in both Europe and the United States. In the case of the four European countries for which the requisite data were available, the results implied that the average unconditional elasticity of a two-digit industry's output with respect to its own output is about 1, which jibes with previous estimates that failed to take into consideration the possibility of external effects. By comparison, at the polar extreme in which all industries increase their production in lockstep, our results imply an elasticity of 1.3, reflecting the significant role of positive external effects. The US results are remarkably similar: the two corresponding elasticities are 1.15 and 1.33.

Our previous work, however, was done on a country by country basis. It did not consequently, shed any light on the question of whether any direct international spillovers existed. Of course, to the extent that there is a relation between aggregate production levels, the previous results imply an important indirect channel through which external effects are propagated. In taking the first steps towards a resolution of the issue of direct international effects, we develop here a model that provides a means of discriminating between country-specific inter-industry and international intra-industry externalities. Though our preliminary estimation lacks power, the results do provide some mild evidence that international external economies are indeed present, over and above the country-specific effects evinced in the earlier work. We describe the evidence regarding these distinctions below, and attempt to evaluate the implications for further European economic integration.

The rest of the study is divided into five sections. Section 2 provides a review of the previous evidence on country-specific external economies in the United States and Europe; section 3 describes briefly the approach for discriminating between external economies of different varieties; section 4 presents the resulting evidence on the different external economies; section 5 addresses the implications of our results for the proposed gains resulting from 1992; and section 6 provides our conclusions. The Data Appendix describes the data used to estimate the various specifications for the various countries.

2   Previous evidence of external economies

Section 2 highlights the core results contained in our previous work on country-specific external economies in the United States and Europe. The brief review serves to clarify the methodology, and to put in perspective the new results presented later.

2.1   Summary of US results

C & L (1989) introduces a method for the joint estimation of the degree of internal returns to scale and the extent of external economies, where 'external economies' refers to country-specific inter-industry external effects. The externality that we estimate is operative between the two-digit industry level and the aggregate level of manufacturing; at the aggregate manufacturing level the externality is thus internalised. Indeed, one of the most persistent results arising throughout our previous work, both in the United States and Europe, is the presence of a systematic ranking: aggregate estimates of indexes of returns to scale are consistently much larger than those at the more disaggregated level.

Consider the following equation, estimated by Hall (1988b) at both the two-digit level and the aggregate level (time subscripts and constants suppressed):

$$dy = \gamma[\alpha_c dl + (1 - \alpha_c) dk] + dw, \tag{1}$$

where dy is the change in the logarithm of aggregate manufacturing value added, γ is the coefficient representing the aggregate returns to scale index, α_c is labour's share in total costs, dl is the change in the logarithm of aggregate labour input, dk is the change in the logarithm of aggregate capital input, and dw is a compound error term that includes external effects and random productivity shocks.[3]

Hall estimates this equation using instrumental variables since one would expect that productivity shocks, contained in dw, would be correlated with the regressor, inducing simultaneity bias.

The above formulation, however, fails to recognise a potentially very important consideration. In our previous work we showed that when the compound error term included an external economy component the estimates of γ at the most aggregate level – denoted by ϕ in order to distinguish it properly from the returns to scale parameter at the more disaggregated level – do not in general represent the degree of homogeneity of the production function with respect to capital and labour, but a composite measure of this homogeneity and external economies. That is, the measure is an upward biased estimate of the average degree of industry-level internal returns when external economies are present, since the external economy is internalised at the aggregate level (see section 3 below).

The core model[4] of external effects we estimate in C & L (1989) is described by the following equations:

$$dy_i = \gamma dx_i + \beta dy + dv_i, \tag{1'}$$

at the industry level and

$$dy = \phi dx + dv, \tag{2}$$

at the aggregate level, where dx_i is defined equal to industry i's cost-weighted input share from equation (1).

Table 3.1 summarises the basic results in C & L (1989) and (1990a). The first row of the table corresponds to estimation of equation (2) at the aggregate level over the period 1953 to 1980 (through 1984 in the case of instrumental variables). As is clear from both the OLS and IV results,[5] the parameter ϕ is significantly greater than 1, implying increasing returns to scale at the level of aggregate manufacturing. Given this as the aggregate result, one should expect that a positive β would accompany a γ that is less than the measured ϕ, which is in accord with what we actually find. Not only is there a very significant external effect with the industry level estimates, there is thus also a very clean correspondence between the estimates at the two different levels of aggregation, lending further support to the model.

Before going on to the European context we should first present evidence concerning the robustness of the external effects interpretation of the above results. There are two main alternative explanations: (1) the coefficient on dy is significant because excess capacity exists and is countercyclical, and (2) there is measurement error in the weighted input measure x_i. First, we consider the excess capacity interpretation. In a similar context, Abbott, Griliches and Hausman (1989) persuasively offer this interpretation as an explanation of Hall's (1988a) finding of a significant markup coefficient for US industry. They argue that his result is an artifact of correlation between his instruments and excess capacity. Using a proxy for both capital and labour utilisation rates – the number of hours worked per employee – they find that the significant markup coefficient disappears and that the capacity measure plays an important role. The same argument could be made here – that is, the external effect could in fact simply be a proxy for changes in capacity utilisation. To evaluate their argument, we include their proxy in our regression (C & L, 1990a) and find that the external economy coefficient remains about the same size and

Table 3.1. *Summary of US results on external economies*

$$dy = \phi[\alpha_c dl + (1 - \alpha_c) dk] + dw$$

$$dy_i = \gamma[\alpha_{ic} dl_i + (1 - \alpha_{ic}) dk_i] + \beta dy + dv_i$$

	OLS	IV
ϕ	1.37	1.33
	$(0.08)^a$	(0.07)
γ	0.78	0.98
	(0.02)	(0.05)
β^b	0.39	0.18
	(NA)	(0.04)

[a] Standard errors in parentheses.
[b] The standard error for β using OLS is not available since OLS precluded direct estimation of β due to simultaneity.

is very significant. The excess capacity view thus does not undermine our result. It is true, however, that changes in capacity utilisation are playing a role: the coefficient on the proxy was both positive and significant at the 5% level.

A second alternative explanation of our results come from the possibility that industry inputs are mismeasured, inducing a correlation between dy and the measurement error. The relevance of this argument turns on the degree of measurement error that would be necessary to replicate our results. We demonstrate (C & L, 1990a) that quite extreme error would be necessary. The argument focuses on the difference in the estimated values for the aggregate returns to scale coefficient, ϕ, and the industry-level composite coefficient, θ, implied by a model with no external effects. We show that the actual difference in these coefficients implies that the portion of the measurement error common to all industries, after projection on the instruments, would have to account for about 60% of the covariance between dx and the instruments. We consider this an unrealistic degree of measurement error.

2.2   Summary of European results

C & L (1990b) investigates the possibility that external effects might be at work in the European context as well. The necessary data were available in adequate length for only four of the twelve EC nations (see Data Appendix): West Germany, France, the United Kingdom, and Belgium. Table 3.2 summarises the results using OLS procedures. Given the similarity between the estimates using OLS and IV in the US context, the

Table 3.2. *Summary of European results on external economies (OLS)*

$$dy = \phi[\alpha_c dl + (1 - \alpha_c) dk] + dw$$
$$dy_i = \gamma[\alpha_{ic} dl_i + (1 - \alpha_{ic}) dk_i] + \beta dy + dv_i$$

	ϕ	γ	β
Average: West Germany, France, United Kingdom, Belgium	1.3	0.7	0.5
Average: West Germany, France, United Kingdom	1.3	0.7	0.5

[a] No standard errors are reported since these are simple averages of country by country estimates.

method of estimation does not appear to be crucial in this setting. (The further work presented below on the presence of an international external effect is done using only IV procedures and the results are consistent with those presented in Table 3.2). The coefficient values reported are the simple averages of the coefficients for the individual countries; since they were estimated on a country by country basis, standard errors of the averages are not available. In summary, all of the point estimates of ϕ were greater than 1.0, though only France's significantly so at the 5% level. In contrast, all of the estimates of γ were significantly less than 1.0. Finally, the external effect parameters were positive and significant in every country.

The story is quite similar to that in the United States. In an average sense, there is some evidence of increasing returns to scale at the level of aggregate manufacturing. At the two-digit industry level, there is evidence of constant or decreasing returns to scale. The boost from the external economy appears larger than that in the United States, however. It should be noted, nonetheless, that the difference between the European average and that in the United States is largely due to France: the average β for the other three countries is 0.33. Finally, the purpose for including the results with Belgium omitted is that in the sections to follow we focus only on the three larger countries among the four in order to maintain some sense of balance in the relative sizes; given that the averages are unchanged, the omission of Belgium does not appear substantive.

The above results provide evidence that external economies are indeed at work; at the same time, they leave a number of questions unanswered. A question central to consideration of the implications for 1992 is whether there exist any international externalities apart from the country-specific interindustry externalities we picked up in the earlier studies. To the extent that there are, one could expect additional reinforcing cross-effects to be operative through the integration process. Below we provide some preliminary evidence evaluating the extent to which this is true.

3   The model

In section 3, we describe the basic ways through which externalities affect different measures of output, and discuss how studying different levels and dimensions of aggregation can contribute to identifying different types of externalities.

For expository simplicity we assume that there is a continuum of countries indexed by j in $[0, 1]$, and of firms indexed by i in $[0, 1]$. In actual estimation, however, we make the necessary corrections in order to take into consideration that we have a finite (and small) number of sectors (13) and of countries (3).[6]

The basic equation, corresponding to the lowest level of aggregation considered, is simply a generalisation of that presented in C & L (1989):

$$dy_{ij} = \gamma dx_{ij} + \beta dy_j + \theta dy_i + dv + dv_i + dv_j, \tag{3}$$

where dy_{ij}, dy_j and dy_i correspond to value-added growth in industry i in country j, value-added growth in country j, and industry i's value-added growth respectively.[7]

The variable dx_{ij} corresponds to the measure of factor growth described above for industry i in country j. The disturbances dv, dv_i and dv_j are: Europe-wide technology shocks (i.e., West Germany, France, and the United Kingdom in this study), industry-specific technology shocks, and country-specific technology shocks, respectively.[8] Time subscripts are omitted.

The coefficient γ represents the index of returns to scale if industry i in country j increases its inputs in isolation. β represents the increase in factor productivity in industry i in country j when country j's manufacturing value-added rises (see C & L, 1989). Finally, θ represents the increase in factor productivity in industry i in country j, when Europe's industry i expands.

It is instructive at this juncture to consider further the role of the different external effects by addressing different aggregate concepts. The first of these is the concept of an individual country's value-added (the most aggregate concept in C & L, 1989); for all j in $[0, 1]$, country j's (manufacturing) value-added is obtained by summing over i:

$$dy_j = \frac{\gamma}{1 - \beta} dx_j + \frac{\theta}{1 - \beta} dy + \frac{1}{1 - \beta} (dv + dv_j) \tag{4}$$

In our previous work we implicitly assumed $\theta = 0$ and highlighted the fact that there was strong evidence of external effects since country-level estimates were consistently larger than industry-level (within country) estimates of internal returns to scale, an inference based on the fact that all the coefficients are now divided by $(1 - \beta)$, which is less than 1 in the presence of external economies. The extension here takes into consideration the possibility of *international* intra-industry cross-effects; this is reflected in the second term describing the dependence of domestic output on Europe-wide output. Note that this effect is also magnified by the intra-country external effect (through the denominator).

On the other hand, when we aggregate over countries in order to obtain industries' value-added we obtain:

$$dy_i = \frac{\gamma}{1 - \theta} dx_i + \frac{\beta}{1 - \theta} dy + \frac{1}{1 - \theta}(dv + dv_i) \tag{5}$$

for all i in $[0, 1]$. Now θ, the intra-industry externality, is internalised; as industry i expands in all countries they raise each other's factor productivity (if $\theta > 0$) yielding a larger return to scale index.

Finally, when we aggregate over both countries and industries, all externalities are internalised:

$$dy = \frac{\gamma}{1 - \beta - \theta} dx + \frac{1}{1 - \beta - \theta} dv \tag{6}$$

Except for equation (6), efficient estimation of the systems of equations implied by equations (3), (4) and (5) require difficult transformations of the data to compute the correct variance–covariance matrices. Alternatively, all the parameters of main concern can be obtained by a simpler method involving the deviations of each of the variables from its aggregate counterpart. For this we let $\tilde{z}_h \equiv z_h - z$ for any subindex h and variable z. Simple algebra shows that the analogues of equations (4) and (5) are now:

$$d\tilde{y}_j = \frac{\gamma}{1 - \beta} d\tilde{x}_j + \frac{1}{1 - \beta} dv_j, \tag{7}$$

and

$$d\tilde{y}_i = \frac{\gamma}{1 - \theta} d\tilde{x}_i + \frac{1}{1 - \theta} dv_i. \tag{8}$$

The three-equation system described by equation (7), and the thirteen-equation system described by equation (8) are now easily estimated with conventional 3SLS techniques.

Table 3.3. *Summary of European results on international external effects*

	$\pi_{(6)}$	$\pi_{(7)}$	$\pi_{(8)}$
Instrument set #1[a]	1.36	1.23	0.95
	(0.51)[b]	(0.23)	(0.07)
Instrument set #2	1.46	1.14	1.16
	(0.45)	(0.25)	(0.08)

[a] Instrument set #1 includes (1) a constant, (2) the real price of oil in each of the three countries, (3) a country-size weighted index of the real price of oil in the three countries, and (4) the growth in real government consumption in each of the three countries. Instrument set #2 does not include (3).
[b] Standard errors in parentheses.

4   Empirical evidence

As described above, estimation proceeds along three different lines: the aggregate equation (6), the set of three differenced equations that isolate the country-specific shock dv_j captured by equation (7), and the set of thirteen differenced equations that isolate the industry-specific shock dv_i captured by equation (8). From these estimates it is then possible to solve to the implied values for the coefficients of interest: γ, β, and θ.

Table 3.3 presents 3SLS estimates (2SLS in the case of equation (6)) of the reduced form coefficients for the three sets of equations, where $\pi_{(i)}$ corresponds to the single coefficient in equation (i). The coefficients in the sets of equations (7) and (8) are constrained to be equal, so they are better interpreted as reflecting averages than as accurate reflections of reduced form parameters for individual countries or industries. The instruments comprising instrument set #1 include: (1) a constant, (2) the real price of oil in each of the three countries, (3) a country-size weighted index of the real price of oil in the three countries, and (4) the growth of real government consumption expenditure in each of the countries. Instrument set #2 does not include instrument (3).[9]

The parameter $\pi_{(6)}$ is the largest of the three using either set of instruments, though it is also (not surprisingly) the least precisely estimated. This would be the natural ordering in the presence of external economies that are internalised at the aggregate level. Nevertheless, as reduced form coefficients they do not individually provide any direct evidence as to the magnitudes of the three parameters of primary concern. Using their structural form equivalents, however, provides us with three equations and three unknowns. Table 3.4 presents the implied coefficient values calculated using results from different sets of equations.[10]

Table 3.4. *Results from international external effect models*

$$dy_{ij} = \gamma dx_{ij} + \beta dy_j + \theta dy_i$$

	γ	β	θ
Implied Coefficient IV 1	0.89	0.28	0.07
	$(0.36)^a$	(0.25)	(0.36)
Implied Coefficient IV 2	0.96	0.16	0.18
	(0.28)	(0.20)	(0.23)

[a] Standard errors in parentheses.

These results corroborate the previous results as far as internal returns to scale at the industry level are concerned: it appears as though constant or slightly decreasing returns to scale is an accurate description of European manufacturing, when interpreted in an *average* sense. Overall, however, the methodology does not provide much resolving power with respect to the external effects: both are positive and of plausible magnitude, but neither is statistically significant. The addition to the earlier story is the suggestion of a cross-country intra-industry effect, summarised by θ. To clarify the economics of its magnitude, it implies that if the aggregate of industry i's output in the rest of Europe increases by 10%, the output of industry i in the home country will increase by roughly 1 to 2%, with no increase in inputs.

It should be stressed that we view these results as a first step in the process of isolating the role of international external effects. Further work is needed at a more disaggregated level before the various channels can be evaluated in an appropriate way. For example, the added dimension of international inter-industry effects merits further attention. Of course, the previous results in and of themselves suggest an indirect channel for the transmission of cross-country inter-industry effects given that β is consistently positive, and given that aggregate production levels are positively correlated. Additionally, more powerful procedures may yield insights into the question of whether (or how) integration and the magnitude of external effects are related.

5   Implications for 1992

In subsection 2.1 we made the point that when external economies are present, estimation using the Hall methodology of the elasticity of output with respect to weighted capital and labour inputs results in an upward biased estimate of the average degree of internal returns to scale. That is, the resulting coefficient is a composite measure that includes both internal returns to scale and external economies. This does not imply, however, that the estimates underlying the Cecchini Report (1988), principally those of Pratten (1987), are composite measures. The methodology Pratten emphasises is based upon engineering estimates of input–output relationships at a fairly micro level. These estimates involved physical production only, not any of the myriad other activities involved in more comprehensive measures of input and output. Our estimates, on the other hand, are quite comprehensive in that we look at the amount of output historically generated with a given amount of total capital and labour input. Thus, unless all external economies are operative at the level of production activities only, which seems unlikely, it would not be justified to conclude that the Pratten survey of estimates are simply composite measures.

Nevertheless, in the end it is fair to say that our results bear both good and bad news. The bad news is that there appears to be little opportunity, at least in an average sense, for further exploitation of internal increasing returns in European manufacturing (at least in the countries we estimate). We do not, however, intend to suggest that certain subindustries will not enjoy significant gains from internal scale economies, particularly those currently shielded by national procurement policies. Yet, these gains do not show up in our more aggregated measures: our instrumental variables estimates for both Europe and the United States do not allow us to reject constant returns to scale as a description of internal returns at the two-digit level.

The good news is that external economies appear to be present. Unfortunately, our estimates for Europe do not give us enough resolving power to conclude that cross-country intra-industry effects are present. The point estimates are positive and are of a reasonable size, but the standard errors are too large for any statistical significance. Yet, while the evidence for an intra-industry effect is mild at best, there is considerable evidence of inter-industry effects in both Europe and the United States. This external economy brings the elasticity of output with respect to total input up from approximately 1.0 at the industry level to 1.3 at the aggregate level.

Quantification in this context is always a bit loose, but it deserves some attention. The Cecchini Report puts the estimated cost savings from economies of scale in manufacturing production at about 61 billion ECU, or about 35% of the total gains of 216 billion ECU (midpoint estimate). Our estimates suggest that as far as internally exploitable returns to scale is concerned, this 61 billion ECU should not appear in the estimated total gains. As for quantifying the external effects channel of further economic integration, it should be emphasised that any conclusions are necessarily conditional on aggregate activity forecasts, since the measured external effects are functions of those levels of activity. Yet, if we assume a balanced adjustment of activity levels across two-digit sectors equal to the remaining estimate gains of 155 billion ECU – which is generous, since these gains are not all concentrated in manufacturing – inter-industry external effects should contribute 47 billion ECU (155×0.3, which includes feedback theories implied by the aggregate elasticity of 1.3). Therefore, the admittedly rough net adjustment is downward by approximately 14 billion ECU, or about 6.5% of the original total).

There is an additional dimension to the Commission's estimated gains from economies of scale that also deserves emphasis. Take, for example, the automobile industry. The Cecchini Report provides rather more detail regarding potential scale economies for this industry than for the others; after outlining some of the significant barriers inhibiting further integration (pp. 55–6), the Report goes on to highlight the sizeable economies of scale that would result through the further rationalisation of supply industries, most notably automobile platform supply: 'Today 30 platforms are used in the EC for passenger volume cars produced by the six majors, but in the fully integrated market conditions sought for 1992 this could be reduced to 21 involving platform-sharing between several manufacturers'. Our estimation of returns to scale indexes, however, does not span periods of structural shift of the degree implied by the 1992 programme. Since added gains from economies of scale are occasioned by the shift itself, our methodology will overlook this type of gains. In this sense, our adjusted estimate of the gains is on the conservative side.

As a final point concerning the benefits of 1992, our preliminary results hint at the possibility that non-European nations may receive gains through the non-traditional channels of external effects. The first of these could work through the direct channel of intra-industry effects, lowering within-industry costs in other nations as a result of heightened activity levels in Europe. The second, more empirically relevant, effect would work through an indirect channel: to the extent that heightened activity levels in Europe induce the same in other countries, other countries would then benefit from their own country-specific inter-industry economies.

6   Conclusions

In the end our results provide some corroboration for our previous results concerning internal returns to scale and the presence of country-specific inter-industry effects. In contrast, our efforts in measuring cross-country intra-industry effects met with resistance: though the coefficient values suggested the presence of a positive international intra-industry effect, they were too imprecisely estimated to draw any definitive conclusion.

As far as the relevance for 1992 is concerned, it appears as though the results bring both good and bad news. The good news is that positive external effects are operative within Europe; the bad news is that there do not appear to be widespread opportunities for further exploitation of internal economies of scale. A rough calculation suggests that these two adjustments to the Cecchini estimates of gains bring the figure down by approximately 6.5%. On the flipside, some of the benefits grouped under economies of scale by the Cecchini Report are occasioned by the structural shift itself; since these gains would not be picked up by our methodology, they should not be netted from the original number. How much of the original economies of scale gains should be maintained is a question beyond the scope of this study. Finally, it is likely that fuller integration will enlarge external economies, but without a better understanding of their source we feel it is premature to conjecture along these lines.

It is clear that considerable further work towards identifying the source of the externalities is essential before any firm basis for policy recommendations can be established; at the current time any proposals must necessarily be extremely speculative. One quite promising line of research stems from the fact that there remain many more disaggregated levels at which external effects may be operative, which are internalised once the two-digit level is reached. Work along this line may provide some of the resolving power needed to attack more directly the question on many people's minds: where are these external effects coming from?

Data appendix

European data

The data for each country are from the Cronos data bank which is compiled and maintained at the Statistical Office of the European Communities (EUROSTAT) in Luxembourg. The data base includes the requisite series in adequate length for only four of the twelve EC countries: West Germany, France, the United Kingdom and Belgium. For each of these four countries the necessary series are available for all thirteen of the NACE two-digit industries at annual frequency. In the case of West Germany the data spanned the period from 1960 to 1986. In the case of each of the other three countries the data spanned the period from 1970 to 1986.

The relevant series included real gross value-added, real fixed capital, and real compensation of employees (includes gross wages and salaries, employers' actual social security contributions, and imputed social security contributions). The European government consumption expenditure series used as instruments were taken from *International Financial Statistics*. The dollar oil price series was from Hall's (1988a and 1988b) data set, described below. In calculating the rental price of capital we used an economic rate of depreciation of 10%. (Our results are not substantively changed by any realistic departure from this rate.) The real interest rate was calculated from the government bond yield and the change in the CPI index, both from *International Financial Statistics*. We checked some of our results in the case of the United Kingdom using the dividend yield as a measure of the real cost of funds, and found very little effect on the estimated coefficients.[11]

The inadequacy of the data for the other EC countries was due to various reasons. For example, in the case of Italy only five observations were available for regressions since the compensation of employees series included only six observations. While both Denmark and Luxembourg had ten observations each, Denmark was missing data for six of the thirteen industries and Luxembourg for three. The data were even less appealing for the remaining five members of the EC.

US data

The data used are the same as those used in Hall (1988a and 1988b) and were obtained from Hall. They cover the twenty two-digit manufacturing industries for the years 1953–84. The series we use include: Y: real value added in 1982 dollars (*US National Income and Product Accounts*, NIPA), K: net real capital stock (Bureau of Economic Analysis), N: hours of work of all employees (NIPA), and W: total compensation divided by N.

We use different sets of instruments to cope with the correlation between regressors and productivity shocks; however, the basic set of instruments includes: (1) the log difference of the relative price of oil in terms of durables, (2) the log difference of the relative price of oil in terms of non-durables, (3) the rate of growth of military purchases of goods and services in real terms, and (4) a dummy variable with the value of 1 when the president is a Democrat and 0 when he is a Republican. None of the US instruments was used in estimating the European equations.

We construct the rental price of capital as Hall did, following Hall and Jorgenson (1967). The rental price is determined as:

$$r = (\rho + \delta)\,\frac{1 - c - \tau d}{1 - \tau}\,p\kappa$$

where ρ is the firm's real cost of funds, measured as the dividend yield of the S & P 500; δ is the economic rate of depreciation, set to 0.127 (see Jorgenson and Sullivan, 1981, hereafter J & S); c is the effective rate of the investment tax credit (J & S); d is the present discounted vaue of tax deductions for depreciation J & S; and $p\kappa$ is the deflator for business fixed investment (NIPA).

NOTES

1 The literatures mentioned here certainly do not exhaust the list of external economy applications. For example, the area of urban economics has frequently made use of external effects, and in particular agglomeration externalities.

2 See also Lucas (1988) for a model with constant returns to scale at the firm level and externalities due to human capital accumulation.

3 Equation (1) establishes the percentage change in output as the weighted percentage changes in inputs, multiplied by the returns to scale index γ, plus some unobservables. The weights for the inputs are the corresponding cost shares. Some intuition for the appropriate weights being the cost shares comes from cost minimisation. Consider a slight substitution of l for k at the marginal rate of technical substitution (i.e., such that $dy = 0$). Given factor prices, the percentage rise in the total labour bill equals dl and the percentage fall in the total capital bill equals dk. The only way these (typically) different percentage changes can result in no change in total cost is to weight them by their corresponding cost shares. Thus $[\alpha_c dl + (1 - \alpha_c)dk] = 0$ when $[F_l dl + F_k dk] = 0$. These two expressions establish a clear link between the cost share and the corresponding marginal product.

4 The equations also include the real price of oil. Other extensions are also considered without altering in any substantive way the main message of this study.

5 Estimation of equation (1) directly using OLS would surely be inappropriate given correlation between dy and dv_i. Our OLS estimation for both the United States and Europe proceeds by utilising the reduced form equivalent for dy from equation (2), making dx the regressor that picks up the externality. The value for β is then recoverable from the coefficient on dx.

6 That is, where aggregated measures of the levels are not available we build the aggregated measures of the changes using value-added share weights. Moreover, the aggregates are netted of the dependent variable.

7 In ongoing research we also consider an externality coming from overall activity, or a cross-country inter-industry effect. Because of the additional econometric complexities implied by this innovation, and due to the fact that the main message of this study is not substantially affected by this omission, we have opted for centring our discussion in the more concise model described in equation (3).

8 Since our estimation proceeds using instruments independent of technological innovations, we are able to distinguish between externalities and technological progress.

9 Because relative country size changes over the period, the three instruments (2) and instrument (3) are not collinear. For justification of the use of the oil price as an instrument see Hall (1988a) p. 933.
10 Standard errors are computed using the delta method, using the fact that under the null of a correctly specified model, the three blocks of disturbances are orthogonal.
11 The United Kingdom was the only country for which dividend yield was readily available.

REFERENCES

Abbott III, T.A., Z. Griliches and J.A. Hausman (1989) 'Short Run Movements in Productivity: Market Power Versus Capacity Utilization' (mimeo).

Arrow, Kenneth J. (1962) 'The Economic Implications of Learning by Doing', *Review of Economic Studies*, **39**, pp. 155–73.

Caballero, R.J. and R.K. Lyons (1989) 'The Role of External Economies in U.S. Manufacturing', NBER working paper, **3033** (July).

(1990a) 'Externalities and Cyclical Factor Productivity', Columbia University Department of Economics discussion paper series, **467** (February).

(1990b) 'Internal versus External Economies in European Manufacturing', *European Economic Review*, **34** (June) pp. 805–30.

Cecchini, P. (1988) *The European Challenge, 1992: The Benefits of a Single Market*, Brookfield, Vermond: Gower.

Chang, W.W. (1981) 'Production Externalities, Variable Returns to Scale, and Theory of Trade', *International Economic Review*, **22**, pp. 511–25.

Commission of the European Communities (1988) 'The Economics of 1992', *European Economy*, **35** (March) pp. 1–222.

Cooper, R. and A. John (1988) 'Coordinating Failures in Keynesian Models', *Quarterly Journal of Economics*, **103**, pp. 441–64.

Diamond, P. (1982) 'Aggregate Demand Management in Search Equilibrium', *Journal of Political Economy*, **90**, pp. 881–94.

Diamond, P. and D. Fudenberg (1989) 'Rational Expectations Business Cycles in Search Equilibrium', *Journal of Political Economy*, **97**, pp. 606–19.

Ethier, W. (1979) 'Internationally Decreasing Costs and World Trade', *Journal of International Economics*, **9**, pp. 1–24.

(1982) 'National and International Returns to Scale in the Modern Theory of International Trade', *American Economic Review*, **72**, pp. 389–405.

Griliches, Z. and F. Lichtenberg (1984) 'Inter-industry Technology Flows and Productivity Growth: A Re-Examination', *Review of Economics and Statistics*, **66–2**, pp. 325–9.

Hall, R.E. (1988a) 'The Relation Between Price and Marginal Cost in US Industry', *Journal of Political Economy*, **96**.

(1988b) 'Increasing Returns: Theory and Measurement With Industry Data', prepared for NBER Program on Economic Fluctuations (October) (mimeo).

Hall, R.E. and D.W. Jorgenson (1967) 'Tax Policy and Investment Behavior', *American Economic Review*, **57**, pp. 391–414.

Helpman, E. and P. Krugman (1985) *Market Structure and Foreign Trade*, Cambridge, MA: MIT Press.

Herberg, H., M.C. Kemp and M. Tawada (1983) 'Further Implications of Variable Returns to Scale', *Journal of International Economics*, **13**, pp. 65–84.

Jorgenson, D.W. and M.A. Sullivan (1981) 'Inflation and Corporate Capital Recovery', in Charles R. Hutton (ed.), *Depreciation, Inflation and the Taxation of Income*, Washington, D.C.: Urban Institute, pp. 171–237.

Krugman, P. (1990) *Rethinking International Trade*, Cambridge, MA: MIT Press.

Lucas, R.E. (1988) 'On the Mechanics of Economic Development', *Journal of Monetary Economics*, **22**, pp. 3–42.

Manning, R. and J. Macmillan (1979) 'Public Intermediate Goods, Production Possibilities, and International Trade', *Canadian Journal of Economics*, **12**, pp. 243–57.

Marshall, A. (1920) *Principles of Economics*, London: Macmillan.

Ohlin, B. (1933) *Interregional and International Trade*, Cambridge, MA: Harvard University Press.

Pratten, C. (1987) 'A Survey of Economies of Scale', in *Research on the Costs of Non-Europe, Basic Findings*, vol. 2, Brussels: Commission of the European Communities.

Romer, P. (1986) 'Increasing Returns and Long-Run Growth', *Journal of Political Economy*, **94**, pp. 1002–37.'

Smith, A. and A. Venables (1988) 'Completing the Internal Market in the European Community: Some Industry Simulations', *European Economic Review*, **32**, pp. 1501–25.

Stigler, G.J. (1951) 'The Division of Labor is Limited by the Extent of the Market', *Journal of Political Economy*, **59**, pp. 185–93.

Discussion

ALASDAIR SMITH

The authors' earlier work (C & L, 1989, 1990, 1990b) reports a successful search for evidence of external economies. In this study they report on an extension of that search in a new direction. The direction is an important one, as we know from the analytical work of Paul Krugman and Bill Ethier that the policy implications of international externalities can be quite different from those of national externalities. The fact that the present search has been essentially unsuccessful should not discourage further work on the issue.

The objective is to look for evidence that output growth in industry i in country j is influenced by growth in 'world' output of industry i, as well as by the effect of the growth of aggregate output in country j on which the earlier work focussed. The evidence for the intra-industry effect is provided by the fact that there is a slightly different relationship between input growth and output growth at the aggregate level (the reduced form coefficient of 1.36 or 1.46 in Table 3.3) than at the country level (the coefficient 1.23 or 1.14). Unfortunately, the difference is not statistically significant, indeed none of the reduced form coefficients in Table 3.3 is significantly different from 1, so we cannot reject the hypothesis that there are no external effects of any kind and that there are constant returns in production. If one were to take the positive intra-industry effect seriously in spite of the lack of statistical significance, I think that one would want to look more closely at the data for the source of the result. One might have a rather different view of the result if it turned out to derive from particular episodes in particular countries.

Failure to reject the hypothesis of no effect could reasonably be taken as a signal to end the discussion, on the grounds of there being nothing to discuss; or it could be taken as an indication that a further search is worth undertaking. It is, after all, very plausible that there should be the kind of international intra-industry effect for which the authors are searchng. However, it is also plausible that such effects might appear with substantial time lags, and I would like to see that possibility explored.

Caballero and Lyons reports that their earlier results are fairly invulnerable to the existence of errors in their variables, but clearly the same cannot be said of the results here, given the lack of significance, and this is another issue deserving further investigation. The results, as I noted above, cannot reject the hypothesis that there is no inter-industry effect either, and this contrasts sharply with Caballero and Lyons' earlier work where strongly significant effects were found for individual European countries. The explanation for the difference must be that the present study, unlike its predecessors, imposes identical coefficients on all countries. The implication seems to be that this restriction is rejected by the data, and it would be desirable to investigate how the model would behave without the restriction.

One should be very cautious about basing any policy discussion on a model with insignificant coefficients and indications of mis-specification. Caballero and Lyons do not, however, resist the temptation to do so. They conclude that returns to scale are less than assumed in the Cecchini work, but that some of the gains that would thereby be lost from the Cecchini estimates can be restored by allowing for external economies. But the results derived here on returns to scale are results at a two-digit industry level estimated over a time period with a relatively stable market structure. The Cecchini calculations are based on *firm-level* economies of scale as market structure changes in the changed policy environment ushered in by 1992. Whatever one thinks of this argument, it cannot be dismissed on the evidence of data at the level of aggregation used here.

REFERENCES

Caballero, R.J. and R.K. Lyons (1989) 'The Role of External Economies in U.S. Manufacturing', NBER working paper, **3033** (July).
(1990a) 'Externalities and Cyclical Factor Productivity', Columbia University Department of Economics discussion paper series, **467** (February).
(1990b) 'Internal versus External Economies in European Manufacturing', *European Economic Review*, **34** (June) pp. 805–30.

4 The quality and production of textiles and clothing and the completion of the internal market

RICCARDO FAINI and ALBERTO HEIMLER

1 Introduction

Regulations in textile trade have a long history. The first multilateral agreement was signed in 1961; the most recent one will expire in 1991 and is most likely to be renewed. During these thirty years there have been major changes in the pattern of textile trade and production; the issue is whether these changes have gone far enough – or perhaps even in the right direction – for textile and clothing (T & C) trade to return to normal trade practices.

In this respect Italy represents an interesting case. As is well known, the Multi-Fibre agreement (MFA) (i.e., the main instrument of regulation in T & C) is of a discriminatory nature. In open violation of GATT principles, it is indeed applied mostly against exports from developing countries and does not interfere with trade flows among industrial countries. It is likely therefore to favour those countries, such as Italy, which within industrial countries hold a comparative advantage in T & C. As a matter of fact a country like Italy will not only benefit from protection in its domestic market, but also from the fact that other industrial countries restrict their market to developing countries.

It is not, therefore, altogether surprising to find that in Italy T & C continues to maintain a large share of industrial production, employment and exports. Unlike the position in other countries, resources have been attracted into the sector – or at the least have been forced to leave it at a relatively slower rate; adjustment by 'down sizing' (to use Cline's, 1987 terminology) has not been clearly prominent. Under these circumstances it is interesting to assess whether the sector has undertaken some of the required adjustment in other forms. By taking a close look at some aspects of the textile sector in Italy, we can probably get some useful insights as to the possible resistance that a return to normal trade practices in T & C will entail.

54

In this study we focus on one particular aspect of the adjustment to protection (i.e., the choice of quality). Since the seminal papers by Falvey (1979) and Rodriguez (1979), there have been several attempts to assess empirically the relationship between protection and quality choice. The conventional presumption is that protection will increase the quality of imports and may have an opposite effect on domestic output; however, it is not clear that this is what will actually happen, since producers from developing countries and Italian producers do not necessarily compete on the same market. The high-quality market covered by Italian production is probably characterised by a lower elasticity of demand than the one which prevails for standard-quality products in which developing countries specialise. Developing countries are also unable to produce for the high-quality market because of lack of capital (or knowledge), and because their reputation for high-quality production is often low.

An analysis of the quality of competing imports from developed and developing countries can provide some understanding of the average degree of differentiation which characterises different markets and different products. From this evidence, some conclusions on the effect of the existence of MFA on Italian industry can be reached; moreover, the hypothesis that quantitative restrictions lead to a quality upgrading of imported goods can be tested.

The Cecchini Report (1988) suggests that completing the internal market will create little intra-EC trade in T & C. But our 'pure' price indices, which have been corrected for quality differences, suggest substantial remaining price differences between different EC markets, and thus that there is scope for further gain from economic integration.

The study is organised as follows. Section 2 gives a brief description of the world market of T & C products. A presentation of a simple model that highlights the determinants of the decision on quality is made in section 3. The literature on the economic theory of index numbers and its relevance for the measurement of the quality of imported goods is summarised in section 4 and applied to the European market of T & C in section 5. After an analysis of the likely impact of 1992 on the T & C industry (section 6) a brief summary (section 7) concludes the study.

2   Production and trade in textiles and clothing

Increasing restrictions to trade have played a major role in influencing the pattern of world trade in T & C. The MFA, the major instrument for regulating trade in T & C, could not (and perhaps was not intended to) offset the evolution in the pattern of comparative advantages between developing and developed countries. The most remarkable change has in fact been the significant reduction in employment and in the levels of production the sector has undergone in the industrial countries, in particular in Europe. Whereas developing countries' production of T & C products increased from 1973 to 1988 by 50% and by 90% respectively (and by 350% and 600% in South Korea!), over the same period production of the developed countries remained virtually flat. Stagnation of production coupled with increasing productivity took a toll on employment; in 1988 T & C employment in Europe declined with respect to 1973 by 44% and by 39% respectively. The same order of magnitude can be found in the United States (23% and 28%).

A look at trade data reveals even more clearly how, despite the MFA, the pattern of revealed comparative advantages has shifted in favour of developing countries. It also shows that developed countries have managed much better in textiles, where the effect of technical progress and of automation has been much stronger, than in clothing. In 1986 developing countries accounted for 34% of world exports of textiles products, up from 30% in 1980 and 26% in 1973; despite the significant loss in market shares, developed countries continue to be the largest exporters of textiles. A somewhat different picture emerges in clothing. Developing countries are now the major world exporters, accounting in 1987 for 63.4% of world exports, compared to 57.7% in 1980 and only 43.1% in 1973.

Italy provides the exception to the pattern by which developed countries steadily lose market shares in the production and export of T & C products. As a single country Italy remains the first world exporter of clothing, with a world market share of 11%,[1] and the second world exporter of textiles after Germany (but with a much better net export performance). The EC represents the most important market for Italian exports. In all EC countries, with the exception of the United Kingdom, imports from Italy account for more than 20% of total imports both in textiles and in clothing. Long-term trends seem to be favourable to Italian exporters; from 1973 to 1986 Italy increased its market shares in the imports of major EC countries by more than 3 percentage points in textiles and by almost 2 percentage points in clothing. To a large extent, therefore, Italy's performance can be assessed in its ability to penetrate OECD – and, in particular, EC – markets. The displacement of LDC producers from the OECD markets caused by the MFA is therefore likely to have favoured Italian producers. Short-run trends, however, are much less reassuring. Whereas in textiles Italy is still strengthening its market leadership, in clothing the relative position of developing countries is steadily improving. This is reflected in the loss of market shares that Italian exporters have suffered since 1982 in the main EC countries.[2]

Table 4.1. *The coverage and restrictiveness of the MFA*

		Trade coverage ratio		Quota utilisation rate	
		T & C	Clothing only	T & C	Clothing only
EC	1981	40.3	54.4	68.3	68.7
	1987	36.2	46.0	82.1	87.7
USA	1981	52.5	68.3	67.7	72.2
	1987	61.9	76.5	81.8	84.4

Source: Erzan, Goto and Holmes (1989).

The rapidly growing import volumes from developing countries may imply that the MFA was not exceedingly restrictive. Unfortunately information on the utilisation rates of the quotas of the different countries is fairly limited. A recent study (Erzan, Goto and Holmes, 1989) suggests a pattern of increasing restrictiveness of the MFA. Both the average quota utilisation rates in the US and in the EC and the trade coverage ratio (i.e., the share of restricted to total imports from LDCs) in the United States show a significant increase (see, e.g. Table 4.1). Perhaps surprisingly, no noticeable differences seem to emerge in this respect between textiles and clothing. If we take South Korea and Hong Kong as two fairly representative developing country exporters of T & C, we find that textiles are protected as much (and sometimes even more) than clothing in the EC market (see Table 4.2). It is true that in absolute terms the extent of protection (as measured by the trade coverage ratio) was larger in clothing than in textiles (see Table 4.1); yet the fact that textiles restrictions were equally binding suggests that protection was a significant factor, in addition to technical change, in allowing developed countries to strengthen their position in textiles trade.

Increasing restrictiveness did not however, impede the penetration of LDC products in the markets of industrial countries. Cline (1987) suggests that the increase in imports into the United States and the EC in the 1980s can be attributed to the flexibility provided by the rules of the MFA. For example, as already mentioned, exporters can 'swing' some portion of an unused quota of a certain product to replenish a binding quota, or 'carry forward' and 'carry over' unused quotas from different years. Product upgrading provides another way for weakening the restrictive effect of MFA. The quotas are fixed in physical terms and the exporting country can find it advantageous to change the product mix, shifting to products

Table 4.2. *EC quota utilisation rates for selected T & C exports from South Korea and Hong Kong*

		Cotton	Man-made fibres	Knitted goods	Other clothing
South Korea					
	1981	115.0	101.9	98.9	72.7
	1982	115.0	97.0	96.5	67.4
	1983	112.8	83.8	87.6	60.6
	1984	98.4	91.2	81.7	59.4
	1985	102.5	103.9	84.8	54.0
	1986	108.8	107.6	101.1	72.5
	1987	109.3	91.8	95.2	78.8
Hong Kong					
	1981	81.5	67.9	79.5	65.3
	1982	66.5	56.3	76.6	63.2
	1983	98.9	70.5	78.8	66.5
	1984	77.5	58.8	79.9	67.3
	1985	71.7	49.6	74.3	56.4
	1986	102.7	50.3	90.8	68.5
	1987	96.7	60.3	100.7	88.5

Source: World Bank, LFA data base.

of higher quality – that is of higher value-added. In section 3 we will try to provide an understanding of the choice on qualities and some order of magnitude for the product upgrading that occurred in the past decade.

3   The impact of protection on the quality of imports and of domestic production

In section 2 it was shown how both tariff and non-tariff barriers have been applied extensively to limit exports of clothing and textile products from developing into the industrial countries. The importance of tariffs has however, been somewhat declining (even if less for T & C than for other manufacturing products) as a reflection of the various GATT-sponsored negotiated tariff reductions. On the other hand, the extent of non-tariff barriers has become more pervasive, as a result of their increasing coverage in terms of both countries and products. One salient feature of most non-tariff barriers, in particular of those applied in the context of the MFA, is that they consist of quotas on physical units. This would not matter if the retricted good was of an homogeneous quality; if, however, allowance is made for a possible quality differential of the restricted good, then protection is likely to influence not only the quantity (and the price) of such a good, but also the choice of quality. This possibility has stimulated several contributions in the trade literature (see, among others, Swan, 1970; Falvey, 1979; Rodriguez, 1980 and, more recently, Krishna, 1987; Das and Donnenfeld, 1987; Main, 1989).

Most of these approaches share the general presumption that the relative quality of imports will increase in response to quantitative protection. Even if import quality declines (as would occur in Krishna's approach if p_{xq} was greater than zero), domestic production would follow suit. We show below that these results may not hold in a more general model. As a matter of fact, if we posit a more general technology, then a quota may cause the quality of domestic production to increase and the quality of imports to decline. We illustrate this result in the context of a simple duopoly model.

Like Krishna (1987), we rely on Spence's approach to the analysis of quality and assume that the demand price for the duopolistic producer is a function of its own production and quality and of its competitor's production and quality – i.e., for producer 1 we have $p_1(x_1, x_2, q_1, q_2)$. An increase in either producer's output is associated with a lower demand price, whereas a rise in own (competitor's) quality raises (decreases) the price. The duopolist is assumed to maximise:

$$p_1(x_1, x_2, q_1, q_2)x_1 - c_1(q_1, x_1)x_1 \tag{1}$$

The duopolist chooses both output and quality taking its competitor's output and quality as fixed. After omitting for notational simplicity the producer's subscript and letting a subscript indicate now a partial derivative, we find that the two first-order conditions for a maximum are:

$$p_x(\quad)x + p(\quad) - c_x(\quad)x - c(\quad) = 0 \tag{2}$$

$$p_q(\quad)x - c_q(\quad)x = 0 \tag{3}$$

In what follows we abstract from all demand effects (which, as mentioned earlier, played a crucial role in previous models) by assuming that $p_{xq} = 0$. However, we allow for the possibility of a non-constant returns to scale technology and for a possible interaction in the cost function between quantity and quality. More specifically, it is assumed that $c_{xq} < 0$ – i.e., average costs of production decline more rapidly (or increase less sharply) for higher-quality goods. This would occur, for instance, if higher-quality goods required higher fixed costs because (say) of design, product development costs, etc. Consider now the last first-order condition. Suppose that the physical quantity of production increases. This induces a reduction in c_q. Marginal revenue from quality is therefore

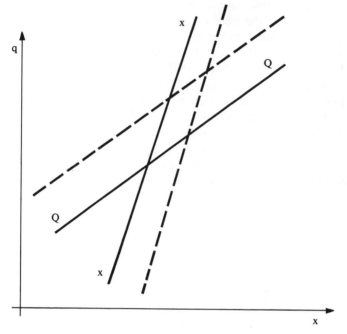

Figure 4.1 The single duopoly equilibrium

higher than its marginal cost and producers will have an incentive to increase quality. Equation (3) therefore implies a positively sloped schedule in the quantity–quality space (*QQ* in Figure 4.1). If we consider the other first-order condition we find that an increase in quality will raise both marginal revenues and marginal costs. By exploiting the second-order condition, we can show, however, that we have again a positively sloped curve (indicated as *xx* in Figure 4.1), whose slope is steeper than the one implied by equation (3).

Suppose now that the (foreign) competitor's output is restrained (say, by the imposition of a quota). As a result, only the second first-order condition (equation (3)), which describes the choice of quality and implies a positive relationship between quantity and quality, will matter for the foreign duopolist. A lower quota level will therefore reduce the quality of foreign production, and will also influence the equilibrium position of the domestic duopolist. Indeed, as a result of the reduction in the other duopolist's output and quality, the curve *xx* for the domestic producer will shift to the right (marginal revenue has increased). Given our assumption that $p_{xq} = 0$, the second schedule *QQ* will not shift provided that p_q

does not change in response to a variation in the quality of production of the foreign duopolist. If, perhaps more reasonably, we assume that the marginal willingness to pay for domestic quality (p_q) is positively affected by a decline in foreign quality, then the QQ schedule will shift upward (p_q increases because of the decline of quantity and quality of foreign production), strengthening the initial effect. Both the quality and the quantity of domestic production will rise in response to a decline in the other duopolist's output. Contrary to earlier analyses, we therefore find that, following the imposition of a more stringent quota, the quality of domestic production increases, while the quality of imports falls. The intuition behind this result is fairly simple. Protection will grant domestic producers a larger market share and provide them, as a result, with an incentive to shift production toward those commodities where increasing (decreasing) returns to scale are more (less) pervasive. Given our assumption that c_{xq} is negative, these happen to be the higher-quality goods.

This very simple model thus highlights the ambiguity of the impact of protection on the choice of quality. It may account for the surprising result (de Melo and Winters, 1989) where the quality of Korean footwear exports was found to decline following the introduction of quantitative restrictions. Of course other explanations, which stress (for instance) the role that foreign exchange targets may play in determining the final outcome (de Melo and Winters, 1989) are equally – or perhaps even more – plausible. The fact remains that it is not possible theoretically to determine in an unambiguous manner the impact of protection on quality choice.

Up to this point, it has been consistently assumed that consumers are perfectly informed about product quality. This assumption, however, is not always tenable and several contributions have explored the implications of the alternative hypothesis where consumers are only imperfectly informed about product quality. For instance Rodrik (1988) shows that the positive effect that the choice of a higher quality level by an individual producer entails will be internalised the more the domestic industry is concentrated. As a result, we should expect that more concentrated sectors would exhibit a higher average level of quality, and Rodrik find encouraging support for this hypothesis from a comparison between the Taiwanese and the Korean case. Of course, trade policy may itself affect the pattern of competition in the domestic industry (Helpman and Krugman, 1989). By increasing the sector's concentration, protection may therefore induce a higher average level of quality in domestic production. It therefore appears that several factors, often moving in opposite directions, are at work to determine the impact of protection on the choice of quality. This theoretical ambiguity can be solved only by empirical analysis.

4   The measurement of the quality of competing imports

Chinloy (1980), Jorgenson, Gollop and Fraumeni (1987) and, more specifically, Aw and Roberts (1988) have distinguished differentiated products according to their quality content without recurring to hedonic equations, which require as a prerequisite a very extensive data set, often impossible to assemble. On the assumption that individual prices of differentiated products differ because of differences in quality, they have utilised the economic theory of index numbers to construct an index of quality.

As Aw and Roberts (1988) acknowledge, import prices vary substantially not only across products within a given industry, but also across supplying countries. Furthermore each supplying country does not necessarily sell the same product to different countries, implying that an analysis of quality upgrading has to take into consideration different products, different supplying countries and different markets. Recent developments in the economic theory of index numbers can be used to construct (for each importing country) industry-level price indices that avoid this aggregation bias.

In recent decades there have been many papers that have approached the theory of index numbers under a new perspective. Following Samuelson and Swamy (1974), the one to one relation between production and utility functions, and the corresponding index numbers, has made index numbers a convenient tool for analysing many phenomena that needed a solid economic underpinning. Diewert (1976) has made a strong case for the generalisation of index numbers; he proved that when the aggregator function provides a second-order approximation to an arbitrary aggregator function, then the corresponding index number is sufficiently general and can be called 'superlative'.

There are two 'superlative' index numbers that are of particular interest, the Fisher Ideal index and the Tornqvist–Theil–Translog index. Diewert (1976) has proved that the Fisher index, which is widely known as the geometric mean of the Laspeyres and the Paasche indices, and which can also be written as:

$$F_{kl} = \{[\Sigma \, S_{li}(Z_{ki}/Z_{li})]/[\Sigma \, S_{ki}(Z_{li}/Z_{ki})]\}^{1/2} \tag{4}$$

where
S_{li} and S_{ki} = value share weights
Z_{li} and Z_{ki} = prices or quantities

is exact for the quadratic mean of an order two aggregator function. Diewert also showed that this aggregator function is flexible, implying that the Fisher Ideal index is superlative and that therefore it differentially approximates to the second order of any other superlative index. The Fisher Ideal index also has the property of being consistent both with a linear aggregator function (perfect substitutability) and a Leontief aggregator function (no substitutability). No other superlative index number has these properties and therefore we decided to conduct our analysis utilising this index rather than the more frequently used Tornqvist–Theil–Translog index.

We assume that in each importing country the consumer is maximising a nested utility function $F(x)$ subject to the expenditure constraint

$$p^T x \equiv \Sigma p_i x_i \le y$$

where $\mathbf{x} \equiv (x_1, x_2, \ldots, x_n)$ is a non-negative vector of quantities of imports and $p \equiv (p_1, p_2, \ldots, p_n)$ is a positive vector of commodity prices and $y > 0$ is expenditure on imports.

The consumer maximisation problem can be divided into two stages: in the first the consumer attempts to minimise the cost of achieving a certain level of utility; in the second stage he chooses the maximum level of utility allowed by his budget constraint. The solution to the first-stage problem defines the consumer cost function C:

$$C(u, p) \equiv \min_x[p^T x: F(x) \ge u, x \ge 0_N] \qquad (5)$$

which under the usual assumptions is assumed to be continuous, concave, linearly homogeneous in p for every u and increasing in u. If F is linear homogeneous in x, the consumer cost function may be written as:

$$C(F(x), p) = F(x)c(p) \qquad (6)$$

where
$c(p) =$ dual unit cost function

The true aggregator function F can be approximated to the second order by a quadratic mean of order two function. The Fisher Ideal quantity and price indices (equation (4) therefore approximates (to the second order) the true ratios of quantities imported and of their unit costs.

Equation (4) can be used to measure the difference in the quantity of the import bundle k and the import bundle l, since the Fisher Ideal index provides a binary comparison between observation k and observation l. However, as Fisher (1922) had already noticed, the index does not satisfy the so-called 'circularity test'. If there is a third observation m, F_{kl}/F_{ml} is not equal to F_{km}. This implies that the ranking of observations is not independent from the order chosen to compare them, the reason being that the bilateral comparisons use information relative to two observations only.

Caves, Christensen and Diewert (1982) introduce the concept of multilateral index numbers which allow for transitive comparisons. Multilateral indices are particularly useful when cross-sectional elements are present; in such a case the time ordering, which is natural for time series comparisons, is no longer valid and transitivity becomes a crucial issue. Caves, Christensen and Diewert (1982) have proposed a Tornqvist–Theil–Translog multilateral index which has also been applied by Aw and Roberts (1988). On the other hand, Drechsler (1973), applying a method already proposed by Elteto and Koves (1964) and Szulc (1964) (the EKS method), proposes a multilateral index where circularity is achieved departing as little as possible from the Fisher Ideal index. Caves, Christensen and Diewert (1982) show that the EKS method provides a second-order approximation to a multilateral translog comparison, therefore assuring flexibility to the index.

The use of multilateral indices is particularly important in the context of international trade data where one wishes to distinguish transactions according to supplying countries and through time. In order to make transitive cross-sectional and time series comparisons the index constructed with the EKS method turns out to be:

$$F_{lm} = \frac{\{[\Sigma S_{li}(Z_{ki}/Z_{li})]/[\Sigma S_{ki}(Z_{li}/Z_{ki})]\}^{1/2}}{\{[\Sigma S_{mi}(Z_{ki}/Z_{mi})]/[\Sigma S_{ki}(Z_{mi}/Z_{ki})]\}^{1/2}} \quad (7)$$

where

S_{ki} = value share weights of the reference observation.

In this case the ratio between F_{lm} and F_{ls} is exactly equal to F_{ms}.

Caves, Christensen and Diewert (1982) and also Aw and Roberts (1988) consider as the reference observation the mean over all observations. In such a circumstance Dinopoulos (1988) observes that these multilateral indices do not maintain the historic fixity of the data – that is, if a new observation is added, then all the calculated indices would differ.

In order to be constructed, these indices further require that all countries trade in the same products. Since we are comparing the price performance of many suppliers of T & C products to that of Italian producers, a natural candidate for the base observation is thus the information on total exports (of T & C products) of Italian producers. The k subscript in equation (3) thus refers to values and prices (or quantities) of Italian exports in the base year, applying the Drechsler (1973) central country solution.

When the multilateral indices are calculated on price data, it is possible to construct industry level indices that differ by importing country and by supplying country, the term of reference always being the price of Italian exports to all countries (which approximates a competitive price for goods of Italian origin).[3]

As suggested by Chinloy (1980), Jorgenson, Gollop and Fraumeni (1987) and applied to import prices by Aw and Roberts (1988), the multilateral price and quantity indices can be used for assessing how the quality of the import bundle varies over time, across supplying and importing countries. One way is to decompose the total quantity of imports into a quality index and an unweighted index of quantity:

$$F(x) = \lambda Q \qquad (8)$$

where

$F(x)$ = index of quantity imported given by equation (4)

λ = index of quality

$W = \Sigma x$ = index of the unweighted total quantity of imports

From equation (8) it can be seen that $F(x)$, the total quantity of imports, can change even if Q, the unweighted quantity, does not change. λ reflects substitution to higher quality (that is, relatively more expensive) products. If quota premia should be present, they would not affect the measurement of λ. The measurement of λ is somewhat arbitrary because prices may rise for many additional reasons other than quality. Nonetheless, since it does not require a very extensive information set, equation (8) may provide some approximate understanding concerning the degree of differentiation of the T & C market in major EC countries.

An alternative is to use equation (6) to create bilateral price indices, $c(p)$, corrected for quality, and to compare these with uncorrected unit value indices, V. Hence:

$$c(p) = V/\lambda \qquad (9)$$

This approach for the measurement of quality is therefore not much affected by quota premia, in that one of the set of observations for such premia will be included in both $c(p)$ and V.

5   International trade data and empirical results

Multilateral price indices have been used for measuring the price and quality of T & C imports of the four major EC countries (Italy, France, Germany and the United Kingdom). T & C are classified according to the NIMEXE classification system which is used for international trade data in the EC; the alternative would have been to utilise the more common

SITC system, which is used for international trade data of the OECD countries, and in UN statistics. However, the level of disaggregation provided by NIMEXE is much larger; NIMEXE has over 1000 products in the T & C categories, while SITC has fewer than 300.

The import supplying countries have been divided into 17 groups:

1   France
2   Germany
3   Italy
4   United Kingdom
5   United States and Canada
6   Belgium, the Netherlands, Denmark and Ireland
7   Spain, Portugal and Greece
8   EFTA countries
9   Yugoslavia and Turkey
10   Eastern European countries
11   Middle East and Mediterranean countries
12   Southern Asian countries
13   Japan
14   Hong Kong
15   South Korea
16   South East Asia
17   Rest of the world

The analysis has been carried out for the four major EEC countries (for the period 1982–7[4]) for 13 chapters of the NIMEXE classification. The results, however, will be presented and discussed for the more common general categories of 'Textiles' and 'Clothing'.[5]

In Tables 4.3 and 4.4 the industry-level unit-value indices for imports of T & C by France, Germany, Italy and the United Kingdom are reported. All values are normalised by the unit value of Italian total exports in 1982 (transformed from fob into cif by multiplying the fob price of every individual product by 1.049, where 4.9% is the share of transport and insurance on the fob value of total Italian imports in 1982). The most evident pattern in Tables 4.3 and 4.4 is that the unit value of Italian imports of T & C is in all years the highest among all importing countries.[6] Again in all importing countries, imports from Southern Asia (i.e., India, Pakistan and Sri Lanka) present the lowest unit values. For textiles, the unit value of Italian exports is 1.19 in 1987 and that of imports from Southern Asian countries is lower than 0.20. The same pattern can be noticed for clothing. The unit value of Italian exports is 1.43 in 1987 and that of imports from Southern Asia is lower than 0.40.

The major supplying countries fall into three groups, based on the level

Table 4.3. *Unit values of imports of textiles products in 1982 and 1987;*
indices, Italian exports 1982 = 1, 1987 = 1.19

Countries of origin	France		Germany		Italy		United Kingdom	
	1982	1987	1982	1987	1982	1987	1982	1987
France	—	—	0.95	1.14	0.75	0.87	0.93	1.01
Germany	0.71	0.81	—	—	0.60	0.69	0.81	0.84
Italy	1.03	1.21	1.16	1.46	—	—	0.87	0.92
United Kingdom	0.79	0.83	0.83	0.89	0.69	0.84	—	—
China	0.40	0.45	0.47	0.23	1.50	1.37	0.20	0.18
South Korea	0.30	0.38	0.34	0.50	0.27	0.24	0.66	0.71
Japan	1.11	2.05	2.09	2.70	1.97	2.51	1.32	1.57
Hong Kong	0.24	0.18	0.31	0.62	1.09	1.40	0.44	0.41
Northern EC	0.75	0.87	0.76	0.76	0.78	0.95	0.65	0.67
Southern EC	0.60	0.65	0.60	0.52	1.02	1.07	0.74	0.83
EFTA	0.64	0.72	0.70	0.90	0.61	0.69	0.73	0.83
Yugoslavia, Turkey	0.39	0.36	0.30	0.33	0.75	0.68	0.26	0.43
Eastern European	0.42	0.20	0.37	0.28	0.42	0.28	0.25	0.33
United States, Canada	0.55	0.36	0.30	0.57	0.50	0.33	0.62	0.68
Latin America	0.67	0.51	0.34	0.35	0.63	0.72	0.48	0.39
Middle East	0.70	0.60	0.52	0.38	1.07	0.94	0.41	0.80
Southern Asia	0.15	0.18	0.18	0.10	0.25	0.14	0.12	0.14
South-East Asia	0.60	0.35	0.43	0.46	0.49	0.46	0.31	0.25
Rest of the world	0.70	0.71	0.61	0.61	1.01	0.85	0.62	0.62

Importing countries

of unit-value indices. EC and (but only for clothing) EFTA countries
present the highest unit values; the United States, Canada and the other
European countries fall into a middle group, while Yugoslavia, Turkey,
Eastern European and the developing countries show the lowest indices.

These unit value indices are not neutralised from differences in commodity prices and differences in the mix of products across countries and
time; they are therefore inherently biased as price indicators. Multilateral
Fisher indices correct for cross-section and time series difference in the
mix of goods supplied.[7] They are reported in Tables 4.5 and 4.6. It can
immediately be seen that the cross-country variation in prices is strongly
reduced when compared to the variation in unit-value indices. Italian
products are no longer the most expensive; in textiles, we can see that
imports from EFTA countries are the most expensive after Japanese
products, and that developing countries continue to supply the least

Table 4.4. *Unit values of imports of clothing products in 1982 and 1987; indices, Italian exports 1982 = 1, 1987 = 1.43*

| | Importing countries | | | | | | | |
| | France | | Germany | | Italy | | United Kingdom | |
Countries of origin	1982	1987	1982	1987	1982	1987	1982	1987
France	—	—	1.46	1.70	1.29	1.69	1.49	1.73
Germany	0.90	1.18	—	—	0.83	1.13	1.14	1.48
Italy	0.83	1.27	1.06	1.38	—	—	1.05	1.52
United Kingdom	0.95	0.89	1.20	1.25	1.59	1.62	—	—
China	0.34	0.34	0.33	0.42	0.54	0.36	0.40	0.38
South Korea	0.71	0.73	0.67	0.69	0.77	0.85	0.69	0.60
Japan	0.58	0.86	1.03	1.17	0.73	0.66	0.74	0.70
Hong Kong	0.72	0.74	0.77	0.78	0.72	0.63	0.61	0.57
Northern EC	0.54	0.66	0.73	0.98	0.46	0.85	0.72	0.89
Southern EC	0.55	0.74	0.71	0.92	0.35	0.44	0.50	0.61
EFTA	1.04	1.05	0.89	1.38	0.76	2.08	0.87	1.54
Yugoslavia, Turkey	0.45	0.59	0.66	0.74	0.41	0.30	0.48	0.48
Eastern European	0.35	0.45	0.56	0.69	0.16	0.21	0.44	0.48
United States, Canada	0.68	0.66	0.97	0.98	0.55	0.36	1.08	0.88
Latin America	0.29	0.30	0.45	0.52	0.75	0.62	0.50	0.37
Middle East	0.55	0.71	0.60	0.85	1.13	1.28	1.18	0.91
Southern Asia	0.23	0.33	0.26	0.32	0.17	0.21	0.50	0.39
South-East Asia	0.75	0.58	0.70	0.57	0.76	0.68	0.70	0.53
Rest of the world	0.48	1.23	0.58	0.73	0.76	0.71	0.54	0.55

expensive items, although charging a price which is only 50% lower than that of the most expensive producer. The same is true for clothing, where Italian products are overtaken by French and German as the most expensive categories.

By comparing unit values and price indices, rates of change also differ. In particular, the dynamics of unit values are usually much stronger than those of the Fisher price indices, because product upgrading is incorrectly interpreted as a change of prices in the calculation of unit values. However, the relative position of the different supplying countries in terms of the Fisher Ideal is very much similar to that found when analysing unit values.

The information on unit values and on the Fisher Ideal price indices can be combined with the equation (4) and provide us, for each importing country, with a measure of the quality of the import bundle of each

Table 4.5. *Multilateral price indices of imports of textiles products in 1982 and 1987; indices, Italian exports 1982 = 1, 1987 = 1.20*

	Importing countries							
	France		Germany		Italy		United Kingdom	
Countries of origin	1982	1987	1982	1987	1982	1987	1982	1987
France	—	—	1.07	1.30	1.14	1.21	1.10	1.19
Germany	0.98	1.13	—	—	1.01	1.14	1.07	1.19
Italy	0.97	1.21	1.06	1.36	—	—	0.91	1.07
United Kingdom	1.12	1.15	1.14	1.18	1.04	1.13	—	—
China	0.60	0.56	0.62	0.57	0.75	0.62	0.48	0.46
South Korea	0.82	0.81	0.69	0.78	0.75	0.66	0.86	0.83
Japan	1.59	1.83	1.85	2.28	1.58	1.44	1.39	1.51
Hong Kong	0.59	0.76	0.79	0.84	1.12	1.21	0.70	0.63
Northern EC	0.81	1.00	0.89	1.08	1.02	1.10	0.90	0.92
Southern EC	0.84	0.94	0.92	1.05	0.93	0.91	0.97	1.04
EFTA	1.12	1.26	1.08	1.34	1.07	1.35	1.12	1.25
Yugoslavia, Turkey	0.66	0.69	0.58	0.61	0.72	0.71	0.53	0.67
Eastern European	0.55	0.55	0.56	0.52	0.88	0.56	0.58	0.59
United States, Canada	1.32	1.15	0.84	1.12	1.07	0.84	0.99	1.02
Latin America	0.82	0.73	0.69	0.64	0.74	0.63	0.84	0.74
Middle East	0.72	0.83	0.80	0.73	0.95	0.80	0.66	0.82
Southern Asia	0.76	0.51	0.64	0.51	0.61	0.56	0.58	0.48
South-East Asia	0.75	0.53	0.68	0.72	0.68	0.67	0.74	0.60
Rest of the world	1.02	1.01	0.90	1.00	1.27	1.01	1.00	0.88

supplying country in each year. Higher (lower) values of the index of quality indicate higher concentration with respect to the quality of total Italian exports in 1982, in the more (less) expensive T & C products. These indices, which are independent of quota premia or of any other imperfection in prices, are reported in Tables 4.7 and 4.8.

In textiles, the quality of Italian and Japanese products is the highest and has remained fairly stable throughout the years. The quality of the products of most developed countries also does not show much variation. As for developing countries, the analysis of the quality content of their production is mixed. South Korea, China and Southern Asian countries improved the quality of their exports to France by 30% while South Korea and Hong Kong improved from 1982 to 1987 the quality of their exports to Germany by 50%. In general, however, the quality of imports from developing countries is much lower than that of imports from Italy.

Table 4.6. *Multilateral price indices of imports of clothing products in 1982 and 1987; indices, Italian exports 1982 = 1, 1987 = 1.22*

	Importing countries							
	France		Germany		Italy		United Kingdom	
Countries of origin	1982	1987	1982	1987	1982	1987	1982	1987
France	—	—	1.52	1.64	1.47	1.74	1.38	1.68
Germany	1.22	1.46	—	—	1.18	1.37	1.09	1.27
Italy	0.86	1.22	1.09	1.33	—	—	1.03	1.25
United Kingdom	1.10	0.85	1.13	1.02	1.38	1.34	—	—
China	0.49	0.46	0.44	0.50	0.68	0.49	0.48	0.43
South Korea	0.67	0.64	0.63	0.63	0.72	0.64	0.61	0.52
Japan	1.00	1.24	0.87	1.15	0.96	1.17	0.69	0.76
Hong Kong	0.70	0.76	0.76	0.72	0.68	0.56	0.64	0.57
Northern EC	0.92	1.02	0.84	1.00	1.41	0.89	0.86	0.96
Southern EC	0.70	0.82	0.67	0.80	0.76	0.91	0.74	0.81
EFTA	1.10	1.16	1.07	1.49	1.35	2.31	1.10	1.49
Yugoslavia, Turkey	0.49	0.54	0.69	0.72	0.49	0.51	0.64	0.56
Eastern European	0.53	0.63	0.53	0.67	0.35	0.40	0.40	0.40
United States, Canada	0.71	0.72	1.95	1.30	0.73	0.58	1.17	1.04
Latin America	0.65	0.81	0.56	0.48	0.66	0.46	0.56	0.44
Middle East	0.63	0.76	0.67	0.76	0.82	0.88	0.88	0.66
Southern Asia	0.56	0.45	0.54	0.44	0.42	0.33	0.46	0.38
South-East Asia	0.61	0.52	0.60	0.52	0.59	0.53	0.58	0.52
Rest of the world	0.85	1.11	0.59	0.54	0.67	0.84	0.67	0.57

This picture is slightly different when the Italian imports of textiles from developing countries are considered (see Table 4.7); these appear to be of a much higher quality, and are competitive with products of Italian origin. These results can be probably explained by the increasing decentralisation of production that has characterised the Italian clothing industry in recent years and that has utilised more and more textiles inputs of foreign origin. It has, however, to be recognised that these results could also be rationalised by the existence of binding constraints to trade.

In clothing, quality upgrading occurs to a greater extent (see Table 4.8). The quality of Italian production improved by 17% from 1982 to 1987. Among the developed countries, Italian products appear to be particularly challenged by those from the United Kingdom, which in general showed a slightly higher level of quality. However, with respect to textiles,

Table 4.7. *Multilateral quality indices of imports of textiles products in 1982 and 1987; indices, Italian exports 1982 = 1, 1987 = 0.99*

Countries of origin	Importing countries							
	France		Germany		Italy		United Kingdom	
	1982	1987	1982	1987	1982	1987	1982	1987
France	—	—	0.89	0.88	0.66	0.72	0.85	0.85
Germany	0.72	0.72	—	—	0.59	0.61	0.76	0.71
Italy	1.06	1.00	1.09	1.07	—	—	0.96	0.86
United Kingdom	0.71	0.72	0.73	0.75	0.66	0.74	—	—
China	0.67	0.80	0.76	0.40	2.00	2.21	0.42	0.39
South Korea	0.37	0.47	0.49	0.64	0.36	0.36	0.77	0.86
Japan	0.70	1.12	1.13	1.18	1.25	1.74	0.95	1.04
Hong Kong	0.41	0.24	0.39	0.74	0.97	1.16	0.63	0.65
Northern EC	0.93	0.87	0.85	0.70	0.76	0.86	0.72	0.73
Southern EC	0.71	0.69	0.65	0.50	1.10	1.18	0.76	0.80
EFTA	0.57	0.57	0.65	0.67	0.57	0.51	0.65	0.66
Yugoslavia, Turkey	0.59	0.52	0.52	0.54	1.04	0.96	0.49	0.64
Eastern European	0.76	0.36	0.66	0.54	0.48	0.50	0.43	0.56
United States, Canada	0.42	0.31	0.36	0.51	0.47	0.39	0.63	0.67
Latin America	0.82	0.70	0.49	0.55	0.85	1.14	0.57	0.53
Middle East	0.97	0.72	0.65	0.52	1.13	1.18	0.62	0.98
Southern Asia	0.20	0.35	0.28	0.20	0.41	0.25	0.21	0.29
South-East Asia	0.80	0.66	0.63	0.64	0.72	0.69	0.42	0.42
Rest of the world	0.69	0.70	0.68	0.61	0.80	0.84	0.62	0.70

production of clothing by developing countries seems to be of a far more homogeneous quality than that of the most successful producers. The range of variation of quality among supplying countries is lower than in textiles, and shows a tendency for reduction. In general, developing countries are improving the quality of their exports to European countries at rates similar to those experienced by Italian producers. South Korea, Yugoslavia and Turkey, the Eastern European countries and (to a lesser extent) Hong Kong, all seem to have strongly ameliorated the quality of their production in recent years. Since constraints from MFA are more likely to have occurred in clothing than in textiles, these results tend to confirm the hypothesis that, at least for these countries, a binding quota leads to quality upgrading. In fact in the case of Italy and (but to a lesser extent) the United Kingdom, where constraints in clothing are likely to have been more binding, the quality of clothing imports from developing

Table 4.8. *Multilateral quality indices of imports of clothing products in 1982 and 1987; indices, Italian exports 1982 = 1, 1987 = 1.17*

Countries of origin	Importing countries							
	France		Germany		Italy		United Kingdom	
	1982	1987	1982	1987	1982	1987	1982	1987
France	—	—	0.96	1.04	0.88	0.97	1.08	1.03
Germany	0.74	0.81	0.97	1.04	0.70	0.82	1.05	1.17
Italy	0.97	1.04	—	—	—	—	1.02	1.22
United Kingdom	0.86	1.05	1.06	1.23	1.15	1.21	—	—
China	0.69	0.74	0.75	0.84	0.79	0.73	0.83	0.88
South Korea	1.06	1.14	1.06	1.10	1.07	1.33	1.13	1.15
Japan	0.58	0.69	1.18	1.02	0.76	0.56	1.07	0.92
Hong Kong	1.03	0.97	1.01	1.08	1.06	1.13	0.95	1.00
Northern EC	0.95	0.65	0.87	0.98	0.33	0.96	0.84	0.93
Southern EC	0.79	0.90	1.06	1.15	0.46	0.48	0.68	0.75
EFTA	0.95	0.91	0.83	0.93	0.56	0.90	0.79	1.03
Yugoslavia, Turkey	0.92	1.09	0.96	1.03	0.84	0.59	0.75	0.86
Eastern European	0.66	0.71	1.06	1.03	0.46	0.53	1.10	1.20
United States, Canada	0.96	0.92	0.50	0.75	0.75	0.62	0.92	0.85
Latin America	0.45	0.37	0.80	1.08	1.14	1.35	0.89	0.84
Middle East	0.87	0.93	0.90	1.12	1.38	1.45	1.34	1.38
Southern Asia	0.41	0.73	0.48	0.73	0.40	0.64	1.09	1.03
South-East Asia	1.23	1.12	1.17	1.10	1.29	1.28	1.21	1.02
Rest of the world	0.56	1.11	0.98	1.35	1.13	0.85	0.81	0.96

countries (in particular from South Korea and from Hong Kong) improved more than in the other European countries.

6   The impact of 1992

Our empirical results provide some useful indications as to the likely impact of the unified European market in 1992 for the T & C sector. Yet some preliminary considerations are in order. Any attempt to assess the effect of 1992 faces a basic difficulty – i.e., that to a large extent such effect will depend on the trade policy stance that the EC adopts, and the latter is very difficult to predict. In what follows, we avoid making projections about the future course of EC trade policy for T & C and consider as a working hypothesis that imports of T & C from developing countries are kept at their present level but, following the dismantling of internal barriers within the EC, national quotas are replaced by an aggregate EC quota.

The impact of even such a limited move may be sizeable on two accounts: (a) the actual opening of domestic markets may weaken existing monopolistic positions held by domestic producers; (b) the abolition of national quotas may involve a redistribution of LDC exports within the EC from presently unconstrained to constrained national markets. Several doubts have been raised about the importance of these two effects. The Cecchini report argues that there are very few remaining barriers to trade in T & C within the EC and that, as a result, the unified market may not lead to much trade creation in that sector. With respect to imports from LDCs, a (1987) GATT report claims that, within the EC, the MFA provision for the almost automatic transfer of unutilised regional quotas from one member state to another has been fairly effective and not much use of Art. 115 of the Treaty of Rome has been made in order to restrict indirect imports from another member state of the products under quotas in a member state. However, as shown in Sapir (1989), the proportion of Art. 115 case acceptances accounted for by the textile sector, while steadily declining since 1979, was still equal to 68% in 1987.

Our results, albeit indirectly, can somewhat clarify both of these issues. First, they allow us to evaluate the importance of discriminatory pricing practices across member states in the EC; price differential may be taken as an indication of monopolistic positions. However, different strands in prices may reflect compositional and quality effects. By controlling for quality we can assess whether price differences are still significant. In this respect, our results suggest that, after controlling for quality differentials, there is evidence of significant price spreads of single EC exporters across several markets. From 1982 to 1987 the coefficient of variation of prices of EC producers in the three markets considered has been fairly constant. However the variability of prices has been much stronger in textiles than in clothing (the coefficient of variation of prices for textiles products was twice as high than that for clothing), implying a much more competitive market in clothing than in textiles (see Table 4.9). A comparison in the size of price spreads between EC and LDC producers provides in turn some indirect evidence of the role that barriers within the EC play in limiting the mobility of imports from LDCs across member states. We find that the variability of prices of T & C products from LDCs are significantly higher than that observed for EC producers. Moreover, while in textiles the difference in the coefficients of variation of prices of LDC and EC imports is very limited, it is very relevant in clothing, suggesting a possible effect on LDC prices of the unequal restrictiveness

Table 4.9. *Average coefficient of variation of import prices on all markets for all years, 1982–7*

Countries of origin	Textiles	Clothing
France	26.7	13.0
Germany	25.1	20.1
Italy	15.8	12.1
United Kingdom	24.1	12.7
China	16.6	82.0
South Korea	7.7	43.8
Japan	35.9	21.2
Hong Kong	10.8	67.7
Northern EC	15.5	10.6
Southern EC	30.2	32.9
EFTA	18.3	13.3
Yugoslavia, Turkey	33.2	45.6
Eastern European	41.7	17.5
United States, Canada	25.2	21.8
Latin America	29.0	25.2
Middle East	27.1	35.5
Southern Asia	34.1	25.1
South-East Asia	13.9	24.9
Rest of the world	16.9	20.3

of MFA quotas among the different countries. In sum, our results indicate that significant price differentials still exist in the EC and that they may be squeezed by the completion of the internal market. Furthermore, if the origin of price differentials of LDC imports is the degree of 'bindingness' of the constraints of the MFA, the abolition of national quotas may be associated with a reduction of the price spreads for LDC imports across EC markets, particularly significant for clothing.

7   Summary and conclusions

The trade literature has recently produced a number of contributions detailing the effect that protection exercises on the choice of quality. The most common result that has been reached is that the quality of production of the constrained country improves with protection. We present a model where this is not necessarily the case, when fixed costs are an important element in production and increasing returns to scale characterise the technology of production of high-quality products. In any case, in order to analyse the choice on quality, it is necessary to provide some quantification of that phenomenon, since not much evidence is available, especially for textiles and clothing.

Recent developments in the economic theory of index numbers can be used to provide an estimate of product quality. We estimated the quality of T & C imports of the four major EC countries with respect to total Italian exports for the period 1982–7. Italy is the major producer of clothing in the world and the second world producer of textiles, so that the decision of considering Italy as the central country of the comparison seems quite natural.

Several results have been reached. Within each industry substantial country specialisation is present. Around a half of unit-values differences among the different supplying countries can be explained by quality differentials. On the other hand, the difference in quality in a time series comparison is much lower, simply because the mix of commodities each single country exports is pretty much stable over time.

If developed and developing countries are compared, a mixed picture emerges. In textiles, the quality of the products of developed countries origin does not change greatly from 1982 to 1987, while the lower quality of the products of developing countries improves for some and remains stable or declines for many others. In clothing, where quotas were more likely to be binding, the process of quality upgrading is stronger. Developing countries tend to export products which are more similar to those in which developed countries specialise, rapidly challenging them in the high-quality segments of the market.

The calculation of quality indices has provided us with 'pure' price indices as well. These in turn were utilised for assessing the extent of price discrimination. In terms of pricing policies of EC producers, our results show the existence of significant price differentials among the different export markets, especially in textiles. The increasing competition brought about by the completion of the internal market will therefore probably tend to eliminate them. On the other hand, pricing policies of LDC producers show much greater variability, both in textiles and in clothing. If these price differences depend upon the degree of 'bindingness' of the constraints of the MFA, the abolition of national quotas associated with 1992 will be a major force for squeezing these substantial price differentials.

However, the possibility of adopting a more liberal posture for the future trade regime in T & C depends, to a large extent, on the adjustment that the sector has already achieved in the EC. Empirical evidence suggests that, in particular for textiles, adjustment has already gone a long way. In some countries, in particular in Italy, the T & C industry seems to have benefited most from the MFA. In such cases it is not possible to rely on export performance as an indicator of successful adjustment insofar even as the latter can be attributed to the operation of the MFA. It would have been interesting in this respect if we could have related the pattern of Italian penetration in T & C in OECD markets to the geographical structure of protection. Unfortunately data on quota utilisation rates for individual EC importing countries were not available and it must be left to future research to determine whether Italian exports performed better in the most constrained markets.

As an indicator of the viability of the T & C sector, we have relied in this study on the degree of product differentiation proxied by the relative level of quality. Theoretical analyses often suggest that quantitative restrictions on imports will result in a process of quality upgrading for imports and quality downgrading for domestic production. Paradoxically, this may allow foreign producers to penetrate market segments which used to be dominated by domestic firms and as a result compound the problems for domestic producers of adjusting to the return to a liberal trade regime. We found, however, that, even for a purely theoretical point of view, the impact of protection on the choice of quality is quite ambiguous and that, under not unreasonable conditions, protections may lead instead to a downgrading of import quality and a quality upgrading for domestic production.

Our empirical results confirm the difficulties in establishing a link between protection and quality choice. Both textiles and clothing appear to enjoy a substantial level of protection in the EC. However, whereas in textiles there still exist significant differences in quality levels between (say) production in Italy and Japan on the one hand, and in LCDs on the other, in clothing the range of variation in quality among supplying countries is lower and furthermore shows a declining trend. This may suggest the existence of more severe adjustment problems in clothing than in textiles; yet the pattern of quality upgrading in clothing in LDCs may simply reflect a process of decentralisation, where developed countries producers have moved some of their production facilities to developing countries.

NOTES

We would like to thank Alan Winters for his stimulating suggestions which substantially improved the content and the presentation of the study. We are very grateful also to Emanuele Fusco for having written the computer programs necessary for the computations, to Ombretta Main and Willem Molle for valuable suggestions on an earlier draft, and to Paula Holmes and Richard Hughes for help with the data.
1 Italy is the first exporter only when Hong Kong exports are netted out of reexports.

2 In any case it has to be recognised that a sizeable proportion of Italian imports of clothing is constituted by products designed by Italian producers.

3 Since import data are reported as cif while export data are fob we homogenised the price of import and exports by assuming for all Italian exports a constant markup for transportation and insurance costs. Furthermore, since Italian producers export world-wide (that is, in restricted and in not restricted countries) it is implicitly assumed that the (possibly unobserved) quota premia are irrelevant over the aggregate.

4 Although the analysis has been carried out for six years, the results reported in all tables refer to 1982 and 1987 only. More detailed tables are available, on request, from the authors.

5 As is well known, the Fisher Ideal index is not consistent in aggregation. The aggregates for Textiles and Clothing therefore have been reconstructed from the original disaggregated data.

6 The only exceptions are imports of textiles from Japan, which have a much higher unit value, the reason being a very specialised production in high-price products.

7 Obviously these indices cannot eliminate the effect on prices of possible quota premia, or any other difference in prices originating from different market structures.

REFERENCES

Aw, Y.B. and M.J. Roberts (1988) 'Price and quality level comparisons for US footwear imports: An application of multilateral index numbers', in Robert C. Feenstra (ed.), *Empirical Methods for International Trade*, Cambridge, Mass.: MIT Press.

Caves, D.W., L.R. Christensen and E.W. Diewert (1982) 'Multilateral comparisons of output, input and productivity using superlative index numbers', *The Economic Journal*, **92**, pp. 73–86.

Chinloy, P. (1980) 'Sources of quality change in labor input', *American Economic Review*, **70**, pp. 108–19.

Cline, W.R. (1987) *World Trade in Textiles and Apparel*, Washington, D.C.: Institute for International Economics.

Das, S. and S. Donnenfeld (1987) 'Trade policy and its impact on quality of imports', *Journal of International Economics*, **23**, pp. 77–95.

Diewert, E.W. (1976) 'Exact and superlative index numbers', *Journal of Econometrics*, **4**, pp. 115–45.

Dinopoulos, E. (1988) 'Comment' (to Y.B. Aw and M.J. Roberts, 1988), in Robert C. Feenstra (ed.), *Empirical Methods for International Trade*, Cambridge, Mass.: MIT Press.

Drechsler, L. (1973) 'Weighting of index numbers in multilateral international comparison', *The Review of Income and Wealth*, **19**, pp. 17–34.

Elteto, O. and P. Koves (1964) 'One index computation problem of international comparison' (in Hungarian), *Statistikai Szemle*, **7**.

Erzan, R., J. Goto and P. Holmes (1989) 'Further evidence on the restrictiveness and other trade effects of MFA on exports of developing countries in the 1980's', paper presented at the workshop on International Textile Trade, the MFA Agreement and the Uruguay Round (Stockholm).

Falvey, R. (1979) 'The composition of trade within import-restricted product categories', *Journal of Political Economy*, **87**(5), pp. 1105–14.

Fisher, I. (1922) *The Making of Index Numbers*, Boston: Houghton-Mifflin.

GATT (various years) *International Trade*, Geneva: GATT.

(1984, 1972) *Textiles and clothing in the World Economy*, Geneva: GATT.

Goto, J. (1988) 'Effects of the Multifibre arrangements on developing countries', PPR working papers, **102**, Washington, D.C.: World Bank.

Helpman, E. and P. Krugman (1989) *Trade Policy and Market Structure*, Cambridge, Mass.: MIT Press.

Jorgenson, D.W., F.M. Gollop and B. Fraumeni (1987) *Productivity and U.S. Economic Growth*, Amsterdam: North-Holland.

Krishna, K. (1987) 'Tariffs versus quotas with endogenous quality', *Journal of International Economics*, **23**, pp. 97–122,

Main, O. (1989) 'Trade restrictions under vertical differentiation', University of Sussex (mimeo).

Melo, J. de and A. Winters (1989) 'Price and quality effects of Ver's – revisited', PPR working paper, **216**, Washington, D.C.: World Bank.

Rodriguez, C.A. (1979) 'The quality of imports and the differential welfare effects of tariffs, quotas and quality controls as protective devices', *Canadian Journal of Economics*, **12**, pp. 439–49.

Rodrik, D. (1988) 'Industrial organization and product quality: evidence from South Korean and Taiwanese exports', NBER working papers, **2722**.

Samuelson, P.A. and S. Swamy (1974) 'Invariant economic index numbers and canonical duality: Survey and synthesis', *American Economic Review*, **64**, pp. 566–93.

Sapir, A. (1989) 'Does 1992 come before or after 1990? On regional versus multilateral integration', CEPR discussion paper, **313**.

Swan, P. (1970) 'Durability of consumption goods', *American Economic Review*, **60**, pp. 844–94.

Szulc, B. (1964) 'Indices for multiregional comparisons' (in Polish), *Przeglad Statystyczny*, **3**.

UNCTAD (1983) *Manual for Textile Negotiators vol. 1*, Geneva: UNCTAD.

Discussion

WILLIAM MOLLE

1   Introduction

The analysis of the effects of 1992 on the structure of production and on the patterns of internal and external trade is an important topic. It can best be tackled by looking at specific industries (see, for example,

Emerson *et al.*, 1988; Molle, 1990). Faini and Heimler (hereafter FH) have picked for their analysis the textile and clothing (T & C) industry. This is generally recognised as a politically very sensitive sector and is still important, particularly in the southern member states of the EC.

2   1992: internal trade changes

1992 means the taking away of the remaining barriers to trade between EC member states. In T & C this applies notably to non-tariff barriers, the most obvious one being the quotas, that are set within the Multi-Fibre Agreement.

In the recent past, some authors have tried to measure the impact of 1992 on the T & C industry. First to be mentioned in this respect is the IFO/PROMETEIA (1988) study on the cost of non-Europe. The conclusion of this study was that only marginally enhanced competition would result from the further opening of markets, because of the advanced state of integration already achieved. The specific influence of the abolition of the country-specific import quotas of the MFA and its replacement by EC-wide quotas would not have much effect either; Davenport (1990) estimates it to be some 3–5% of total imports. The impact is likely to be concentrated on Southern European countries.

In view of the theme of the 1990 conference, my first point of critique of the FH study is that it does not go into these effects more deeply: although of limited importance overall, these effects may in fact be sufficiently important for specific countries as to warrant further analysis.

3   External trade aspects

The many (IFO/PROMETEIA; Davenport; Ackermann and Lindquist, 1989) who agree that the effects of 1992 *per se* are fairly limited for the T & C sector, also agree that a very significant impact may be expected from the changes in the external trade regime of the EC (Uruguay Round) that are likely to follow the 1992 programme: the further liberalisation of the MFA is likely to accelerate the external pressures from developing countries on EC producers.

The usual response of home producers to such a challenge by imports is twofold:

1   The cutting of cost. There are several ways to do this: in the T & C sector flexible automation for cutting capital cost is well known; for labour, cost cutting by relying on the black market ('sweat shops') is one method increasingly observed in the EC, outward processing or

the relocation of parts of the production process to low-wage countries being another.

2   The selection of market niches, where price is not the main factor so
competition from low-wage producers is less. In T & C many firms
have moved into such well-known niches as products for which
design, fashion, etc. are the most important motives for consumer
choice.

FH isolate the latter point for further analysis (calling it the 'upgrading of
quality'!). They ask themselves the question whether this phenomenon
has occurred in the EC in the recent past, and take into account that
external producers, faced with quantitative restrictions, may also have
followed a strategy of upgrading quality.

4   Quality upgrading patterns

By examining the concept of 'quality', FH enter an area full of snares and
pitfalls. They know this, and prepare for a safe journey through the land
by devising a method based on indices. My point is that this method does
not do away with the basic difficulty that 'quality' in this way is measured
only by the price. Now prices of imports do not differ only due to
differences in quality of the goods; they may differ also due to differential
responses to exchange rate movements, trade restrictions, quota premia,
income distribution patterns, tastes, and market structures.

The results of the FH analysis suggest that – notably for clothing – EC
producers have followed a strategy of quality upgrading, and that this has
been even more the case for producers in developing countries. There is,
however, a great variety of developments in sub-markets (import and
export countries), making it difficult to come up with generally valid
conclusions.

Combining the presence of question marks in the methodology with the
absence of exclamation marks in the result of the FH analysis, we may say
that a firm conclusion as to quality upgrading is not warranted without
providing further evidence on the order of magnitude of the influence on
prices of the other factors such as market structures, etc.

5   What lessons for the future?

The patterns revealed by the FH analysis for the period 1982–7 do not
seem to give many leads for the analysis of a possible impact of a further
liberalisation of external EC trade in the future, as no explanatory model
including trade measures as independent variables is estimated. I think

that FH therefore, wisely abstain from making a forecasting exercise on this point in the final part of their study.

FH are less reticent as to the relevance of their findings for the impact of 1992. I have, however, some problem with their approach here also. First, they give no explanatory factor of the price differences between different markets of the same EC exporter they observe in their figures. Second, they give no idea of the degree to which the 1992 programme will affect these factors (and, hence, the observed price differences). In the absence of such an analysis, an indication of the significance of the reported price differences in T & C in the light of 1992 could have been given by a comparison of T & C price differences with those prevailing in markets that are competitive, and where it is known that 1992 will have almost no impact. Unfortunately these indications are also not provided.

6   Conclusions

To summarise I feel that the FH analysis is very interesting but would gain considerably if a number of elements could be added that are essential for an assessment of the changes in the trade and production patterns (and welfare) of the T & C sector that can be expected to follow from the completion of the 1992 programme. The same holds for the analysis of the potential impact of the changes in the EC external trade regime.

REFERENCES

Ackerman, C. and J. Lindquist (1989) '1992: implication of the EC textile and clothing industry', *Textile Outlook International, The Economist* Intelligence Unit, **21**, pp. 82–95.

Davenport, M. (1990) 'The external policy of the Community and its effects upon manufactured exports of the LDC's', *Journal of Common Market Studies*, special issue on 1992 and the developing countries.

Emerson, M. *et al.* (1988) 'The economics of 1992; an assessment of the potential effects of completing the internal market of the European Community', *European Economy*, **35**(3), pp. 5–22 (now also *The Economics of 1992*, Oxford: Oxford University Press).

Molle, W. (1990) *The Economics of European Integration; Theory, Practice, Policy*, Aldershot: Dartmouth.

IFO/PROMETEIA (1988) 'The cost of non-Europe in the textile clothing industry', *Research on the Cost of Non-Europe, Basic Findings*, **14**, Brussels: IFO-PROMETEIA).

5 Competition and imports in the European market

ALEXIS JACQUEMIN and ANDRÉ SAPIR

The completion of the European Community's (EC) internal market, by removing the barriers still affecting intra-EC trade, is expected to strengthen European competition. Theoretical and empirical research indeed suggest that import competition within European markets imposes a major constraint on domestic firms' price–cost margins. According to the European Commission's assessment of the economic effects of the 1992 liberalisation programme (Emerson *et al.*, 1988), import competition should result in significant welfare gains.

The removal of intra-EC trade barriers is also likely, however, to generate merger activities within the Community. And although concentration of European industries may prompt greater efficiency and raise social welfare, it may also create or foster dominant positions that lower overall welfare. The completion of the internal market may, therefore, require the strengthening of European competition policy in order to ensure a lowering of domestic prices (see Jacquemin, 1990, for an analysis of mergers and competition policy in the EC). But lowering trade barriers against imports from the rest of the world could be as powerful a tool for promoting competition in the EC, or at least play an essential complementary role. Indeed, there are various arguments suggesting that the trade discipline effect of extra-EC imports on European market performance could be stronger than that of intra-EC imports. A further opening of the EC to world imports could then lead to an even stronger competitive impact on EC industrial price–cost margins than expected from the 1992 programme alone (see Sapir, 1989, for a discussion of the external impact of 1992 and the possible links between internal and external trade liberalisation).

This study investigates empirically the relative trade discipline effect of intra-EC and extra-EC imports on European industry performance. Section 1 examines the theoretical arguments for the role of trade – actual and potential – as a discipline factor and the possible influence of the

82

origin of imports. Section 2 sets out the econometric model and presents the empirical results. Sectoral aspects of trade liberalisation are discussed in section 3, and the study concludes in section 4 with some policy comments.

1   Imports as a discipline factor[1]

Various oligopoly models have incorporated international factors and derived equilibrium relations where the role of imports has been identified (see Caves, 1980; Jacquemin, 1982). The Cournot–Nash case with homogeneous products is straightforward in establishing a negative association between the domestic price–cost margin (or, with constant variable costs, the industry rate of gross return on domestic sales) and the rate of imports. Contrasting with this model – in which each firm calculates its optimal policy, treating parametrically the outputs of rivals (importers as well as domestic producer) – the dominant firm solution concept distinguishes between a fringe of small firms, taking price as parametric, and members of the dominant group of firms, taking the fringe's reaction function as parametric. Here again the various equilibria show a negative link between the price–cost margin and the rate of imports. However, the interpretation of the variables depends on the identity of the members belonging respectively to the dominant group and the competitive fringe. If foreign producers are treated as the competitive fringe and the domestic industry forms the cartel, trade as a discipline factor results immediately. But when foreign producers form the dominant group (usually of multinationals) and domestic firms make up the fringe, discipline is imposed not by imports but by domestic firms' output (Geroski and Jacquemin, 1981). This leads to a basic implication: the causal mechanism which produces a profit–import penetration joint outcome depends on the nature of imports and the origin of trade discipline.

Concerning the *nature of imports*, several characteristics can have a restrictive impact on the strength of this pro-competitive force. One important one is the existence of product differentiation at the level of firms and industries, implying the existence of monopolistic competition. Such a differentiation tends to reduce the intensity of import discipline and to favour intra-industry trade. Also important is the role of intra-firm trade that happens when the domestic firms have a multinational base that controls imports, therefore increasing the prospects of effective market cartelisation. A second factor is the role of barriers to trade, natural or artificial. Among natural barriers are the existence of important scale economies, differences in preferences, habits, language, culture and incomes, that can all limit the entry of imports. Artificial barriers include various tariff and non-tariff obstacles, such as technical norms and public procurement policies. More generally, trade as a discipline factor depends on the elasticity of foreign supply with respect to domestic price, this elasticity being only partly reflected in the current flow of imports since the latter can be restricted by various barriers to entry.

Concerning the role of the *origin of trade discipline*, the question to be tested is the possibility that the discipline of extra-EC imports on European industrial profitability is stronger than the discipline of imports of Community origin. *A priori* reasons for this expectation can be based on evidence that European integration has been associated with a growing complementarity and division of labour as well as intra-industry and intra-firm trade (Greenaway, 1987). The relative intensity of intra-EC imports of an intra-industry nature is one factor that could explain the lesser competitive effect of intra-EC imports. A second factor is the existence of market behaviours successfully adopted within the Common Market in order to reduce competition: various horizontal and vertical agreements, dominant positions leading to price leadership, intra-firm trade, and corresponding restrictive practices including transfer pricing. These behaviours can be expected to be less effective for imports coming from the rest of the world.

To identify the specific role of imports on industrial price–cost margins, it is finally necessary to disentangle it from the role of various industry features, such as capital intensity and the technological factors that are also expected to be related to profitability.

Given the non-uniqueness of market behaviour and structure configurations, a single model encompassing all possible alternatives cannot be provided. Our empirical analysis seeks merely to determine the extent to which intra- and extra-EC imports exercise a different impact on profit margins, taking into account the interaction between profits and imports. The flow of imports will be endogenously determined by various structural features of industry, and these features must also be expected to exercise an impact, differing according to the origin of imports. In addition, the effects of trade on industry performance will vary according to the source of the threat or discipline.

2   Methodology and empirical results

To test whether intra-EC imports and extra-EC imports exert a differing disciplinary effect on price–cost margins, we postulate the following structure–performance equation:

$$\pi_i = \alpha + \beta_1 m_i^i + \beta_2 m_i^e + \sum_{j=1}^{J} \gamma_j X_{ij} + \epsilon \tag{1}$$

where i denotes the industry, π is the price–cost margin, m^i is intra-EC import penetration, m^e is extra-EC import penetration, X is a set of variables characterising industry performance, and ϵ is a zero mean, normally distributed error.

Ordinary least-squares (OLS) estimation of equation (1) is likely to lead to biased and inconsistent parameter estimates since, as noted by Pugel (1980), there is a simultaneity problem in considering price–cost margins and import penetration. Not only is import penetration expected to influence (negatively) profits, but profits are also expected to influence (positively) import penetration: the higher the level of profits in a domestic industry, the greater the attraction for foreign firms to supply the domestic market. An instrumental variable procedure is used to solve this simultaneity problem, whereby m^i and m^e in equation (1) are replaced by their estimated values.

The empirical analysis is conducted for the 'big Four' EC member states i.e., France, Germany, Italy, and the United Kingdom) for 1983. It relies on a recently developed data bank allowing research to be conducted on European industry at a somewhat disaggregated level (three-digit NACE) that distinguishes over 100 manufacturing sectors.

Profitability, the dependent variable of the structure–performance equations, is the price–cost margin, defined as value-added at factor cost minus payroll cost divided by total sales. It is computed as an average of three years centred on 1983.

Following the conventional literature on industry performance, we associate the level of price–cost margins with a number of variables reflecting industry structure and conduct, including import competition. As discussed in section 1, above, this study distinguishes two separate effects of trade on profitability: the effect of actual imports and the effect of potential imports. In both cases, a further distinction is made between intra-EC and extra-EC imports. Actual import competition is measured by means of *import intensity*, defined as the ratio between imports and apparent consumption. The potential pressure of imports is measured with the help of existing trade barriers. *Non-tariff barriers* (NTBs) that affect intra-EC trade are captured by two dummy variables, which take the value 1 for sectors characterised, respectively, by strong NTBs and medium NTBs, and 0 for other sectors. These two variables were constructed on the basis of a study by Buigues and Ilzkovitz (1988), identifying the most fragmented EC markets.[2] Barriers against extra-EC imports are reflected by the *common external tariff*, measured by the ratio between the amount collected by Belgian customs and the value of extra-EC imports. On the basis of our earlier discussion, we expect that import intensity will have a negative impact on price–cost margins, with a stronger effect on extra- than intra-EC imports. By contrast, trade barriers (both NTBs and the external tariff) are expected to reinforce the market power of domestic firms and, hence, to be positively associated with profitability.

The remaining explanatory variables of the industry–performance equations are traditional indicators of structure and conduct: the extent of industry demand, the importance of economies of scale, the intensity of R & D and the degree of product differentiation. The rate of growth of consumption in OECD countries is used to identify *areas of fast growing world demand*; this variable is expected to exert a negative influence as market growth facilitates entry. As regard to *economies of scale*, we have used British data on the output achieved in each industry by the largest plants which account for 50% of total output; large-scale economies are likely to have positive impact on profitability as it is positively correlated with concentration, and may also reflect barriers to small-scale entry.[3] The intensity of R & D is measured by the ratio between R & D staff and total staff. R & D activities are clearly important to maintaining profitability in an international context, as world-wide competition is increasingly technological. *Product differentiation* is captured by dummy variable which takes the value 1 for consumer goods and 0 otherwise. We expect that the intensity of competition will be reduced, and profits increased, by greater product differentiation.

Finally, as is customary in studies that employ the price–cost margin to measure profitability, the *ratio of capital to revenue* is included among the independent variables, in order to correct for sectoral differences in capital intensity.

The regression analysis covers all the available observations ($n = 258$), which are obtained by pooling the observations for each of the 'big Four' countries;[4] the pooling was necessary because several explanatory variables were missing for some industries in some countries. However, preliminary testing of the data indicated the necessity of introducing *country dummies* in order to capture differences in profitability among the four large EC members in 1983 not accounted for by the other explanatory variables.

The results of the profit regression appear in Table 5.1. This reports on the instrumental variable estimation of structural equation (1).[5] The estimates of the coefficients are generally consistent with our expectations and the summary statistics (R^2 and F) are relatively high. Trade barriers, economies of scale, R & D, and product differentiation are all conducive to a high level of price–cost margins. In contrast, the intensity of imports and the growth of demand tend to impose a constraint on profitability. The estimates also indicate that industries in Italy and the United

Table 5.1. *Regression analysis of determinants in EC industrial price–cost margins*

Constant	15.780
	(10.07)*
Intra-EC imports	0.075
	(0.54)
Extra-EC imports	− 0.431
	(− 3.61)
Intra-EC: strong NTBs	2.717
	(2.37)
Intra-EC: medium NTBs	0.718
	(0.68)
Common external tariff	0.184
	(1.67)
Demand growth	− 0.365
	(− 2.07)
Economies of scale	18.049
	(2.63)
R & D	0.413
	(4.27)
Product differentiation	2.899
	(2.22)
Capital–revenue ratio	17.564
	(0.85)
France	1.623
	(1.01)
Italy	4.407
	(4.62)
United Kingdom	3.317
	(4.42)
R^2 (adjusted)	0.333
F	10.89

* Figures in brackets are t-statistics.

Kingdom had significantly higher price–cost margins than German industries.

The major result of the study concerns the respective roles of intra-EC and extra-EC imports. The estimates reveal that only extra-EC imports exert a significant disciplinary effect on price–cost margins. Intra-EC imports seem to exert no disciplinary effect at all. Another interesting result concerns the potential effect on price–cost margins of removing the common external tariff and intra-EC trade barriers. As far as the latter effect is concerned, the estimated coefficients show that potentially important barriers to trade within the EC do indeed protect European producers and, consequently, raise their profit margins. However, such protection is limited to those sectors subject to the highest NTBs.[6] In the study sample, the average price–cost margins for these sectors is about 19%, three percentage points higher than in other sectors. The estimated regression coefficients suggest that the removal of internal barriers would reduce price–cost margins by about 15% in the sectors presently affected by strong NTBs.

3   Sectoral aspects of trade liberalisation

Increased competition in the European market will produce not only efficiency gains, but also adjustment costs. In order to make the gains possible, policy measures need to be devised to reduce the costs. In this respect, a possible distinction could be made between traditional and high-tech sectors. In the *traditional sectors*, specialisation is based on comparative advantages and production is undertaken by a large number of firms. In the *high-tech sectors*, on the other hand, there are significant economies of scale, learning and scope, and the competition is between a limited number of large firms. If products are differentiated, trade remains largely within the same industry and can be increased by competition. Conversely, if products are homogeneous, competition results in an expansion in production in certain firms and certain countries, and in a contraction of activity – or even closures – in others.

For the first type of sectors, a better world-wide division of labour is desirable, although it may lead to considerable structural adjustment costs, especially in certain labour-intensive industries. Empirical studies of the textiles and clothing sector, for instance, suggest that the removal of tariff and non-tariff barriers would enhance the welfare of developing countries and industrialised nations, but by bringing about important costs of adjustment to labour.

As far as the high-tech sectors are concerned, open policies towards the outside world are also desirable as they will improve efficiency in production by lowering unit costs, reducing the threat of monopoly power on the domestic market and extending the product range. Such policies may, however, also facilitate the creation of global dominant positions and the transfer of monopoly rents to specific oligopolists and countries. Empirical studies suggest that in sectors such as aviation or electronic components, strategic commercial policies can secure net gains for those who initiate them, but often at the expense of the rest of the world. In view of the possible gains in terms of national – and sometimes even international – welfare, it is inevitable that the authorities, already under pressure from various lobby groups, will be tempted to have increasing recourse to such policies. This risk is especially great in the present climate of drift towards the formation of economic blocs and the adoption of non-cooperative attitudes. While a simultaneous process of internal and external liberalisation of the single market is a source of increased potential benefits, these can thus materialise only if there is consensus as regards the long-term outlook and the accompanying policies to be adopted, both internally and externally.

For the traditional sectors, there must be acceptance of a gradual shift in specialisations and methods of production, in order to create a worldwide division of labour in line with the dynamics of comparative advantage. Far-reaching structural adjustment policies must be implemented at the sectoral level, designed to encourage rather than to hinder change. This will involve either pulling out of certain areas, or retargeting production towards the upper end of the market. These policies are particularly urgent in southern Europe, where adjustments have been very limited despite the increasing competition from developing nations in labour-intensive activities which these countries face.

In high-tech sectors, a policy of international consultation should be implemented to ensure genuine world-wide cooperation and avoid the pitfalls of bilateralism or anti-competitive behaviours. Here, too, urgent action is called for, since Europe's relative position in growth sectors has slipped in recent years, constrasting with the particularly effective export policies conducted by Japan and the newly-industrialised countries of South-East Asia. There must be no retreat into isolation; on the contrary, an outward-looking strategy must be developed in conjunction with the liberalisation of the internal market.

The message that emerges from this analysis is clear: in both the traditional and the high-tech sectors, it is important for the Community to supplement and balance its trade concerns with longer-term structural policies, which alone will ensure that its international relations are based on stable multilateral cooperation.

4 Concluding comments

This study has argued that extra-EC imports already exercise a strong disciplinary effect on European industry, and that further external liberalisation would be helpful in reinforcing such an effect, especially given the oligopolistic nature of most sectors presently subject to the highest EC internal barriers. In the first part, an empirical model to measure the relative strength of import discipline of European industrial price–cost margins has been developed; a general result is that both potential and actual competition induced by imports prove to be effective in the narrowing of such margins. Trade discipline also proves to vary not only according to different features of industry but also according to the origin of imports: only extra-EC imports were found to exercise a significant impact.

The liberalisation of the European market will indeed increase the competitive pressure on European industry and exert a constraint on the exercise of market power. A main competitive pressure today comes from the discipline imposed by extra-EC imports and tomorrow will come from the removal of intra-EC barriers to potential competition. Concerning the second effect, a recent study by Neven and Röller (1989) suggests that the elimination of these barriers should increase extra-EC more than intra-EC imports. Hence, even in the case of potential competition, the main pressure could come from the rest of the world rather than from within the Community itself. External trade liberalisation is, however, far from being a perfect substitute for domestic competition and could even have perverse effects – for instance, when a small number of foreign firms dominate the market (see Ross, 1988, for a theoretical treatment of this issue). Although the EC should use multilateral trade negotiations to strive towards freer trade in order to complement its 1992 programme, it should thus also set up a strong competition policy.

The second part of the study has presented a strategy for making acceptable such dual (internal and external) liberalisation, that distinguishes between traditional and high-tech sectors. It is argued that combining the completion of the internal market with a further opening of it to the rest of the world will result in further efficiency gains compared to the single strategy of suppression of internal trade barriers. At the same time, however, external liberalisation in traditional as well as high-tech sectors could lead to further adjustment costs that would require appropriate international cooperative policies.

NOTES

We are grateful to Isabelle Pouplier for excellent research assistance. We also wish to thank Victor Ginsburgh, Victor Norman, Pier Carlo Padoan, Lars-Hendrik Röller, Khalid Sekkat and Alan Winters for helpful comments and suggestions on earlier drafts.
1 Section 1 and part of section 2 are based on Jacquemin and Sapir (1990).
2 This study uses two indicators of market fragmentation. This first is a set of eight trade barriers: technical standards and regulations, public procurement, administrative barriers, frontier formalities, differences in VAT and excise duties, transport regulations, capital market controls, and implementation of Community law. The second is a measure of price discrepancies between member states.
3 Recent studies suggest that, contrary to traditional wisdom, concentration as

such is not generally correlated with price–cost margins (see Schmalensee, 1989). Our own data do not allow us to use concentration over a sufficiently large sample; nonetheless, a simple correlation analysis over a reduced set of observations shows a rather strong link between concentration and economies of scale.

4 All (processed) agricultural sectors have been omitted from the sample because profitability there was thought to be conditioned by a rather different set of factors than is the case for manufacturing industries.

5 The exogenous variable used in the instrumental variable estimation are, in addition to those reported in Table 5.1, transportation costs and human capital (see Jacquemin and Sapir, 1988, for the definition of these two variables).

6 According to Buigues and Ilzkovitz (1988), these sectors include activities with important public procurement features (such as boilermaking, railway equipment, and shipbuilding). The removal of these barriers should result in a significant lowering of price–cost margins.

REFERENCES

Buigues, P. and F. Ilzkovitz (1988) 'Les enjeux sectoriels du marché intérieur', *Revue d'Economie Industrielle*, **45**.

Caves, R. (1980) 'Symposium on International Trade and Industrial Organization', *Journal of Industrial Economics*, **29**, pp. 113–218.

Emerson, M. (1988) *The Economics of 1992*, Oxford: Oxford University Press.

Geroski, P. and A. Jacquemin (1981) 'Imports as a competitive discipline', *Recherches Economiques de Louvain*, **47**, pp. 197–208.

Greenaway, D. (1987) 'Intra-industry trade, intra-firm trade and European integration: Evidence, gains and policy aspects', *Journal of Common Market Studies*, **26**, pp. 154–72.

Jacquemin, A. (1982) 'Imperfect market structure and international trade: Some recent research', *Kyklos*, **35**, pp. 75–93.

——(1990) 'Horizontal concentration and European merger policy', *European Economic Review*, **34**, pp. 539–50.

Jacquemin, A. and A. Sapir (1988) 'International trade and integration of the European Community: An econometric analysis', *European Economic Review*, **32**, pp. 1439–49.

——(1990) 'The discipline of imports in the European market', in J. de Melo and A. Sapir (eds), *Trade Theory and Economic Reform – North, South and East*, Oxford: Basil Blackwell.

Neven, D. and L.H. Röller (1989) 'European integration and trade flows', Fontainebleau: INSEAD (mimeo).

Pugel, T.A. (1980) 'Foreign trade and U.S. market performance', *Journal of Industrial Economics*, **29**, pp. 119–30.

Ross, T.W. (1988) 'On the price effects of mergers with free trade', *International Journal of Industrial Organization*, **6**, pp. 233–46.

Sapir, A. (1989) 'Does 1992 come before or after 1990? On regional versus multilateral integration', in R. Jones and A.O. Krueger (eds), *The Political Economy of International Trade*, Oxford: Basil Blackwell.

Schmalensee, R. (1989) 'Inter-industry studies of structure and performance', in R. Schmalensee and R. Willig (eds), *Handbook of Industrial Organization*, Amsterdam: North-Holland.

Discussion

PIER CARLO PADOAN

This study reconsiders the traditional argument that imports deliver a competitive effect to a national economy by lowering profit margins, and applies it to the creation of the European Internal Market (EIM). From this argument the authors draw the policy implication that lowering trade barriers against imports from the rest of the world could be a powerful tool for promoting competition within the European Community (EC). Hence, internal and external liberalisation in the EC should be pursued jointly to reinforce the effects of the creation of the EIM.

The study first considers the theoretical aspects in some detail and then provides some empirical support; the conclusions the authors draw, however, are somewhat more cautious than their opening statements. Following the structure of the study, I shall first consider the theoretical aspects and then the empirical ones, and suggest additional caution in deriving straightforward policy implications.

1   The theoretical framework

The main theoretical point in the literature is that there is a negative relationship between domestic price–cost margins and the rate of imports. Such a relationship, however, apart from the Cournot–Nash case, is not always straightforward if one distinguishes between a dominant group of firms and a competitive fringe. If this is the case Geroski and Jacquemin (1981) consider three different possibilities: (a) domestic firms are in the dominant cartel while foreign firms are the competitive fringe; (b) the opposite situation, foreign firms make the cartel while domestic firms compose the competitive fringe; (c) a mix of the two possibilities. In case (b) imports do not represent a discipline on domestic firms; indeed not only is the direction of discipline reversed but its extent is 'inversely associated with import penetration' (Geroski and Jacquemin, 1981, p. 200). One of the major theoretical issues is hence not whether imports are a discipline factor, but rather who disciplines whom in international markets. The answer clearly depends on the industry structure, and on the nature of imports.

A second theoretical point relates to the method of deriving the relationship between discipline and import penetration. As Geroski and Jacquemin (1981) suggest profitability, domestic concentration, and import shares should be jointly determined – i.e., a multi-equation approach should be followed. If a single-equation approach is followed it might be dangerous to derive simple causal relationships between imports and profit discipline.

One final comment in this section relates to the impact of exchange rates changes on industrial behaviour. Recent developments in the literature on exchange rate pass-through and pricing to market (see, e.g., Baldwin, 1988; Dixit, 1987; Baldwin and Krugman, 1986; Froot and Klemperer, 1989) suggest that exchange rate expectations are very important in determining pricing and profit policies. Froot and Klemperer (1989), for instance, show that expected earnings from investment aimed at increasing market shares depend on whether exchange rate changes are expected to be permanent or transitory. Similarly, pricing policies can either be aggressive (i.e., prices in the currency of the importing country are lowered when the exchange rate appreciates) or passive (i.e., prices in the currency of the importing country are not changed), depending on the judgement on the nature of the exchange rate movement. Obviously the discipline effect would, accordingly, be different.

This point is quite relevant to the argument investigated by Jacquemin and Sapir, as they discuss the possible discipline effect on EC firms coming from non-EC imports, and it suggests (at least) one possible policy implication. External trade liberalisation could produce different discipline effects according to European exchange rate policy – i.e., the degree of global monetary coordination.

2 Empirical aspects

The empirical test of the argument is based on a structure–performance equation (equation (1)). While this follows a well consolidated literature one general comment on the approach is required. As recalled above, the theoretical literature calls for a simultaneous determination of import shares, profit margins and concentration, consequently one would expect a multi-equation simultaneous approach to be followed also in empirical analysis.

Turning back to the estimated equation, the crucial parameters are β_1, the parameter which relates profits to intra-EC import penetration and, especially, β_2, the parameter which relates profits to extra-EC import penetration. Geroski and Jacquemin (1981) suggest caution in the interpretation of the parameter associated with import penetration as an indicator of discipline, as such a parameter does not clearly identify the basic conduct of the industry and it is not possible, therefore, to determine who is disciplining whom. However, with a somewhat different explanation, which should be mentioned by the authors, the coefficient can be taken as a measure – but not as an explanation – of discipline.

The joint determination of import penetration and profit margins implies a simultaneity problem which is solved through 2SLS techniques. As already mentioned, given the specification of the theoretical model, simultaneous estimation techniques would be better suited and provide greater consistency between theory and empirical testing.

Let us now take a look at the empirical results. Extra-EC imports are significantly negatively correlated with profits and the size of the parameters is roughly the size suggested by Geroski and Jacquemin (1981). However non-tariff barriers to trade do seem strongly to influence imports, while country dummies hint at important national differences. This last point leads to the following question. Is data limitation so bad that the same exercise cannot be carried out at a national level?

A further point relates to the use of R & D expenditure as a proxy for technological competition effects. While the R & D variable is significantly related to profits one should look at the effects of the other main variable influencing technological competitiveness (namely, patents), perhaps through a technology index which includes both input and output technology variables as in Fagerberg (1988).

3   Sectoral aspects of trade liberalisation

This is a somewhat looser and less well argued part of the study. It contains policy recommendations based on the distinction between traditional and high-tech sectors. This distinction is used to warn of the need for a more cautious strategy of liberalisation. While traditional sectors could incur relevant adjustment costs after liberalisation, Jacquemin and Sapir maintain that lowering barriers in high-tech sectors requires 'consensus as regards . . . long-term outlook and the accompanying policies' and 'international consultation . . . to ensure genuine world-wide cooperation' (pp. 88 and 89). While I agree that a closer look at accompanying competition and industrial policies should be taken, I fail to see the link with the analysis in the previous paragraphs. How does import discipline influence different industrial sectors, apart from the industry structure argument recalled above? A better understanding of the argument could benefit from a closer empirical look. This, in turn, could be better carried out by choosing an industry classification more detailed with respect to the high-tech–traditional distinction followed in the study. One possibility is to consider a macro-sectoral classification following Pavitt (1984), which includes four sectors for manufactured goods: traditional, specialised suppliers, scale-intensive and science-based. This classification is more helpful in determining the influence of different structural determinants of competitiveness, and hence of import discipline.

4 Concluding comments

The general conclusions of the study are much more cautious than one would expect from its opening lines. I share this cautious approach and conclude by reiterating two caveats. The theory of import discipline, as it stands, remains ambiguous as to who is disciplining whom, and by how much. External trade liberalisation is far from a perfect substitute for domestic competition, and could even lead to perverse results. While the EC should exploit the opportunity afforded by the Uruguay Round – as the authors suggest – to complement the EIM programme, it should also define an effective competition policy and appropriate cooperative agreements to deal with adjustment costs.

REFERENCES

Baldwin, Richard (1988) 'Hysteresis in import prices: the beach-head effect', *American Economic Review*, **78**.

Baldwin, Richard and Paul Krugman (1986) 'Persistent trade effects of large exchange rate shocks', NBER working paper, **2017**.

Dixit, Avinash (1987) 'Hysteresis, import penetration and exchange rate pass-through', Princeton University (mimeo).

Fagerberg, Jan (1988) 'International competitiveness', *Economic Journal*, **98**, pp. 355–74.

Froot, Kenneth and Paul Klemperer (1989) 'Exchange rate pass-through when market shares matter', *American Economic Review*, **79**, pp. 637–54.

Geroski, Paul and Alexis Jacquemin (1981) 'Imports as a competitive discipline', *Recherches Economiques de Louvain*, **47**, pp. 197–208.

Pavitt, Keith (1984) 'Sectoral patterns of technical change. Towards a taxonomy and a theory', *Research Policy*, **6**.

6 The structure and determinants of East–West trade: a preliminary analysis of the manufacturing sector

DAMIEN J. NEVEN and LARS-HENDRIK RÖLLER

1 Introduction

Since the autumn of 1989, important political changes have taken place in eastern European countries and in the USSR. These changes are far from completed and much uncertainty remains with respect to the speed at which reforms will proceed, as well as to the content of the reforms. However, it is uncontroversial at this point to presume that some form of a market system for goods and factors will be established and that trade between eastern European countries and the rest of the world is likely to be liberalised. In this study, we shall assume that this reform has indeed been implemented and we shall focus on its consequences for western European countries. We will try to assess how the liberalisation of trade will affect the EC countries and whether the '1992' programme of integration could be jeopardised by such liberalisation.

The consequences for western Europe of liberalising trade with the East are, in principle, relatively straightforward (see Smith and Venables, 1988, or Norman, 1989): as barriers to trade between the East and western Europe are removed, one can expect that the comparative advantage between the East and western Europe will be further exploited and accordingly that inter-industry trade will develop between the two areas. Between countries having similar factor endowments, one can also expect that scale economies will be further exhausted and hence that intra-industry trade will increase. In order to assess the consequences of trade liberalisation with the East for western Europe in terms of exports potential, competition from imports and associated restructuring, a useful approach will thus consist of trying to assess the comparative advantage of eastern Europe which is currently unexhausted, as well as the potential for further intra-industry trade.

A significant part of the benefits associated with the '1992' programme will also stem from a better exploitation of the comparative advantage of the southern European countries within the EC, namely Portugal, Spain and Greece (see Neven, 1990 for an estimate of these gains). These countries have a relatively large endowment of labour and should therefore benefit from further specialisation in labour-intensive commodities. In turn, northern European countries will specialise further in capital- and human capital-intensive commodities; given their modest size, relative to the North, southern European countries should still appropriate most of the benefit from specialisation. The potential conflict between the 1992 programme and trade liberalisation with the East could then rise to the extent that the eastern European countries share many characteristics in terms of factor endowments with the southern EC members. From the prospective of southern European countries, the simultaneous liberalisation with the East and the South would reduce the extent to which specialisation could occur and the extent to which factor prices could be expected to change. The benefits from EC integration in the south would thus be reduced.

The likelihood of actually realising the potential benefits of integration might also be affected; the process through which comparative advantage in the South will actually be exploited could indeed be somewhat jeopardised. The reallocation of resources across industries associated with the exploitation of comparative advantage will require investments which in many cases would be undertaken more effectively by northern European companies – i.e., through foreign direct investment. If a premium is attached to foreign direct investment in the East, the process of restructuring in the South could be impaired. Such a course of events is thought to be particularly likely as far as German companies are concerned: given the political and economic links between West Germany and the East, German companies might give a premium to investment in the East.

Needless to say, the simultaneous liberalisation of trade with the East and the South can only benefit the northern European countries, given that the scope for specialisation and changes in factor prices will be enhanced in the North. The unskilled labour force should, however, be expected to lose out in those countries.

To sum up, this study will try to identify the comparative advantage of eastern European countries and thereby characterise the trade that will take place between the East and western Europe. We proceed by analysing the factor content of the actual trade between the East and Western Europe, which should 'reveal' such comparative advantage. As mentioned above, whether a conflict can arise for southern EC members between the implementation of the 1992 programme and trade liberalisation with the East will depend on the relative labour endowment and comparative advantage of eastern Europe. Our analysis of the comparative advantage revealed in East–West trade will thus shed some light on the issue of whether the 1992 programme could be jeopardised by East–West trade liberalisation.

The study is organised as follows. In section 2, we provide a brief description of trade patterns in manufactures between the East and Western Europe; we will characterise these trade patterns in terms of direction and size. In section 3, we will look more specifically at revealed comparative advantage between the northern European countries on the one hand and eastern and southern European countries on the other (presuming that the revealed comparative advantage is a good guide to the actual one). In section 3, we explicitly compare intra-industry trade indices between North–East and South–North trade. In section 4, we present an econometric study of the trade flows between Germany, France, Italy and the United Kingdom on the one hand and the COMECON countries on the other. The objective of this study is to explain actual trade balances at the industry level, in terms of a variety of variables, including the factor intensity of production in those industries. A summary of results and some conclusions will follow in section 5.

2   Trade patterns between western Europe and COMECON

In section 2, we shall describe the trade flows in manufacture between the western European countries, which include eleven EC countries (Belgium and Luxemburg being taken together) and five EFTA members, and the European COMECON countries as a block (that is, East Germany, Poland, Bulgaria, Albania, Czechoslovakia, Hungary, Romania, Yugoslavia and the USSR). We obtained data from the OECD on exports and imports as recorded in the Western countries, at the three-digit level of the ISIC industrial classification, for the period 1960–87.[1] In what follows, we shall focus on three dimensions of East–West trade, namely the evolution of trade balances, the relative importance of Western countries as markets and sources of supply for COMECON and finally the relative importance of COMECON trade for Western countries. At the outset, an important caveat is in order. Quite to our surprise, there is no data available on trade flows between East and West Germany. The appropriate information is, so it seems, not communicated to the OECD (or the EC) by the West German authorities. At the same time, these trade flows are likely to be fairly large. When making comparisons between western countries in terms of their respective trade flows with the East, the absence of intra-German trade flows should be kept in mind.[2]

First, with respect to trade balance (as a percentage of total exports), we observe that the trade balance of most western European countries with

Table 6.1. *Importance of western countries for the East*

	Market share of exports			Market share of imports		
	1975	1980	1987	1975	1980	1987
Austria	5.32	6.07	8.17	3.85	4.15	5.42
Belgium–Luxemburg	3.27	3.30	2.05	3.35	2.83	2.53
Finland	4.89	7.04	11.29	4.31	3.44	3.82
France	10.44	11.78	6.94	9.64	10.34	8.03
Federal Republic of Germany	31.63	29.72	28.93	27.17	28.60	27.22
Italy	10.66	9.33	9.43	10.47	12.37	9.68
Netherlands	2.68	3.34	2.69	4.66	4.04	3.77
Sweden	3.69	3.06	3.02	4.31	3.44	3.82
Switzerland	3.42	3.21	5.27	2.44	2.39	2.73
United Kingdom	5.31	6.04	4.24	9.55	7.11	7.33

COMECON has deteriorated since 1975 (for the sake of brevity, the data is not reported here). Most of the deterioration actually occurs after 1983 and in some cases, the deficit is now substantial. This timing suggests that the deterioration is probably due to the fall in the price of oil in the early 1980s, which has reduced the foreign exchange earnings of COMECON countries, and of the USSR in particular; facing a sharp reduction of oil exports, COMECON countries have presumably reduced their imports of manufactures. Interestingly, Finland, Austria and Germany have a surplus with COMECON, which is stable over time. This patterns might simply reflect the geographical (and cultural) proximity of these countries with the East. Alternatively, it could possibly indicate a conscious policy on behalf of COMECON of favouring those suppliers (i.e., of not restricting imports from those sources).

Table 6.1 assesses the relative importance of western countries as markets and sources of supply for COMECON. The left-hand side of Table 6.1 presents the market shares of the various European countries in the total exports of the main non-communist trading partners of COMECON (EC, EFTA, Japan and the United States), to the COMECON market, for 1975, 1980 and 1987. Similarly, the right-hand side of Table 6.1 presents the market shares of European countries in the total imports from COMECON to its main trading partners. The first observation is that the FRG has about one-third of the export as well as the import market with COMECON. Of course, this does not imply that the FRG is going to keep this relative dominance *vis-à-vis* the East, but it says something about the relative starting position, and may be more

Table 6.2. *Importance of the East for western countries*

	Share of exports to COMECON			Share of imports from COMECON		
	1975	1980	1987	1975	1980	1987
Austria	21.54	15.68	10.65	5.01	4.53	3.93
Belgium–Luxemburg	3.78	2.59	1.36	1.69	1.31	1.26
Denmark	3.99	2.43	1.76	2.9	2.30	2.24
Finland	24.44	21.48	17.87	6.41	7.06	5.43
France	6.32	5.05	2.57	2.70	2.39	1.90
Federal Republic of Germany	9.85	6.63	4.53	4.83	4.24	4.00
Greece	12.12	8.27	3.70	5.01	8.63	4.57
Ireland	1.51	1.41	0.73	1.34	0.78	0.94
Italy	9.17	5.44	4.55	4.41	3.96	3.30
Netherlands	3.21	2.92	1.87	2.00	1.71	1.62
Norway	4.43	3.05	1.85	2.37	2.13	1.66
Portugal	2.52	2.36	1.10	0.92	1.17	0.69
Spain	3.91	3.26	1.79	3.02	1.59	1.27
Sweden	6.76	4.73	2.45	3.57	3.31	2.56
Switzerland	7.77	5.24	4.35	2.24	1.71	1.36
United Kingdom	3.89	2.92	1.67	2.61	1.75	1.59

relevant in the short to medium run. Focusing on exports, we observe that a number of countries experience a decline in their market share; this is the case for Belgium, France (with a decrease of some 30%), Sweden, the United Kingdon, Germany and Italy (a 10% fall). Countries which experience a rise in their market shares include Finland (some 130% increase), Austria (up by some 50%) and Switzerland (54%). Finally, the Netherlands maintains a more or less constant market share.

Next, we observe that Belgium, France, Italy, Netherlands, Sweden, Finland and the United Kingdom experience a decline in their relative importance as import markets from COMECON. Germany and Switzerland tend to absorb a constant share of COMECON imports, whereas Austria takes an increasing share.

On the whole, the geographical pattern of trade with COMECON has tended to change, away from the EC countries and in favour of Finland and the alpine EFTA countries. For our purpose, it is particularly significant that the EC has become less important, both as a supplier to COMECON and as a market for COMECON.

Table 6.2 presents the exports to (imports from) COMECON for the western European countries, as a percentage of their total exports (imports) for 1975, 1980 and 1987. We observe that the eastern European countries are not very significant export markets for most Western countries; only in Finland and Austria do total exports to the East represent more than 10% of total exports (in 1987). More importantly, the relative importance of the East as an export market has tended to decline over time: except for Finland (where the decrease is less pronounced), the share of western countries' exports to the East has declined by some 50% since 1975. Looking at imports from the East, a similar pattern emerges: the COMECON countries are a relatively less important source of supply than they were 15 years go. By comparison with the fall in export shares, the fall in import shares is however less pronounced (as would be expected, given the trend in trade balances described above).

On the whole, we find that eastern trade is rather unimportant for most European countries, and particularly small for EC countries. To the extent that the effects of trade liberalisation would presumably take some time to come through, this evidence therefore suggests that, at least initially, the overall consequences of the Eastern European liberalisation on Western Europe should not be overestimated.

3 Factor intensity of trade with COMECON

The objective of section 3 is to assess the comparative advantage of COMECON countries as a block relative to western European countries. A standard approach to assess comparative advantage would consist of estimating differences in factor prices and productivity across countries. Such an approach is unlikely to be successful for eastern European countries for at least two reasons. First, reliable information on factor prices and productivity is hard to come by. Second, in the absence of well organised labour and capital markets in the East, recorded factor prices might not be very meaningful. An alternative approach to assessing comparative advantage would be to estimate differences in factor endowments. Such an exercise is again likely to be difficult because of a shortage of reliable data. Finally, comparative advantage can also be estimated from actual trade flows; the factor content of trade flows will indeed 'reveal' the comparative advantage underlying actual trade. This revealed comparative advantage will provide insight into the effect of trade liberalisation only to the extent that the revealed advantage is a fair guide to the actual comparative advantage. This would also be a natural priority for market economies. To the extent that trade in COMECON countries has been 'managed' away from what comparative advantage would dictate, revealed comparative advantage with COMECON might have to be interpreted rather cautiously; it is, however, unlikely that revealed comparative advantage will be totally misleading: it would be irrational on the

Table 6.3. *Composition of exports, % of total exports*

	1	2	3	4	5
Austria	3.56	9.96	2.66	28.21	55.61
Belgium–Luxemburg	4.39	14.18	0.68	26.18	54.56
Denmark	9.16	10.82	1.11	4.83	74.07
Finland	6.45	3.61	10.66	26.89	52.39
France	3.72	7.07	2.05	18.12	69.04
Federal Republic of Germany	3.60	13.27	2.45	16.90	63.77
Greece	33.10	13.81	14.33	19.94	18.82
Ireland	59.95	5.99	1.51	19.94	18.82
Italy	2.24	14.72	3.32	19.28	60.44
Netherlands	17.92	11.79	1.94	3.91	64.44
Norway	8.30	6.93	0.34	49.69	34.74
Portugal	39.03	11.33	13.54	5.06	31.04
Spain	3.79	8.31	0.79	30.32	56.80
Sweden	4.17	5.99	0.22	21.80	67.81
Switzerland	1.56	3.48	0.32	2.50	92.13
United Kingdom	2.82	11.00	0.82	11.53	73.92

1 = Natural resources
2 = Average labour–capital
3 = Labour-intensive
4 = Capital-intensive
5 = Human capital-intensive

part of central planners managing trade in Eastern Europe to try to export commodities for which they have a comparative disadvantage.

As mentioned above, our data uses the three-digit ISIC industrial classification (29 industries). We have sorted out these industries into five categories according to their factor intensity. The classification of industries that we use can be found in Neven (1990) and it contains the following classes: industries intensive in natural resources, industries with an average labour and capital intensity, industries highly intensive in labour, industries highly intensive in capital and industries with a high content of human capital. The classification of the 29 ISIC industries into these five classes is presented in Appendix B.

Table 6.3 presents the allocation of the total exports of each western European country to COMECON over the five categories of industries for 1987; the commodity composition of imports is presented in Table 6.4. Table 6.5 presents, for each category of industries, the net exports of each western European country as a proportion of its total trade (sum of exports and imports) with COMECON.

Focusing first on trade in commodities intensive in natural resources, we

Table 6.4. *Composition of imports, % of total imports*

	1	2	3	4	5
Austria	23.17	14.89	5.96	20.04	35.94
Belgium–Luxemburg	19.61	17.17	8.02	11.53	43.67
Denmark	16.79	14.84	15.61	17.86	34.89
Finland	4.15	18.78	7.09	13.56	56.42
France	12.92	20.10	11.32	9.66	46.00
Federal Republic of Germany	13.49	19.94	28.89	11.67	25.02
Greece	18.54	8.31	1.16	23.07	48.92
Ireland	13.95	14.49	11.71	8.91	50.94
Italy	23.29	16.89	5.64	22.00	32.19
Netherlands	16.42	18.53	23.52	11.04	30.48
Norway	4.89	29.91	8.27	9.65	47.28
Portugal	3.90	11.74	0.30	22.26	61.80
Spain	17.58	10.08	1.59	16.83	53.91
Sweden	14.17	20.87	7.84	14.06	43.06
Switzerland	18.90	29.36	9.90	12.00	29.84
United Kingdom	16.05	20.65	8.18	12.86	34.54

1 = Natural resources
2 = Average labour–capital
3 = Labour-intensive
4 = Capital-intensive
5 = Human capital-intensive

observe that the exports of such commodities out of Ireland, Portugal and Greece account for some 35 to 60% of their total trade. A significant, albeit lower, share of imports from COMECON in Ireland and Greece also occurs in those commodities (to such an extent, however, that Greece has a trade deficit). The Netherlands has also a surprisingly large share of (bilateral) trade in this category. Finally, we observe that the other countries have a larger share of imports than exports and substantial trade deficits in those commodities; this is somewhat surprising, given the widespread belief that the agricultural sector in eastern Europe is somewhat ineffective and that shortages occur in food markets. The evidence presented here might suggest that food production is directed towards exports markets, despite shortages in the domestic economy; it also accords with the intuition that the specialisation of imports in such commodities is somewhat higher in Switzerland and Austria, which should indeed have a relatively low endowment of natural resources.

Turning to the second category of industries, with an average capital and labour content, we observe that for EC countries the proportion of imports and exports in this category is rather similar. Northern European

Table 6.5. *Net exports by commodity, % of total trade*

	1	2	3	4	5
Austria	− 0.45	0.25	0.05	0.55	0.58
Belgium–Luxemburg	− 0.58	− 0.02	− 0.82	0.45	0.19
Denmark	− 0.40	− 0.28	− 0.89	− 0.65	0.25
Finland	0.72	− 0.13	0.71	0.77	0.57
France	− 0.44	− 0.36	− 0.61	0.43	0.34
Federal Republic of Germany	− 0.37	0.07	− 0.75	0.43	0.63
Greece	− 0.18	− 0.22	0.65	− 0.50	− 0.74
Ireland	0.62	− 0.42	− 0.77	− 0.63	− 0.25
Italy	− 0.74	0.15	− 0.04	0.16	0.49
Netherlands	0.12	− 0.15	− 0.83	− 0.42	0.42
Norway	0.05	− 0.74	− 0.95	0.54	− 0.35
Portugal	0.86	0.11	0.97	− 0.54	− 0.21
Spain	− 0.62	− 0.05	− 0.30	0.33	0.07
Sweden	− 0.49	− 0.50	− 0.94	0.29	0.29
Switzerland	− 0.59	− 0.46	− 0.81	− 0.21	0.81
United Kingdom	− 0.82	− 0.37	− 0.84	− 0.13	0.30

1 = Natural resources
2 = Average labour–capital
3 = Labour-intensive
4 = Capital-intensive
5 = Human capital-intensive

countries tend, however, to have a higher share in imports than exports, whereas the opposite holds for southern European countries. Net trade accounts for a significant proportion of total trade, especially in northern European countries (with the exception of Germany and Austria). On the whole, this suggests that there is some intra-industry trade in this category, especially strong with the southern European countries, and that COMECON has some comparative advantage in those products relative to the northern European countries.

The trade pattern for labour-intensive commodities is also revealing. First, there is no western country which specialises in the export of such commodities to the East. Portugal and Greece come first, with some 14% of their exports, and exhibit a significant positive net trade. In terms of imports, however, it is striking that only Germany and the Netherlands exhibit a significant specialisation in those industries. These two countries seem to be the only ones to use eastern Europe as a source of labour-intensive commodities. Given that countries like Belgium, France or the United Kingdom should have similar factor endowments to those found in Germany and the Netherlands, this observation is somewhat surprising. It may be the reflection either of highly managed trade or of the existence of trade barriers.

With respect to commodities intensive in physical capital, we observe the following: northern EC countries (except for Denmark and the Netherlands), Sweden, Finland, Austria and Spain exhibit some intra-industry trade in those industries, while still maintaining a relative specialisation (as indicated by their positive net exports). Greece, Portugal and Ireland tend to import these commodities.

Finally, we observe that the majority of exports out of northern European countries and EFTA countries occur in human capital-intensive industries (up to 92% for Switzerland). Interestingly, imports of human capital-intensive products in these countries are also significant; the import share is always in excess of 30% and the positive net exports of Western countries in most cases does not exceed 50%. Hence, for those countries, even though there is a relative specialisation in human capital-intensive industries, there is still evidence of a significant intra-industry trade. In accord with our intuition, Greece, Portugal and Ireland are characterised by a relative specialisation out of those industries.

On the whole, the commodity composition of trade with eastern Europe is somewhat surprising; trade between the North of Europe and EFTA and COMECON is characterised by a surprising share of intra-industry trade, especially in human capital-intensive industries but also in capital-intensive industries. The share of imports in labour-intensive products is rather low, and such imports are really limited to the Netherlands and Germany. Finally, eastern Europe tends to specialise in the production of natural resource-intensive products. These findings do not support the common intuition that eastern Europe has a comparative advantage in labour-intensive products. To the extent that southern EC countries have a comparative advantage in labour-intensive commodities (see Neven, 1990), this evidence also suggests that the potential conflict between the integration of southern countries in the EC and trade liberalisation with the East could very well be limited. In order to assess this question further, we shall now explicitly compare the trade flows between some northern European countries (Germany, France and the United Kingdom) and COMECON on the one hand, and between the same northern European countries and Greece, Portugal and Spain on the other.

Table 6.6 reports average intra-industry trade indices (adjusted for total trade imbalances) across the 29 ISIC industries (in 1985) for North–South and North–East trade. It is apparent that intra-industry trade is more important between the North and the East than between the North and Portugal and Greece. Intra-industry trade indices between the North and

Table 6.6. *Average intra-industry trade indices, 1985*

	Germany	France	United Kingdom
COMECON	0.49	0.52	0.55
Portugal	0.36	0.39	0.40
Greece	0.35	0.37	0.41
Spain	0.58	0.63	0.57

Spain are, however, closer to those observed between the North and the East.

In order to assess further the extent to which North–East and North–South trade might conflict, we report in Table 6.7 the average intra-industry trade indices for the labour-intensive commodities. The contrast between the East and the South of Europe is again apparent. Portugal and Greece are much more specialised in labour-intensive commodities, relative to the North, than COMECON countries; trade patterns with Spain are also somewhat closer to those observed for eastern Europe.

On the whole, the comparison of intra-industry trade indices for North–East and North–South trade suggests that the conflict between EC and European integration should not be exaggerated for Portugal and Greece. At least by this measure, North–South and North–East trade flows are somewhat different: Spain, so it seems, has most to worry about; it has a trade pattern which is closer to the pattern observed in COMECON.

4   The determinants of trade between the EC and COMECON

In section 4 we complement the descriptive analysis of section 3 by estimating an econometric model which tries to identify the factors underlying trade between the four 'big' EC members (France (F), Italy (I), the United Kingdom (UK) and West Germany (G)) and the COMECON countries. The objective is to explain the trade balances at the sectoral level in terms of a variety of variables representing determinants of classical trade, variables pertaining to intra-industry trade, trade barriers and policy variables. Our dependent variable is the trade balance as a proportion of apparent consumption, at the sectoral level. This should be some measure of relative competitiveness of the COMECON countries *vis-à-vis* the EC.

The analysis is carried out with a panel data set covering 29 manufacturing industries from 1975 to 1987, for the four 'big' European countries. It is worth recalling at this point that the intra-German trade flows are not

Table 6.7. *Average intra-industry trade indices, 1985, labour-intensive industries*

	Germany	France	United Kingdom
COMECON	0.51	0.40	0.39
Portugal	0.07	0.08	0.05
Greece	0.17		0.22
Spain	0.26	0.27	0.43

reported, whereas trade flows between East Germany and France, Italy, and the United Kingdom are available. As a result, one should be cautious regarding cross-country comparison involving Germany. In order to compare trade structures across EC countries we specify a separate equation for each country, leading to the following system of equations,

$$TB_{kti} = a_k + \mathbf{b}_k \mathbf{X}_{kti} + e_{kti}, \qquad k = F, G, I, UK \qquad (1)$$

where TB_{ti} is the trade balance as a proportion of apparent consumption in country k at time t in sector i.

Notice that this specification is a system of four equations, one for each country, where the parameter vector $(a_k, \mathbf{b}_k)$ varies across countries. The vector $\mathbf{X}$ is a set of twelve explanatory variables representing inter-industry and intra-industry determinants of trade, as well as trade barriers. These variables include proxies for the intensity of human and physical capital in production, the R & D intensity, a measure of the degree of scale economies, a proxy for non-tariff barriers, the Community common external tariff, a measure of product differentiation, the rate of growth of demand, a measure of transportation costs, dummies for the agricultural and wood sectors, as well as a dummy for industries with high public procurement. The data and the proxies used for these variables are described further in Appendix C. There are 29 sectors for the time period 1975–87 (see Appendix A for a list of sectors).

Notice that human and physical capital intensities, as well as the R & D intensity, attempt to capture the factors underlying inter-industry trade. Scale economies and product differentiation try to capture the factors underlying intra-industry trade. The common external tariff, the public procurement, and the non-tariff barriers variables, as well as transportation cost measure the extent of protection (natural or policy-induced).

Table 6.8.. *Seemingly unrelated regression results (t-statistics in parenthesis)*

	France	Italy	UK	West Germany
Intercept	− 0.014	0.281	− 0.014	0.019
	(− 1.81)	(7.48)	(− 0.86)	(1.21)
Human capital	0.021	− 0.166	0.010	0.019
	(3.36)	(− 5.50)	(0.67)	(1.45)
Investment	0.076	− 0.166	0.187	0.022
	(1.76)	(− 2.95)	(1.57)	(0.30)
R & D	0.040	0.172	0.099	0.388
	(0.59)	(0.40)	(1.12)	(3.50)
Scale	− 0.197	− 1.604	0.117	− 0.204
	(− 2.13)	(− 4.30)	(0.78)	(− 1.16)
NTB	0.003	0.005	− 0.002	− 0.003
	(1.52)	(0.65)	(− 0.78)	(− 0.72)
Tariff	− 0.020	− 0.263	− 0.009	− 0.112
	(− 1.81)	(− 5.92)	(− 0.47)	(− 5.22)
Product Diff.	− 0.004	0.023	0.003	− 0.014
	(− 1.61)	(3.41)	(0.77)	(− 3.06)
Growth	0.011	− 0.052	− 0.012	− 0.004
	(0.11)	(− 1.57)	(− 0.90)	(− 0.24)
Transportation	− 0.003	− 0.029	− 0.013	− 0.001
	(− 2.23)	(− 4.55)	(− 5.38)	(− 0.45)
Agriculture	− 0.000	− 0.021	0.002	0.019
	(− 0.05)	(− 1.10)	(0.30)	(2.28)
Wood	− 0.022	− 0.137	− 0.046	− 0.034
	(− 5.38)	(− 8.23)	(− 7.49)	(− 4.58)
Public proc.	0.004	− 0.053	0.010	0.017
	(0.95)	(− 3.35)	(1.71)	(2.30)
R^2	0.35	0.32	0.38	0.42

We assume that the additive error terms e_{ti} are temporally uncorrelated (within as well as across equations), contemporaneously correlated, and multinormally distributed with,

$$E[e_{it}] = 0, \quad E[e_{it}, e_{it}] = s_{kl}, \quad E[e_{it}, e'_{it}] = 0, \qquad k = F, G, I, UK \quad (2)$$

With the above stochastic assumptions we estimate the system by seemingly unrelated regression (SUR). Table 6.8 reports the SUR estimates for the four countries. It is interesting to note that the determinants of trade with COMECON, despite some commonality, are somewhat differentiated across EC members. Among the common effects, we observe that non-tariff barriers seem rather unimportant as a determinant of trade balance with the East. This is somewhat puzzling. Our NTB variable captures the barriers to intra-EC trade, which presumably also apply to imports from the rest of the world. In previous work (see Neven and Röller, 1990), we found that NTBs, as represented by this variable, do indeed reduce trade within the EC and between the EC and the rest of the world. The lack of significance that we obtain here might suggest that COMECON manages to restrict imports from the EC, possibly through NTB's in the same industries as those where NTBs are prevalent in the EC. Barriers in COMECON would then balance those of the EC, with no effect on the trade balance. Other trade barriers such as the common external tariff also turn out to be much more significant, and there is a remarkable consistency across countries regarding the effect of the common external tariff. The role that these barriers play is very similar to what we have observed regarding trade between the EC and the rest of the world (see again Neven and Röller, 1990), namely that a high common external tariff is associated with increased imports. This suggests that the common external tariff is used as an instrument to counterbalance Europe's comparative disadvantage. This may be particularly relevant for labour-intensive industries where the common external tariff is indeed quite high. Regarding the other policy variable – i.e., public procurement – it seems that in West Germany and the United Kingdom industries with high degree of public procurement are indicative of a positive trade balance with the East, whereas in Italy the reverse is observed.

A large degree of similarity across countries also exists regarding the impact of high transportation costs. In all countries except West Germany industries with large transportation costs favour western exports over eastern imports. This empirical finding might be explained by the still rather poor transportation technology available to COMECON exporters. Since this sector is expected to be developing rather rapidly in the coming years, one might expect some increased exports from the East in sectors where transportation costs are substantial.

Turning to the classical determinant of inter-industry trade – namely human and physical capital, as well as R & D intensity – no clear picture emerges. Indeed the only significant pattern is that none of these variables seems to be significant in explaining trade balances between the West and the East. The exceptions are Italy, where human and physical capital intensity is associated with a negative trade balance, and France, where the opposite occurs. West Germany is also somewhat of an outlier with respect to R & D-intensive industries, which are indicative of a large West German trade surplus.[3] On the whole, we do not find much consistent empirical evidence for inter-industry trade along the classical factor endowments. Notice that these results are also consistent with the descriptive analysis of the trade patterns in section 4.

Economies of scale are either insignificant (i.e., in West Germany and the United Kingdon) or impact negatively on the EC members trade surplus with COMECON (i.e., in France and Italy). The relative advantage of COMECON countries in industries with significant scale economies could be related to the industrial structure of COMECON during the time period under investigation. Large worker cooperatives dominated the industrial landscape and the small businesses were almost exclusively absent. This regulated industry structure, inefficient as it may be from a managerial point of view, will presumably have allowed for a full exploitation of technical scale economies.

A consistent picture emerges for all of the four EC countries in the wood industry, where COMECON has a large trade surplus. This is again consistent with the earlier observation that COMECON exports in natural resources have been significant over the last two decades. it is not clear, however, whether this trade pattern is indicative of a future comparative advantage of COMECON in the wood sector. To the extent that their wood exports are associated with a lack of a proper accounting of environmental costs, a change of policy regarding the management of environmental resources could reduce these exports.

Finally, in the food sector a rather homogeneous picture emerges. In all EC countries trade is fairly balanced, except for West Germany which has a surplus. This is rather surprising since one might expect more exports of agricultural products into COMECON, especially in light of the frequently reported food shortages. One might argue that these exports out of the West have not happened for political reasons, and will expand now that political systems have changed. On the other hand, it could be argued that eastern Europe may have a comparative advantage in agricultural production which could be realised under the new political and economic system (this is due to fertile land and lower population density). In this case, one may expect a large surplus in agricultural commodities for COMECON countries. Under this scenario a dismantling of the protectionist practices within the EC (within the CAP) may be vital to allow the COMECON countries to exploit their comparative advantage.

5   Conclusions

The main conclusion which emerges from this preliminary analysis of East–West trade is that the extent to which trade arises out of comparative advantage might be rather limited. Indeed, there is some evidence of significant intra-industry trade in capital and human capital-intensive sectors. As a result, the conflict between EC integration and integration with the East should not be overestimated for southern European countries.

Our analysis, of course, presumes that East–West trade has not been systematically managed away from what market forces would dictate. This assumption may not be appropriate, and it should be examined further. In particular, it would be quite informative to compare factor prices and the distribution of industrial output across sectors between eastern and western countries. This might, however, be difficult because of the scarcity of comparable data.

In this study, we have focused on the COMECON countries as a block. There is, however, presumably a large diversity of factor endowments across COMECON countries and a more detailed analysis would be very useful. In particular, East Germany is likely to integrate with the EC much faster than the other COMECON countries. A detailed analysis of East German trade is thus especially pressing.

Appendix A: data overview and list of industries

Data overview

The period selected for the analysis includes the years 1975–87. The data are available for all EC countries, with Belgium and Luxemburg regrouped as one country. The currency retained is the ECU (in thousands and constant in the base year 1980). In order to obtain a coherent final data set, the conversion of foreign currencies into ECUs (R & D data, trade data) and the use of deflators (trade data, economics variable data) to obtain 1980 ECUs had to be performed. The classification of industries used is the International Standard Industrial Classification System (ISIC) (United Nations statistical Studies Series M #4/REV.2,1969).

In our analysis, we used manufacturing (sector 3), which represents 29 industries. The level of aggregation used is the ISIC three-digit level. Industries from other data sources were therefore matched to the ISIC three-digit level classification.

List of industries

ISIC code	Industry
311	Foodstuff
312	Foodstuff – Other
313	Beverage
314	Tobacco
321	Textile
322	Textile – Clothing

ISIC code	Industry
323	Leather – Fur
324	Leather – Footwear
331	Wood
332	Wood – Furniture
341	Paper
342	Printing – Publishing
351	Chemical
352	Chemical – Other
353	Oil Refineries
354	Products derived from petroleum
355	Rubber
356	Rubber – Other
361	Ceramic goods
362	Glass & glassware
369	Stone & non-metallic mineral products
371	Steel
372	Production & transformation of non-ferrous metals
381	Tools & finished metal goods
382	Mechanical machinery
383	Electrical machinery
384	Motor vehicles, Railway, Aerospace
385	Chirurgical, Optical instruments
390	Other manufacturing

Appendix B: classification of industries according to factor intensities

Natural resources	Average capital and average labour intensity	High labour intensity
Foodstuff	Metallic products	Clothing
Wood	Printing	Shoes
	Leather	Ceramic
	Wood furniture	

Appendix B: classification of industries according to factor intensities

Natural resources	Average capital and average labour intensity	High labour intensity
	Non-ferrous products Printing Rubber Textile	

High capital intensity	High human capital intensity
Plastics	Chemicals
Glass	Pharmaceuticals
Other mineral products	Mechanical machinery
Beverage	Electrical machinery
Paper	Transportation equipment
Steel	Medical/Optical instrument

Appendix C: Sources for data for section 3

Number of employees, gross wages, production values (value-added taxes excluded), total investments for the years 1975–86: Statistical Office of the European Communities, magnetic tape, extracted from Domaine:In-de:Enquete Industrielle Annuelle, Collection:01, Données Globales (Luxemburg:SOEC 06/07/88). The NACE three-digit classification used there was converted to the ISIC three-digit classification. The variables, expressed in million ECU, have been deflated to thousand constant 1980 ECU with unpublished deflator factors obtained at the Statistical Office of the European Communities in Luxemburg.

Imports and exports for individual countries for the years 1961 to 1987 were obtained from: The Organisation for Economic Cooperation and Development, National Economics Statistics and National Accounts Division, magnetic tape, extracted from International Trade by Products System (Paris: OECD).

Imports are expressed cif (cost, insurance and freight) and exports are expressed fob (free on board). The currency used was thousand dollars, which has been converted (conversion rate tables: EUROSTAT, EC) to thousand ECU and deflated similarly to the data obtained through the SOEC in Luxemburg.

R & D expenditures were obtained at the Organisation of Economic Cooperation and Development from unpublished sources for the years

1975–85. Data was made available to us by the Administrator of the Scientific, Technological and Industrial Indicators Division at the OECD office in Paris. In order to expand the data base some data points had to be created when years and industries were missing for some countries. When a year was missing in a particular industry for a particular country the previous year was used, and when an industry for a particular country was missing the average of existing country data for that industry was substituted. In addition, the ISIC four-digit classification used there was converted to the ISIC three-digit classification. Constant 1980 million dollars have been converted with unpublished conversion rate tables provided by the same source at the OECD in Paris into constant 1980 ECU. There are no data available for Greece.

Tariffs data was produced from the Bulletin International des Douanes, European Economic Community, Year 1986–1988 (International Customs Tariffs Bureau, Brussels). Averages were created within industries for the ISIC three-digit classification.

Non-tarrif barriers data for each sector's data were created based on the article by Pierre Buigues and Fabienne Ilzkovitz, 'The Sectoral Impact of the Internal Market'. Commission of the European Communities, 1988 (the NACE three-digit classification used there was converted to the ISIC three-digit classification). In this article industrial sectors are classified into high, medium, and low intra-EC NTB sectors. Our NTB variable thus ranges from 0 to 3. On the other hand, one could argue that sectors with an NTB ranking of 3, which are typically characterised by a large degree of public procurement, direct those NTB's to the same degree at other EC member countries as at non-EC countries. Sectors with a lower NTB classification may be more characteristic of larger extra-EC than intra-EC NTBs.

Price per kilo of Belgian imports: Belgium Ministry of Foreign Trade.

Economics of scale data, measured by the relative size of the mid-point plant for the German industry, for the years 1978–84: Scherer (1980, p. 66). The SYPRO four-digit classification used there was first converted into NACE three-digit and secondly into ISIC three-digit classification. A regression model was performed to create data for the years 1975, 1976, 1977 and 1985.

A dummy variable is used for the agricultural and wood sectors, as well as for product differentiation where the dummy is 1 for the consumer industry and 0 otherwise. The human capital variable is proxied by the deviation of industry wages from the country mean wage. Demand growth is computed as the percentage growth in apparent consumption.

NOTES

This study was prepared for presentation at the CEPR/INI conference at Urbino on 15–16 March 1990. We are grateful to the participants of the conference for useful comments on an earlier draft, and in particular to one of the editors of this volume, A. Winters, who provided numerous and detailed suggestions for improvement. We also wish to thank Carole A. Bonanni for excellent research assistance. The financial support of INSEAD under grant No. 2139R is gratefully acknowledged.

1 Further details on data sources and manipulations are provided in Appendices A–C.
2 Another minor remark is in order: exports are reported on a fob basis, whereas imports are reported on a cif basis. Given that the COMECON countries are not part of the OECD (and hence do not provide information on their imports), it is not possible to construct data for imports and exports on a common basis. In the data that we use here, the value for exports is thus biased upwards. This bias is, however, likely to be rather small and should be consistent across countries.
3 It should also be mentioned that the lack of R & D results may be due to Cocom, which restricts technology exports to the East.

REFERENCES

Neven, D.J. and L.-H. Röller (1990) 'European Integration and Trade Flows', CEPR discussion paper, **367**.
Neven, D.J. (1990) 'EC Integration Towards 1992; Some Distributional Aspects', *Economic Policy*, **10**, pp. 13–63.
Norman, V. (1989) 'EFTA and the Internal European Market', *Economic Policy*, **9**, pp. 424–65.
Scherer, F.M. (1980) *Industrial Market Structure and Economic Performance*, Chicago: Rand-McNally.
Smith, A. and A. Venables (1988) 'Completing the Internal Market in the European Community: Some Industry Simulations', *European Economic Review*, **32**, pp. 1501–25.

Discussion

FABRIZIO ONIDA

This study makes a valuable and timely effort to analyse patterns of trade between countries expected to integrate rapidly during the 1990s. I fully share the authors' (hereafter NR) expectation of net gains from trade from East–West integration, owing to fuller exploitation of comparative advantages and economies of scale, leading to greater inter-industry as well as intra-industry specialisation.

I do, however, not really share NR's trust in the analytical and econometric apparatus funding their conclusions. Inferences about gains–losses from integration drawn from 'revealed factor abundance' (see also Neven, 1990) seem to me rather weak. While I agree that trade data must be a fair guide to the actual comparative advantage even in a state trading setting (section 3), I stay rather sceptical about neoclassical factor intensities according to standard measures being meaningful and reliable sources, or even determinants, of actual absolute and comparative advantages. We should not forget that the factor abundance–intensity apparatus, even in its weaker form, implies the notion of pure elastic demand for factors as homogeneous inputs substitutable on the basis of freely available technologies. True, in their econometric tests of patterns of trade between the EC and COMECON NR go well beyond the standard Heckscher–Ohlin scheme, taking a standard multivariate approach dating from Baldwin (1971) and Hufbauer (1970), and widely employed thereafter. However a multivariate eclectic approach raises a number of theoretical and methodological issues, so that traditional gains from trade can hardly be inferred and factoral and neofactoral abundance becomes blurred. Econometric estimates from these multivariate regressions can usefully point to the impact of technology gaps, industrial structure (average firm size), natural resource abundance, institutional barriers and other items that appear more related to specific factor availability, economies of scale and economic–institutional infrastructure than to relative abundance or scarcity of internationally immobile original 'factors': for earlier in-depth discussions see Stern (1975), Deardorff (1984) and Leamer (1984).

Neven (1990) himself concludes that 'trade arising from "classical" factors is fairly limited between European countries' and that Heckscher–Ohlin assumptions are unwarranted within the EC, which are basically market economies. What then about EC trade with non-market economies such as COMECON countries?

I shall now make some more specific comments about the study.

1   *COMECON trade*, including the USSR as in this study, is dominated by primary sectors (agriculture, mining, energy): think of Soviet oil and gas and precious metals, Polish wood and coal, live animals and meat and so on. This study focusses on manufacturers (ISIC 3), whose subset of natural resource-intensive sectors is not fully computed by NR. They rather define a relatively tiny subset of 'natural resource-intensive' manufacturers including only foodstuff (which incidentally has very little to do with agricultural food storages referred to by NR

in section 3) and wood. Other typically resource-intensive manufacturers are included in the sub groups of high capital intensity (plastics, steel, glass, stone and non-metallic products) or of average capital–labour intensity (leather, non-ferrous products). NR results thus do not clearly spell out to what extent COMECON (not only the USSR, which is a well-known case) still relies upon exporting resource-intensive semifinished and finished products in exchange for other manufacturers. Given COMECON countries' rather low average ratio of population to natural resources, I do not share NR's 'common intuition that eastern Europe has a comparative advantage in labour-intensive products' (section 3).

3 In these non-market economies, *fixed capital* is largely obsolete and underutilised, owing to inefficient process organisation (think of Trabant cars!), lack of civilian technology domestic input and import from abroad, labour ridigities, climatic conditions, and so on. How, then, can revealed capital intensity explain neoclassical patterns of trade and potential conflict or complementarity with Western production?

3 *Human capital-intensive sectors*, as defined by NR and Neven (1990), include the bulk of practically all modern manufacturing – i.e., chemicals, pharmaceutical, electrical and non-electrical mechanical goods and transport equipment (both consumer and producer goods). Indeed NR's Tables 6.3 and 6.4 clearly how that this category accounts for an average of between a half and two-thirds of Western exports of COMECON (with lower percentages only for small agricultural or primary producing countries such as Greece, Portugal, Norway and Ireland) and between a third and a half of Western imports from COMECON.

   Given its huge statistical coverage, we should not wonder if this highly heterogeneous grade category includes a substantial 'within' variance of neoclassical factor intensity (Hufbauer, 1970; Rayment, 1976). This implicitly follows from NR data showing predominantly net export of western Europe to COMECON in this category (Table 6.5) but at the same time a wide variety of regression signs and their significance when various industrial characteristics typical of modern manufacturing are introduced as regressors (Table 6.8) for explaining net trade balances of major European countries with COMECON: R & D, scale economies, product differentiation and wage proxies for human capital intensity. Interpretation of trade patterns thus become rather difficult. Further disaggregation might help in discriminating among simultaneous effects. Incidentally, multicollinearity biases traditionally loom behind these multivariate regressions, but NR do not publish their correlation matrix to help the reader remove doubts about the robustness of regression results to different specifications.

4   The choice of *sectoral grouping* for descriptive and regression results is always somewhat arbitrary. Personally I would feel inclined to analyse patterns of East–West trade in terms of the fourfold Pavitt (1984) taxonomy, which has the disadvantage of omitting a quantitative clearcut criterion for assigning each sector to the four classes, but shows the advantage of suggesting a framework far more suitable to a technology-minded and potentially dynamic approach to industrial patterns of growth and trade. Pavitt uses (1) science-based; (2) scale-intensive; (3) specialised equipment and intermediate product supplies; (4) traditional consumer goods. This taxonomy suggests a simultaneous interplay of two crucial characteristics of industrial structures:
   (a)   direction of technology generation and use (e.g., 'science-based' industry providing a net generation of innovation for use in downstream sectors, down to net technology users such as traditional manufacturing);
   (b)   prevailing market structure (e.g., oligopoly dominating in 'scale-intensive' and most 'science-based', whereas imperfect competition is the rule among specialised suppliers and traditional consumer manufacturers).

5   Some minor remarks on *econometric specification* can also be made:
   (a)   The dummying for 'product differentiation' as 'consumer good' is very popular, but seems to me highly misleading. Product differentiation in technological (not only in consumer variety) terms dominates producer durable equipment and several sophisticated intermediate goods ('customised' demand).
   (b)   It would be interesting to know how NR have attributed the dummying of 'public procurement' to their 29 industries. To the best of my knowledge, public procurement plays a crucial role *within* specific 3-digits ISIC industries rather than across industries: e.g., electricity generation and transmission and telecommunication belong to ISIC 383 together with domestic appliances, most electronics and standard electrical engines; railway equipment, air transport and aerospace take a relatively small share of ISIC 384 (together with passenger cars and trucks and shipbuilding); large office equipment is included in ISIC 382, together with all mechanical engineering.

6   Finally, NR choose to discuss gains–losses from trade in terms of *standard static comparative advantages*. This is all too legitimate. However, given the very peculiar institutional and historical frame-

work, I would suggest that a greater emphasis should be given to potential dynamic gains from trade. Modern international trade theory convincingly suggests that both static and dynamic gains from trade flow from greater exploitation of scale economies, learning by doing, technology diffusion and wider product variety availability. The Cecchini Report (1988) has made remarkable efforts in estimating potential scale economy gains from integration at *industry* level. Similar calculations at country-industry level are much harder to perform, but may be important in order to evaluate potential COMECON competitiveness in some intermediate and final manufacturing suitable for mass production (say, plastics, fertilisers, car components, steel, non-ferrous metals, etc.). Of course, one has to assume huge inflows of capital and technology from the West (a very non-neoclassical assumption!), but scenarios of gains and losses from trade should not rule out precisely those elements that most intelligent business decision-makers and policy-makers would rate of the utmost importance to evaluate *their* potential gains and losses in dealing with East–West integration.

REFERENCES

Baldwin, R.E. (1971) 'Determinants of the commodity structure of U.S. trade', *American Economic Review* (March).

Deardorff, A.V. (1984) 'Testing trade theories and predicting trade flows', in R.W. Jones and P.B. Kenen (eds), *Handbook of International Economies*, Amsterdam: North-Holland.

Hufbauer, G.C. (1970) 'The impact of national characteristics and technology on the commodity composition of trade in manufactured goods', in R. Vernon (ed.), *The Technology Factor in International Trade*, New York: Columbia University Press.

Leamer, E.E. (1984) *Sources of International Comparative Advantage. Theory and Evidence*, Cambridge, Mass.: MIT Press.

Neven, D.J. (1990) 'EEC integration towards 1992: some distributional aspects', *Economic Policy*, **10** (April).

Pavitt, K. (1984) 'Patterns of technical change: towards a taxonomy and a theory', *Research Policy*, **6**.

Rayment, P.B.W. (1976) 'The homogeneity of manufacturing industries with respect to factor intensity: the case of U.K.', *Oxford Bulletin of Economics and Statistics* (August).

Stern, R.M. (1975) 'Testing trade theories', in P.B. Kenen (ed.), *International Trade and Finance. Frontiers for Research*, Cambridge: Cambridge University Press.

7 1992 and EFTA

VICTOR D. NORMAN

1 Introduction

The EFTA countries differ from most EC countries in three important respects. One is size: each EFTA country is very small, in sum their production amounts only to that of Britain or France. The second is openness: all EFTA countries trade extensively with the rest of the world; the EC is the largest trading partner, but they also have a large volume of trade with non-European countries. The third is reliance on comparative advantage: net trade is a substantial part of their total trade, and there is a high degree of commodity concentration in their exports.

These aspects are important in relation to the effects of 1992. It seems likely that EFTA and the EC will agree on a programme which will integrate EFTA in the internal market, at least as regards manufactured goods and services. As part of the agreement, the EFTA countries will probably have to accept (and copy) the common external trade policy of the Community. Alternatively, if an EFTA–EC agreement does not come about, most of the EFTA countries will probably join the Community. In either case, therefore, EFTA countries will become part of the internal market, and their external trade policies will have to be modified.

The internal market should give participating countries gains through (a) fuller exploitation of economies of scale, (b) increased competition, and (c) more complete exploitation of comparative advantage. Studies, in particular Smith and Venables (1988) and Neven (1990), have concluded that (a) and (b) are the most important effects for the 'Northern' EC, while (c) could be important to the Mediterranean EC countries.

For the EFTA countries, the smallness of their domestic markets would suggest that scale and competition effects could be significant. Given their openness, however, some of their gains may have already been reaped. The same may be true for comparative advantage gains: with the extensive foreign trade of EFTA countries, there might not be very large additional gains to be made.

A particular question arises in relation to the external trade policy of the EC, as compared to that of EFTA countries. For many manufactured goods, the EFTA countries today practise freer trade than does the EC. An example is motor vehicles, where countries such as Sweden and Norway have close to free imports from Japan, in contrast to the VERs of EC countries; this difference is reflected in very high Japanese market shares in the Scandinavian car markets. If EFTA countries have to accept EC trade barriers towards third countries, the gains from integration in Europe could be offset by losses in relation to third-country trade.

The issues involved in assessing the consequences of 1992 for EFTA countries, therefore, are (1) To what extent will scale and competition gains remain unexploited? (2) To what extent is there remaining comparative advantage at the margin? (3) To what extent will more protectionist policies towards third countries reduce the EFTA gains from integration in Europe? These are the three questions addressed in this study. The analysis draws on Krugman (1988), Lundberg (1989), Norman (1989), Flam and Horn (1989), Norman and Orvedal (1990), and Norman and Strandenes (forthcoming).

2   Scale and competition gains

EFTA markets are small. In the absence of international trade, therefore, EFTA countries face a more severe trade-off between competition and scale economies than do the larger countries of the Community. Typically, a smaller market will give both fewer and smaller firms. As an illustration for Norway and Sweden, Table 7.1 gives Herfindahl concentration indexes and average firm size for five industries, and compares these with the corresponding figures for the average EC country. In these industries, the typical EC firm is 5–10 times as large as the typical Norwegian firm, and about twice as large as the typical Swedish firm. The Herfindahl index is 3–5 times as high in Norway as in the average EC country, with Sweden generally in between.

International trade is, of course, a means by which small countries can exploit scale economies more fully, and at the same achieve a high degree of competition in domestic markets. The relative openness of the EFTA countries therefore suggests that scale and competition problems are less severe than the size of their domestic markets would indicate. That is reflected in the relatively high market shares of imports for Norway and Sweden, also shown in Table 7.1: while the average of the import shares for the five industries is only 32% in the EC, it is 53% in Sweden and 68%

Table 7.1. *Concentration, firm size and import ratios, selected industries*

	Norway	Sweden	EC
Household appliances			
Import share	0.68	0.49	0.26
Share of ROW in imports	0.09	0.16	0.20
Herfindahl index	0.40	0.41	0.11
Average firm size (relative to EC)	0.17	0.58	1.00
Pharmaceuticals			
Import share	0.62	0.57	0.21
Share of ROW in imports	0.17	0.31	0.39
Herfindahl index	0.33	0.17	0.06
Average firm size (relative to EC)	0.12	0.26	1.00
Motor vehicles			
Import share	1.00	0.37	0.50
Share of ROW in imports	0.27	0.31	0.16
Herfindahl index		0.50	0.28
Average firm size (relative to EC)		0.47	1.00
Office machinery			
Import share	0.83	0.91	0.49
Share of ROW in imports	0.51	0.52	0.49
Herfindahl index	0.32	0.18	0.12
Average firm size (relative to EC)	0.10	0.21	1.00
Generators and electric motors			
Import share	0.29	0.31	0.15
Share of ROW in imports	0.30	0.40	0.41
Herfindahl index	0.10	0.75	0.02
Average firm size (relative to EC)	0.19	3.71	1.00

Sources: EC based on data provided by Smith and Venables (1988).
Norway and Sweden based on unpublished data from Norman and Orvedal (1990).

in Norway. It is not immediately obvious, therefore, whether remaining scale and competition gains through international trade are larger for EFTA than for the EC countries.

In Norman (1989), I report simulation results for two of the industries (motor vehicles and pharmaceuticals) analysed by Smith and Venables (1988) in their study of the impact of 1992 on European industries. I used the Smith–Venables methodology (i.e., a simulation model with product differentiation and oligopolistic interaction between firms). The simulation model is described in Smith and Venables (1988) and Norman (1989), so only a brief sketch need be given here. European markets are initially segmented along national lies; in each market segment, domestic firms compete with firms from all other EC and EFTA countries, and with firms from the rest of the world. Trade barriers take the form of real trade costs, modelled as *ad valorem* tariff equivalents.

Firms exercise market power in part through product differentiation, in part through significant total market shares. Product varieties are firm-specific, and each firm produces a given number of varieties. Product demand in each country is generated from a Spence–Dixit–Stiglitz utility function (with a constant elasticity of substitution between product varieties). The utility functions allow for differences in preferences across countries, to accommodate the strong home-market bias apparent in all data. In the simulations reported here, industry equilibria are taken to be of the Nash–Cournot type. Smith and Venables also report simulations assuming Nash–Bertrand equilibrium. The model coefficients are found by calibrating the model to actual data on production, trade, and the population of firms, and exogenously specified trade barriers (set at 10% tariff equivalents). It is assumed that the data reflect an initial, zero-profit, free-entry equilibrium.

The effects of 1992 are simulated by assuming that the 1992 programme (a) will give a reduction in real trade costs equivalent to a 2.5 percentage point reduction in *ad valorem* tariffs, and (b) will give fully integrated European markets (i.e., will end market segmentation along national lines). The results for motor vehicles and pharmaceuticals give somewhat larger 1992 welfare gains to Norway and Sweden than to the typical EC country. In Norman and Orvedal (1990), we have looked at three more of the Smith and Venables industries – generators and electric motors, office machinery, and household appliances. For those, the estimated Norwegian and Swedish gains are in some cases smaller and in other cases significantly larger than the estimated gains to the typical EC country. The results for all five industries, compared to the estimated gains to the typical EC country, are shown in Table 7.2. The differences in estimated EC and Scandinavian gains are in general directly related to differences in the degree of domestic competition. If the Herfindahl index adjusted for imports (i.e., the Herfindahl index × (1 − import share)) is used as the measure of concentration, the ranking of countries according to welfare gains coincides almost completely with the ranking according to concentration, as is seen from Figure 7.1.

No general conclusion regarding EFTA scale and competition gains can be drawn on the basis of these results – the gains (both absolutely and relatively to those of EC countries) will differ from industry to industry, depending on domestic concentration and the role of import competition initially. By and large, however, imports shares are quite high in EFTA

Table 7.2. *Welfare gains for the EC and Norway from the 1992 programme, effects of complete market integration; Cournot competition; fixed numbers of firms, % of initial consumer expenditures*

	Pharmaceuticals	Office machinery	Generators and electr. motors	Household appliances	Motor vehicles
Smith–Venables results, EC	1.11	3.88	0.52	1.79	4.09
Norman–Orvedal results:					
EC	1.71	2.49	0.56	1.52	2.78
Norway	3.97	1.41	0.93	1.98	2.02
Sweden	2.28	1.55	17.30	4.70	6.03

Sources: Smith and Venables (1988), Norman (1989), Norman and Orvedal (1990) and unpublished simulation results.

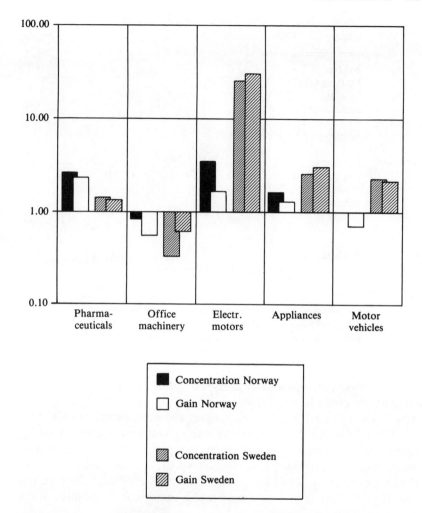

Figure 7.1 Domestic concentration and gains from integration (relative to EC average)

markets, suggesting that the overall scale and competition gains, while significant, could be relatively modest. This is true only for manufactured products, however. In service industries, EFTA markets are generally at least as closed to international competition as are the markets of the Community countries. The Nordic EFTA countries, in particular, have service sectors with very limited international competition, largely protected through government regulation. With small domestic markets, the

Table 7.3. *Share of five largest banks in total bank assets, %, 1984*

Austria	36
Finland (1987)	97
Sweden	89
Norway (1988)	69
Average 4 EFTA countries	73
Germany	26
France (1987)	52
Spain	43
Belgium (3 largest banks)	45
Denmark	57
Ireland	69
Italy	36
Netherlands	97
Portugal (4 largest banks)	55
Average 9 EC countries	53

Sources: Norway: NOS.
Other countries: OECD, *Competition in Banking*, Paris (1989).

scope for scale and competition gains through European integration and deregulation could be very large.

For the Nordic EFTA countries, banking can serve as an example. As is seen from Table 7.3, Nordic banking is more concentrated than banking in most EC countries. Moreover, there is significantly less international competition in the banking sectors in the Nordic countries than in the rest of Europe. Norway permitted no foreign banks until 1984; Sweden not until 1988; in both countries, there are still important constraints on the operation of foreign banks.

The financial sectors in the Nordic countries were generally deregulated in the early 1980s, when interest rate regulation was removed, constraints on competition between different types of financial institutions were relaxed, and international capital movements were liberalised. The Norwegian experience provides an interesting case: the initial effect was a marked increase in competition and declining interest rate margins. The second-round effect was very severe bank losses, a wave of mergers and acquisitions, and rising interest rate margins. At present, the interest rate margin is higher than it was prior to deregulation. This supports the notion that effective competition in banking requires much larger markets

Table 7.4. *Norway, domestic transportation, 1984, percentage distribution*

		Passenger km	Ton km	
Sea	Car ferries	3.5	1.2	Regulated private
	Other regular service	3.6	4.1	Regulated private
	Other	0.0	52.8	Unregulated
Railways		28.8	8.8	Public monopoly
Road	Scheduled	42.2	3.9	Regulated private/public
	Other (excl. private cars)	0.0	29.1	Unregulated
Air		21.9	0.1	Regulated private
Sum regulated		100.0	18.1	

Source: NOS transport statistics.

than those of the individual EFTA countries. If so, participation in the 1992 programme is a prerequisite for a competitive banking sector in the EFTA countries.

Another example is transportation. Like most European countries, the Nordic EFTA countries allow no international competition in domestic transportation, and the industry is thoroughly regulated – in some cases through public monopolies, in other cases through a concession system with monopoly rights for private carriers. Table 7.4 shows the distribution of domestic transportation in Norway across carriers. As is seen, all passenger transportation and almost 20% of goods transportation is subject to regulation. Competition to and from Scandinavia is similarly severely constrained through regulation and international agreements. Regulation of air transportation is particularly rigorous: through the consortium agreement between Denmark, Norway and Sweden which forms the basis for Scandinavian Airlines, SAS is granted the national carrier rights for international air transportation for the three Scandinavian governments. That gives the company a virtual monopoly on inter-Scandinavian routes, and the right to 50% of all routes out of Scandinavia. In Norman and Strandenes (forthcoming), we have looked at the possible effects of international competition on inter-Scandinavian routes, using the Oslo–Stockholm route as an example (see Table 7.5). We use a simulation model in which consumers have preferences for time of departures, so that different flights are imperfect subsitutes. The model is calibrated to an initial SAS monopoly, and then used to simulate the effects of competition. We assume that the resulting equilibrium would be one of Bertrand competition in the pricing of tickets, and a Cournot

Table 7.5. *Effects of competition, Oslo–Stockholm air route*

	Duopoly	3-firm oligopoly	4-firm oligopoly
% change, price	− 29.7	− 39.5	− 42.1
Change, as % of initial consumer expenditures			
Consumer surplus	45.8	67.0	73.3
World real income	36.1	47.1	49.9
Scandinavian real income*	16.9	28.3	31.4

* Assuming new carriers to be non-Scandinavian.
Source: Norman and Strandenes (forthcoming).

equilibrium in the number of flights offered by each carrier. The estimated gains are very large; in our base case, a duopoly would give a consumer gain of more than 45% of initial consumer expenditures and a welfare gain to the world of around 36%. Competition would also shift profits from SAS to the new carriers, reducing the Scandinavian welfare gain if the new carriers come from outside Scandinavia. Even so, Scandinavia would be left with a substantial net welfare gain.

The Oslo–Stockholm gains are probably not entirely representative of the gains from competition in Scandinavian air transportation more generally, as there is some competition today both domestically and on routes to and from Scandinavia. All traffic is thoroughly regulated, however, so the scope for price and frequency competition is severely limited. Even though the Oslo–Stockholm figures represent an upper bound to the gains from increased competition, therefore, we should expect very substantial gains in the other parts of the Scandinavian air transport network as well.

To sum up, there is thus reason to expect EFTA countries to reap significant, but modest, gains from integration of European markets in manufactures, and to reap quite substantial gains from international competition in the markets for services. Moreover, international competition might be a prerequisite for domestic deregulation of key service industries.

3   Comparative advantage

The other potential source of EFTA gains from European integration is unexploited comparative advantage.

'Comparative advantage' is a broad, and somewhat elusive, concept, so when applying it considerable care should be taken to be precise. Generally, it simply means differences in relative ability to produce different goods, and in this sense, much of the industry-level work on the effects of 1992 is concerned with comparative advantage. When Smith and Venables find that market integration will make French firms sell more in France, and German firms more in Germany, and that this will make both countries better off, they thus demonstrate comparative advantage gains: given the menu of products and national tastes, French firms have a comparative advantage in producing goods for the French market (as opposed to producing for the German market), and German firms have a corresponding comparative advantage in catering to German tastes. Market segmentation gives artificial export incentives; the establishment of the internal market could thus have the paradoxical effect that less international trade is needed to exploit comparative advantage more fully.

This way of applying the concept of comparative advantage is in some respect illuminating; nevertheless, it is in many contexts more instructive to distinguish between trade arising because of consumer preferences and the output characteristics of goods, and trade which derives from production technology and the input characteristics of goods, and to restrict the use of the comparative advantage concept to the latter. The question is then to what extent 1992 will affect the allocation of resources between production of goods with different input characteristics.

This question of intersectoral comparative advantage is not unrelated to the issue of scale and competition gains. Generally, if there is significant imperfect competition, high-cost producers will retain positive market shares, so international trade will not equalise marginal costs across countries; as a result, some comparative advantage will remain unexploited. To the extent that there are important elements of imperfect competition in EFTA and EC markets which will be reduced as a result of the 1992 programme, therefore, we should expect significant comparative advantage gains. Some such gains are also captured in the Smith and Venables-type industry simulations discussed above. It can be seen from Table 7.6, which gives the simulated production effects for Norway and Sweden of European integration, and which also shows the initial net exports (in % of total trade) for the two countries. As is seen, the simulated effects generally imply increased production of (net) export goods and reduced production of (net) imported goods. To the extent that initial (net) trade patterns reveal comparative advantages, therefore, the simulated production effects imply fuller exploitation of those advantages.

Table 7.6. *Comparative advantage and effects of market integration*

	Norway		Sweden	
	Net exports* initially	Production effect of 1992	Net exports* initially	Production effect of 1992
Generators and electric motors	− 13.1	− 0.7	10.8	57.2
Office machinery	− 56.6	− 37.5	− 17.6	− 21.6
Appliances	− 42.6	− 12.6	6.4	18.8
Pharmaceuticals	− 57.6	6.5	− 1.3	2.5
Motor vehicles	− 100.0	0.0	34.1	7.3

* Net exports in % of total trade; production effect in %.

If significant intersectoral comparative advantage remains unexploited with Europe, however, this should also be reflected in factor price differences between European countries. Neven (1990) considered this question by looking at wage differences within the Community; he concluded that the remaining differences in wages between the 'Northern' EC countries were too small to indicate significant unexploited comparative advantage. He did, however, find indications of remaining comparative advantage at the margin between 'Northern' and 'Southern' EC countries. A similar comparison between the Nordic EFTA countries and the 'Northern' EC countries is shown in Figures 7.2 and 7.3. Figure 7.2 shows the 1984 relative levels of economy-wide wage costs (including social security contributions) per employee, based on national income accounts. Figure 7.3 shows the development, over the 1976–84 period, in relative hourly wages in manufacturing (excluding social security contributions). It clearly appears that there are no substantial differences between the Nordic countries and the 'Northern' EC: in terms of total costs per employee, Norway and Sweden are about 10% above the average of the 7 EC countries, while Finland is slightly below the EC average. In terms of hourly wages in manufacturing, Sweden and Finland have converged towards the EC average since the mid-1970s; the relative Norwegian wage, on the other hand, has risen, presumably reflecting the effects of the oil industry and domestic spending of oil revenues.

There is something of a puzzle here: if factor prices are, in fact, equalised across European countries, it must mean that there is close to free trade and perfect competition in a 'sufficient' number of European industries.

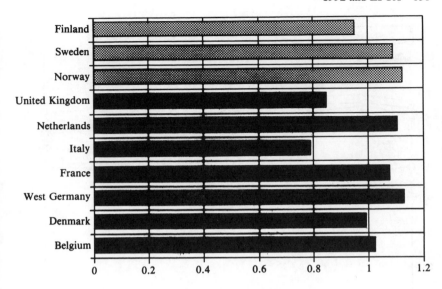

Figure 7.2 Labour costs (national accounts) per employee, 1984 (average for 7 EC countries = 1)

But that contradicts the premise of the 1992 programme, that there are substantial scale and competition gains to be made in a large number of European industries. In the context of EFTA, the puzzle can be formulated more precisely: the nordic EFTA countries have a clear comparative advantage in the production of capital- and raw materials-intensive products like metals and paper. To exploit this, they have to shift resources out of other industries. The fact that Nordic wages are close to the Northern European average suggests that they have done so, and that there would be little gain from increased specialisation.

At the same time, however, the industry studies discussed above suggest that the Nordic countries would gain from increased international competition in services and manufactured products other than metals and forest products. But if so, does it not follow that the imperfectly competitive industries in the Nordic countries are too large – i.e., that high-cost Scandinavian producers (in industries where the Nordic countries do not have a comparative advantage) are protected, through trade barriers and imperfect competition, from low-cost producers abroad? If so, should not increased international competition shift resources into metals and paper?

The apparent paradox should not, however, be oversold. First, the labour cost data does not show complete wage-rate equalisation. Within

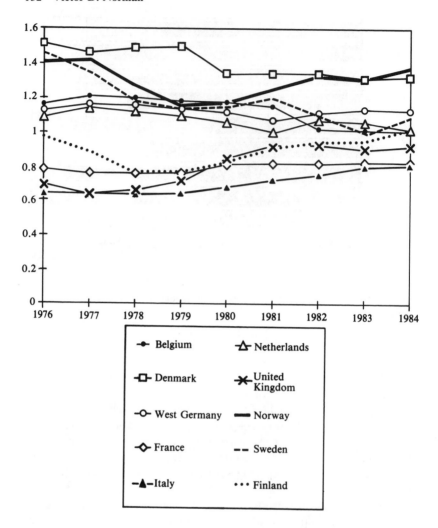

Figure 7.3 Relative hourly earnings, males, manufacturing (average of 7 EC countries = 1)

the Community, labour costs remain higher in Germany, France, and the Netherlands than in the rest of the EC; of the EFTA countries, Norwegian and Swedish wages remain higher than the European average. Moreover, even if the remaining wage difference is small, complete integration could still have significant effects on production and trade.

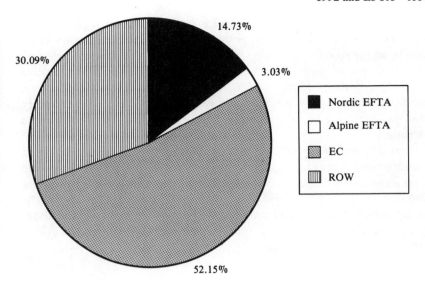

14.73%

30.09%

3.03%

52.15%

Nordic EFTA
Alpine EFTA
EC
ROW

Figure 7.4 Composition of Nordic EFTA trade, 1987

The crucial question is how elastic production and trade patterns are with respect to relative costs; if we take traditional trade theory at face value, the elasticities could be very large. As an illustration, consider the text-book example of a two-factor small, open economy producing labour- and capital-intensive goods with CES production functions. Suppose that for some reason (trade barriers or imperfectly competitive product markets), the wage rate is 10% higher in this country than in the rest of the world. By how much will production be distorted? The answer obviously depends on factor intensities and substitution possibilities. Using reasonable figures of an initial labour cost share of 0.8 for the labour-intensive good and 0.6 for the capital-intensive good, and an elasticity of substitution between capital and labour of 0.8 for both, the production distortion (the increase in production of the labour-intensive good consistent with 10% higher wages) is as high as 58.7%.

Second, the conflicting evidence from wage data and indicators of competition at the industry level can be reconciled by thinking of com-parative advantage at different levels of aggregation. In terms of broad factor and goods aggregates, the Nordic countries undoubtedly have a comparative advantage in capital- and raw materials-intensive products such as metals and forest products – and a corresponding comparative disadvantage in labour-intensive services and manufactured goods. That does not, however, preclude important differences at the industry level, due to sector-specific knowhow, sunk costs in R & D and product design, etc. It is, for example, fully possible that Norway has a comparative advantage in the production of marine equipment, derived from a long tradition of equipping merchant and fishing vessels, even if the country has a comparative disadvantage in engineering products more generally.

Even if it should be the case that the Nordic countries have exploited their comparative advantage at the aggregate level, it is therefore possible that significant comparative advantage gains remain unexploited at the industry level. If so, the 1992 programme could have large effects on the composition of services and manufactured goods production at the disaggregate level (which is exactly what Table 7.6 shows), but modest effects on the broad pattern of resource allocation.

4   Third-country effects

As is seen from Figure 7.4, countries outside the Community are important trading partners for the EFTA countries. The effects of 1992 on trade with (and trade policy towards) non-EC countries is therefore an important question. There are two issues here. One concerns the interdependence between the various EFTA countries: to what extent are the EFTA countries dependent on free trade with other EFTA countries, and thus on complete EFTA–EC integration? The other concerns trade policy towards the rest of the world. Some observers, notably Flam and Horn (1989), have expressed concern that the gains to be made from EFTA integration in the Community could be offset by losses from the more protectionist external trade policy of the EC.

In general, as is apparent from Figure 7.4, intra-EFTA trade is relatively unimportant. There are two important exceptions, however – Swedish–Norwegian and Swedish–Finnish trade. To Norway and Finland the effects of 1992 could depend critically on whether or not Sweden also becomes part of the internal market. Conversely, Norway and Finland could be important to Sweden.

To see how important Nordic interdependence is, we have used the industry model to simulate the effects of unilateral integration in the EC (Norman and Orvedal, 1990). Specifically, for one industry (household appliances) we have simulated the effects for Norway and Sweden of one of the two becoming part of the internal market, while the other remains outside. The results are summarised in Table 7.7. As is seen, there would

Table 7.7. *Effects for Norway of the 1992 programme (complete integration), household appliances, % changes*

	Production	Welfare
Norway and Sweden outside	− 4.13	− 0.20
Norway outside, Sweden inside	− 11.85	− 0.73
Norway inside, Sweden outside	− 4.49	1.03
Norway and Sweden inside	− 12.56	1.98

Welfare change in % of initial consumer expenditures.
Source: Norman and Orvedal (1990).

be a significant welfare loss to Norway if Sweden became part of the internal market and Norway stayed outside; similarly, the gain to Norway from joining would be halved if Sweden stayed outside. It seems fair to conclude therefore that, for the Nordic countries at least, it is important (a) that a joint agreement with the EC is achieved, and (b) that the agreement involves intra-Nordic integration as well as Nordic–EC integration.

The question of external trade policy is also important. At present, it is generally believed that the EFTA countries practise freer trade in manufactures than does the EC (or, more correctly, the EC countries – as far as nontariff barriers are generally national rather than Community barriers). If 1992 were to give a common external trade policy reflecting current EC practices, therefore, the EFTA countries would be likely to suffer a loss in its trade with the rest of the world. To see how important this may be, I have used the industry model for office machinery to simulate the effects of Scandinavian integration in the internal market if this also involves an increase in real trade costs from the rest of the world of 10% of the import price. Office machinery was chosen because imports to Scandinavia from outside Europe for this product group amount to more than 50% of total imports (see Table 7.1). Note also that an *ad valorem* increase in external trade barriers of 10 percentage points is a very high estimate. It is interesting to note from the results in Table 7.8, therefore, that even with such a substantial increase in external protection, the net effect of integration in Europe remains positive.

If even with a high estimate of increased external protection, integration for an industry with very substantial imports from outside the Commu-

Table 7.8. *Effects of integration, with or without changes in external trade policy, office machinery*

	Norway		Sweden	
	No change external trade policy	10% increase real trade costs ROW	No change external trade policy	10% increase real trade costs ROW
Production (%)	− 37.53	− 31.66	− 21.62	− 16.66
Exports (%)	− 54.91	− 54.54	− 21.77	− 20.02
Imports (%)	4.63	2.76	4.15	2.45
Change in domestic markup (% points)	− 1.67	− 1.03	− 1.21	− 0.99
Profits (million ECU)	− 2.97	− 1.64	− 5.48	− 3.53
Consumer surplus (million ECU)	9.89	4.52	20.30	7.93
Welfare (million ECU)	6.92	2.88	14.82	4.40
Welfare (% of initial expenditure)	1.40	0.58	1.49	0.44

nity is beneficial to the Scandinavian countries, it seems likely that the conclusion can be generalised. If so, the EFTA countries are likely to benefit from integration in Europe, even if they have to pay a price in terms of less free trade with the rest of the world. They would, of course, gain even more if the Community decided to practice free trade *vis-à-vis* the rest of the world.

5   Conclusions

This study posed three questions: (1) To what extent can the EFTA countries reap scale and competition gains from European integration? (2) To what extent is there remaining comparative advantage at the margin to be reaped from integration? (3) To what extent will more protectionist policies towards third countries reduce the EFTA gains from integration in Europe? The answers seem fairly clear: there are significant scale and competition gains to be made; particularly in service industries. For manufacturers, some of the possible gains have already been reaped. As regards comparative advantage, there may be little more to be gained at the aggregate level, but quite significant gains relating to the composition of production within broadly defined industries. Finally, more protectionist external trade policy will reduce – but not eliminate – the gains to the EFTA countries.

One important question which has not been addressed in the study is whether formal participation in the European integration process is necessary for the EFTA countries to realise the gains. Economically, this is not clear. Most of the gains discussed in the study derive from deregulation of domestic markets and the opening up of those markets for foreign competition (through simplification of border formalities, changes in product standards, and an end to discriminatory public procurement). All of this can be achieved unilaterally; one could therefore argue, as Flam and Horn (1989) do, that the EFTA countries would be better off through a combination of unilateral deregulation and adoption of desirable elements in the 1992 programme on the one hand and free trade with the non-EC world on the other. In that way, the EFTA countries could realise all the benefits from European integration without paying a price in terms of more protectionist policies *vis-à-vis* the rest of the world.

There are two possible flaws in this line of argument – one economic and one political. Economically, the Flam–Horn argument neglects the question of access to export markets. EFTA countries can unilaterally ensure foreign access to their home markets; they cannot unilaterally ensure access for their own exports to EC markets. To the extent that a unilateral course means that EFTA exports would face barriers in EC markets, therefore, there could be an economic argument for a formal integration agreement. It is unclear how important this argument is. The current free trade agreement between the individual EFTA countries and the EC, which presumably would remain in force, ensures a minimum of market access. For major Nordic EFTA exports such as metals and paper, the free trade agreement is probably enough; for other exports, such as Swedish cars, non-tariff barriers constitute important access restrictions, and a unilateral policy could therefore give significant losses of export profits.

The airline study can serve as an illustration. As noted above, competition on Scandinavian air routes could give very large welfare gains, but it would also involve substantial profit shifting. If the Scandinavian countries unilaterally decided to open up air transportation for European competition, therefore, a significant portion of the welfare gains would 'leak out' in the form of increased profits for non-Scandinavian carriers. With airline deregulation on a European basis, on the other hand, with equal access to all markets for EC and Scandinavian carriers, the loss of domestic profits could be offset by increased profits on intra-EC routes. The potential political flaw in the Flam–Horn argument concerns the likelihood that liberalisation will, in fact, take place. It can be posed in a simple way by asking why, if deregulation and increased international competition are so obviously in the national interest, and if they can be achieved unilaterally, such policies have not been pursued already. The answer presumably has to do with public choice and the political economy of protection. If so, we know that some form of constitutional restraint is called for: an EFTA–EC agreement is exactly that.

NOTE

The research for this study was financed in part through a grant from the shipping research programme of the Norwegian Research Council for Science and Technology. The study draws heavily on joint work with Linda Orvedal, and to some extent also on joint work with Siri P. Strandenes. I am grateful to both; and also to Jan I. Haaland, Carl Hamilton and Anthony Venables for valuable comments and to Gerhard Stoltz and Tore Nilsen for data on banking.

REFERENCES

Flam, H. and H. Horn (1989) 'Ekonomiska konsekvenser för Sverige av EGs inre marknad', *Svensk ekonomi och Europaintegrationen*, Stockholm.
Krugman, P.R. (1988) 'EFTA and 1992', *EFTA Occasional Papers*, **23**.
Lundberg, L. (1989) 'Svenskt näringsliv och den europeiska integrationen', *Svensk ekonomi och Europaintegrationen*, Stockholm.

Neven, D. (1990) 'EC integration towards 1992: some distributional aspects', *Economic Policy* (April) pp. 14–62).

Norman, V. (1989) 'EFTA and the internal European market', *Economic Policy*. (October) pp. 424–65.

Norman, V. and L. Orvedal (1990) 'Stordriftsfordeler, konkurranse og marked-sintegrasjon', *SAF-rapport*, **1/1990**.

Norman, V. and S.P. Strandenes (forthcoming) 'Deregulating Scandinavian air-lines; a case study of the Oslo–Stockholm route', in P. Krugman and A. Smith (eds), *Empirical Studies of Strategic Trade Policy*, Chicago: University of Chicago Press for NBER.

Smith, A. and A.J. Venables (1988) 'Completing the internal market in the European Community: Some Industry Simulations', *European Economic Review*, **32**, pp. 1501–25.

Discussion

CARL B. HAMILTON

Victor Norman's study is clear and well argued, and I agree with his conclusions. These conclusions also serve as an agenda for future research: less emphasis on trade in manufactures and more on the many other aspects of EFTA's integration with the EC. I think this in fact is the most important message of Norman's study. So let me expand somewhat on this theme.

The European Free Trade Association (EFTA) is an association of states, each one of which has its own free trade agreement in manufactures with the EC. EFTA has no supranational institutions, and no long-run political aims. There are no EFTA–EC free trade agreements covering agricultural products, or services, or labour mobility, or capital mobility. In short, the 1992 Internal Market programme covers many more issues than does the present EFTA Charter.

A starting point of Victor Norman is the assumption that the upcoming agreements on the European Economic Space (EES) probably imply that the EFTA countries will have to accept the Community's common external trade policy. This seems to me very unlikely, especially since both sides agree that agriculture is not to be included in any EES agreement. Border controls will consequently have to be kept for this reason, if for no other. However, the preconditions for the EES negotiations changed during 1989, and it now seems plausible to assume that during the 1990s all the EFTA countries – possibly with the exception of Switzerland – will become full EC members. Then, of course, these EFTA countries will also be members of the EC's common policies, including the external commercial policy.

This should have implications for today's, and for any future, research agenda. We must avoid barking under the wrong tree – concentrating on relatively conventional issues of integration for which there exists a developed theory and empirical methods, rather than on the more tricky aspects of EFTA countries' integration into the Internal Market (and the EC), including issues falling in the border zone of law and economics such as integration into the common competition policy (a subset of this is Norman's market segmentation issues). More work is needed on the effects of freer services trade; of agricultural deregulation, trade and EFTA integration into the CAP; of effects on location and quality of investment in EFTA countries; of the common fisheries policy (Iceland's economic base); of migration; of EFTA countries' integration into the common public procurement policy; and of the system of indirect taxation (tax rates and tax base). On many occasions researchers may not be able to give very precise answers on these questions, or to provide simulations, but at least we would be barking under the right trees.

In his study, Victor Norman certainly barks under one of the right trees when he analyses the service sector, a sector where large economic gains and structural changes are likely to appear. His example of airline deregulation is striking, and his discussion of banking deregulation thought-provoking. They point to the possibility of a *'four-phased regulation cycle'*: they would start off with (1) a service sector being regulated. (2) The sector is deregulated which leads to fiercer competition and lower prices through the entry of new firms and imports. (3) There is an autonomous move back towards more concentration, higher prices and a stable market solution, possibly with fewer firms than in stage (1). This – in stage 4 – may then call forth public demands for new regulation aiming at lower prices through guaranteed survival of a larger number of firms. After a period when this regulation has matured or been derailed it is yet again time for deregulation, etc. (Incidentally, the road haulage industry of the Nordic countries is already partly deregulated – just as in the Benelux countries – providing us with a possible *anti-monde* for studies of the effects of deregulation of this large service industry.)

In the area of EFTA's manufacturing production I would not primarily stress trade, but rather investment issues, such as the consequences of the continued uncertainty of the precise future relations of EFTA countries with the EC – i.e., the shadow of potential future EC trade barriers against EFTA exports possibly resulting in more investments being located in the EC. What effects will this have on traded volumes (trade and foreign direct investment being complements, according to Birgitta Swedenborg, 1979), and on imports to the EFTA countries of embodied new technology and management knowledge, wages, and national welfare?

The 1990s promises to be a wonderful decade for European economists!

REFERENCES

Swedenborg, B. (1979) *The Multinational Operations of Swedish Firms. An analysis of determinants and effects*, Stockholm: Industrial Institute for Economic and Social Research, and Almqvist & Wiksell.

8 Technology policy in the completed European market

DAVID ULPH

1 Introduction

While the major aim of completing the European market is the removal of a plethora of barriers to the free movement of goods and factors in order to realise significant *static* improvements in resource allocation, a clear secondary aim is the enhancement of *dynamic* efficiency, and these are clearly seen as *complementary* rather than *competing* objectives.

The Cecchini Report (1988) thus paints a glowing picture of a virtuous circle whereby market liberalisation spurs greater innovative activity, which in turn leads to enhanced competition and the regaining of technological leadership:

> Market integration brings with it a number of factors giving European firms the chance to regain technological leadership. Among these factors [are]: European market liberalization and growth; the removal of market entry barriers (e.g. standards); the creation of new companies, particularly in the high tech sectors; and the rapid development of cross-frontier business cooperation. Only when European companies regain this leadership can they call the shots – or, in the language of economics, go from being 'price takers' to 'price makers'.
>
> In short, strengthening European competitivity (*sic*) leads, so to speak, to the reconquest of the European market.

The emphasis on cooperative R & D arrangements reflects this new-found enthusiasm for cooperation. Thus while Art. 85 of the Treaty of Rome condemns agreements between firms and collusive practices which may restrict trade, the White Paper on the single market, *Completing the Internal Market*, states that 'the removal of internal boundaries and the establishment of free movement of goods and capital and the freedom to provide services are clearly fundamental to the creation of the internal market. Nevertheless, Community action must go further and create an environment or conditions likely to favour the development of cooperation between undertakings'. On p. 86 of the Cecchini Report we are told

142

that 'cooperative behaviour for R & D coupled with tough competition in the end market, might further the general welfare more than totally non-cooperative behaviour'. Moreover, in March 1985, a block exemption regulation on R & D agreements came into force. This new regulation leaves intact a 1968 Notice on cooperation between enterprises, which states that cooperative agreements relating *only* to R & D do not normally fall under Art. 85. It does, however, extend this favourable treatment to R & D agreements that include joint manufacturing of the joint venture product and licensing to third parties. However this can take place only if the knowledge acquired through R & D is integral to the production knowhow, and joint *marketing* of the product is not allowed.

Thus the 'technology policy in the completed European market' that seems to emerge from this is that of encouraging – or at least not discouraging – Research Joint Ventures (RJVs), the presumption being that firms will then be lead to combine to regain technological leadership.

There are three major points I would like to raise about this, and these will take me into the substance of the study.

The first is that discussing technology policy in terms of simply regaining technological leadership is not very sensible. Policy should be geared to increasing some better-founded notion of welfare, and we should be trying to identify ways in which the market might fail, and designing policy to correct that failure. If, in the process, we regain technological leadership, well and good, but that should not be the aim of policy. To illustrate this point, in Beath, Katsoulacos and Ulph (1989), we have a model of two firms, each located in a different country, engaged in a strategic race to be first to innovate. A government, through a policy of subsidising R & D, can certainly increase the probability that 'its' firm will be the likely winner. Yet, even if we assume that all the government is interested in doing is maximising the expected rents accruing to that country, it turns out that in a wide class of cases giving such a subsidy is undesirable.

The second issue I would like to raise is whether, if we do have some wider framework within which to examine technology policy, encouraging cooperation is likely to be desirable. This is an issue on which economic theory is surprisingly uninformative. While there has been a considerable upsurge of interest in innovation over the last ten or so years, particularly in the theory of strategic innovation, the welfare aspects of the work have not been given a great deal of attention. In section 2 I will briefly review what I think can be said.

The final issue I want to raise is whether, if cooperation is desirable, simply creating a permissive regime in which research cooperation is allowed, and then letting market forces dictate the outcome, will produce the right amount of cooperation. Is there a role for a more activist tech-nology policy to encourage or perhaps discourage the market in forming cooperative ventures? This is the subject of sections 2 and 3 of the study.

2   R & D, welfare and cooperation

In section 2 I want briefly to consider what economic theory has to say about the desirability of encouraging cooperation in the form of RJVs.

There are three main gains that RJVs are thought to bring about.

The first is that, by encouraging firms to act in a cooperative fashion of maximising joint profits, rather than act in a non-cooperative fashion of trying to gain some advantage over each other, they can improve their profits. There is nothing here that specifically depends on RJVs – these are just the standard gains from cooperation. However, there are two quali-fications that have to be made. The first is that for this cooperation to be socially desirable there should be no detrimental consequences (e.g., on consumer surplus) which offset the increased profits. I will assume that with RJVs we can ignore any offsetting factors. A more important point is that this argument about the gains from cooperation works in general only when everyone cooperates. We know from the 'paradox of mergers' that simply having a subset of firms merge can lead to their all having lower profits. Moreover, even if those inside the cooperative arrangement gain, those outside might lose and if we are interested in the totality of profits, a partial collaboration might be undesirable. This issue will be taken up more extensively in sections 3 and 4.

A second gain RJVs are thought to bring is that of cost sharing. The idea here is that, under non-cooperative behaviour, firms will engage in need-less duplication of research effort. So it may be possible that by, for example, setting up a single lab, sharing the costs, and disseminating the results to everyone else, the RJV can undertake research much more cheaply than individual firms.

Is excessive duplication a feature of market equilibrium that greater cooperation could help us avoid? In a classic study, Dasgupta and Stiglitz (1980) argued that it was. However, in their model they assumed that firms produced an identical product, and it is easy to see how that could gener-ate a presumption in favour of excessive duplication. However, in a more recent study, Katsoulacos and Ulph (1990) have examined a differentiated products model, in which R & D is product-specific. They show that if consumers' taste for variety is sufficiently small then all the Dasgupta and Stiglitz conclusions hold. However, if consumers' taste for variety is suffi-ciently large, and if we deal with a market in which there are a large number of firms and consumers then

(1)   individual firms will do approximately the right amount of research;
(2)   the market as a whole will do too little, and will have too few
       research labs.

So while there are potential gains to be had from cooperation on this
front, they are by no means universal.

In many circumstances running a single lab is not the best way of
conducting research, and it pays to have different labs trying different
lines of research; in these circumstances, the RJV is thought to offer
benefits from *coordinating research effort*. Dasgupta and Maskin (1987)
analyse the nature of market failure when firms pursue independent
research strategies, and show that the market can lead firms to undertake
the wrong kinds of research. There are again potential gains from
cooperation.

Economic theory does thus suggest that there are potential welfare gains
from forming RJVs though these are not universal, and under some
circumstances it is not obvious that cooperation is desirable.

In the remainder of the study I want to consider the question of whether,
if cooperation is desirable, the market will achieve the right amount of it.

3   A model of market and optimal formation of RJVs

In section 3 and 4 I want to consider whether, in a model where there are
potential gains from the formation of RJVs, the market will always get the
right amount of cooperation. The model I use is one in which firms are
competing to produce a homogeneous product which, from the discussion
of the Dasgupta and Stiglitz (1980) model of section 2, certainly creates a
presumption that there are gains from cooperation. In section 3 I set the
model out, and in section 4 I undertake the comparison between the
equilibrium and the market degree of cooperation.

3.1   The model

The model in this section is a simple extension of that contained in
d'Aspremont and Jacquemin (1988) and in Beath and Ulph (1989), both
of which consider a model with just two identical firms who form an RJV.

There are $n + m$ firms, n of them are 'European', the remaining m
'Japanese', which I will use as a term to cover all outside competitors.
These firms produce a homogeneous product which is sold on an integra-
ted international market. Demand for this product is given by

$$p = D - \sum_{j=1}^{n+m} q_j \tag{1}$$

where $D > 0$ is a constant, and q_j is the output of firm j.

I assume that equilibrium in the product market is a Cournot equilibrium. Then, if c_j is the unit cost of production of firm j, the *production profits* made by firm i in a Cournot equilibrium in which all firms produce positive output are given by

$$
\pi_i = \left[\frac{D + \sum_{\substack{j=1 \\ j \neq i}}^{n+m} c_j - (n+m)c_i}{(n+m+1)} \right]^2 \tag{2}
$$

A proof of this result is given in the Appendix.

I now suppose that, in the absence of any R & D, the unit production costs of the n 'European' firms will be a, those of the m 'Japanese' firms b, where $a > b > 0$. Thus the Japanese already have an advantage.

If we consider first the case where there are no cooperative ventures, then I assume that if a 'European' firm wishes to reduce its costs by an amount x, it will have to spend an amount γx^2 on R & D, whereas if a 'Japanese' firm wishes to reduce its costs by y, it will have to spend γy^2 on R & D. There are no spillovers.

Before proceeding, let me make three remarks on these assumptions:

(1)   The assumption of a quadratic cost function for R & D is crucial for some of the results that follow – in particular, for the result that, in the absence of cooperation, 'Japanese' firms will spend more on R & D than their rival 'European' firms and so will pull further ahead.

It is possible to show that if the relationship between unit production costs had been,

$$
c = a(1 + x)^{-\gamma} \tag{3}
$$

then, at least for some parameter values, the 'European' firms do more R & D than the 'Japanese', though not enough to eliminate the initial cost differences. On the other hand, had the relationship been

$$
c = ae^{-\gamma x} \tag{4}
$$

then initial cost asymmetries are eliminated. However I have retained the quadratic cost assumption of the d'Aspremont and Jacquemin study because it captures in a clear way the concern that if firms continue to act non-cooperatively, 'Europe' will fall further behind.

(2)   I have assumed that all firms have identical R & D technologies. This clearly ignores two possibilities. The first is that because

'success breeds success' the 'Japanese' not only have better production technologies than 'European' firms, but also better R & D
technologies. The second is that the 'Japanese' have a cost advantage
because they already organise their R & D in more cooperative
fashion. However I will ignore these possibilities, in part because I
want to focus on how other asymmetries such as initial cost differences and the way R & D is organised within 'Europe' can affect the
amount of R & D each type of firm does, and in part because I think
it would be a fairly trivial exercise to extend the current study to take
account of these possibilities, and would affect the conclusions in a
fairly obvious way.

(3)   I have ignored spillovers partly because they have been fairly
exhaustively discussed in the two studies referred to at the start of
this section, and I do not think they add much to the present
analysis, though they clearly strengthen the rationale for RJVs to
form to internalise the externality. However I have also ignored
them because taking them seriously would involve discussing
whether there was any difference in the spillovers within 'Europe',
within 'Japan' and between 'Europe' and 'Japan'.

In deciding on the amount of R & D to undertake, each firm takes as
given the amount of R & D done by everyone else. Thus a typical
'European' firm would take as given the amount of R & D, $\bar{x}$, done by
each of the other 'European' firms and the amount $\bar{y}$ done by each of the
'Japanese' firms and will choose its own x to maximise its *overall operating
profits*, Π, defined as its production profits, π, minus its R & D costs.
These are given by

$$\Pi = \left[\frac{D + (m-1)(a + \bar{x}) + m(b - \bar{y}) - (n+m)(a-x)}{(n+m+1)} \right]^2 - \gamma x^2$$

$$(5)$$

It then follows that, in a symmetric equilibrium where all 'European'
firms choose the same x, and all 'Japanese' firms the same y, the equilibrium levels of x and y satisfy the equations

$$\left[\frac{\gamma(n+m+1)^2}{(n+m)} - (m+1) \right] x + my = D + mb - (m+1)a \qquad (6)$$

and

$$nx + \left[\frac{\gamma(n+m+1)^2}{(n+m)} - (n+1) \right] y = D + na - (n+1)b \qquad (7)$$

If we subtract these two equations we find

$$\left[\frac{\gamma(n+m+1)^2}{(n+m)} - 1 \right] (x - y) = (b - a) \qquad (8)$$

In order for the model to satisfy all the relevant second-order and stability conditions, the term in square brackets must be positive, hence we have

Theorem 1 If $b < a$, then $x < y$

The firms with the higher initial costs do less R & D than those with the lower initial costs, and thus fall further behind. This result captures clearly the concern expressed in the Cecchini Report that, in the absence of integration and its associated pursuit of cross-border cooperative research ventures, European firms will fall further behind their rivals.

I want now to examine the formation of RJVs in Europe. By an 'RJV' I will mean a cooperative arrangement covering R & D alone, with production taking place in a purely non-cooperative fashion. Of course there are important policy issues surrounding the question of how far one might want to encourage RJVs by giving them some degree of immunity from competition policy, and allowing some degree of cooperative behaviour in the product market. However, this relates to the question of *how* one might like to encourage cooperation, whereas I am focusing on the prior question of *whether* one wants to encourage it at all. So I will leave these policy issues aside for further work.

The question I want to ask is whether market forces can be relied upon to achieve the socially optimal degree of cooperation, or whether there is a role for policy to encourage or discourage cooperation. More precisely, I am going to assume that only one RJV forms in Europe, and ask whether market forces lead to this being too large or too small. There is of course no reason why only one RJV should form, but answering the question of whether the right number of RJVs form requires a significant extension of the current analysis.

Suppose then that k of the n 'European' firms form an RJV. Later on, I will determine the value of k, but for the moment it is given.

Furthermore, for expositional purposes, I will treat the case where $2 \leq k < n$. The case where $k = n$ is an obvious special case of this analysis.

Let z be the amount of cost reduction achieved by each member of the RJV; x that achieved by each 'European' firm outside the RJV; and y that achieved by each 'Japanese' firm. Then the *production profits* made by a typical firm in the RJV are

$$\pi^r = \left[\frac{\begin{array}{c} D + (n - k)(a - x) + (k - 1)(a - z) \\ + m(b - y) - (n + m)(a - z) \end{array}}{(n + m + 1)} \right]^2 \tag{9}$$

I want now to examine the *overall operating profits*, Π^r, of a firm in the RJV. I want to contrast three different assumptions about R & D costs that can be made; these correspond to three increasingly favourable views of the advantages of forming an RJV.

C1   No cost sharing

Here each firm essentially carries on doing its own R & D and incurs, as before, an R & D cost γz^2. In this case the only feature that distinguishes the RJV is that it maximizes joint profits. Put differently, each firm realises that its choice of z will be the same as that of every other firm in the RJV, and no longer tries to get a competitive advantage over its colleagues. This is the assumption about RJVs made by d'Aspremont and Jacquemin.

C2   Cost sharing

This can be thought of as the case where the RJV operates a single research lab to generate the cost reduction z. The total R & D associated with this is as before γz^2, but now this is shared out within the RJV so that each member of the RJV has an R & D cost of only $(\gamma/k)z^2$. Thus under this type of arrangement the RJV is able to go beyond just the maximisation of joint profits and can also eliminate *needless duplication*.

C3   Full coordination

Here the RJV is able fully to coordinate the research strategies of the individual members, so that the overall cost reduction of z is achieved by having each firm undertake research leading to a cost reduction of z/k. The cost to each firm of this is therefore

$$\left[\frac{\gamma}{k^2}\right] z^2$$

As we will see, in understanding the nature of the equilibrium vs optimal RJV formation, it is critically important to distinguish these three cases. In setting out the formal analysis, I will focus on the case where costs satisfy C3. The other two cases follow with obvious changes.

Firms in the RJV choose z to maximise their *overall operating profit*, recognising that all other firms in the RJV will choose the same z; however, they take as given the values of x and y chosen by firms outside the RJV. Firms outside the RJV choose their own R & D to maximise their *overall operating profit*, taking as given the R & D choices of everyone else. The equations characterising the symmetric equilibrium values of x, y and z are derived from the first-order conditions for profit maximisation for (1) a typical member of the RJV; (2) a typical 'European' firm outside the RJV; (3) a typical 'Japanese' firm. These equations are, respectively:

$$(n - k)x + my + \left[\frac{\gamma(n + m + 1)^2}{k^2(n + m + 1 - k)} - (n + m + 1 - k)\right]z$$

$$= D + mb - (m + 1)a \tag{10}$$

$$\left[\frac{\gamma(n + m + 1)^2}{(n + m)} - (m + k + 1)\right]x + my + kz$$

$$= D + mb - (m + 1)a \tag{11}$$

$$(n - k)x + \left[\frac{\gamma(n + m + 1)^2}{(n + m)} - (n + 1)\right]y + kz$$

$$= D + na - (n + 1)b \tag{12}$$

If we subtract equations (10) and (11) we find

$$\left[\frac{\gamma(n + m + 1)}{k^2(n + m + 1 - k)} - 1\right]z = \left[\frac{\gamma(n + m + 1)}{(n + m)} - 1)\right].x \tag{13}$$

Again, for stability purposes, both square brackets must be positive. Moreover, it is easily checked that $k^2(n + m + 1 - k) > (n + m)$, from which it follows that $z > x$, so that firms in the RJV achieve greater cost reductions than those 'European' ones outside the RJV.

If C2 were to hold then the denominator in the coefficient on z would be $k(n + m + 1 - k)$, which again is $> (n + m)$ and so once again $z > x$. However if C1 were to hold then the denominator in the coefficient on z becomes $n + m + 1 - k < n + m$, and so $z < x$.

Thus if the RJV has no innate cost advantages, the fact that firms are cooperating and not trying to use R & D to get an advantage over some of their rivals means that they do less R & D than the non-cooperative 'European' firms. However, if the RJV does confer some cost advantage, then this outweighs the joint profit maximising consideration and leads firms in the RJV to engage in more cost cutting then their non-cooperative counterparts. Whether, given that their R & D costs are lower, they actually spend more on R & D is unclear, but is not an issue I wish to pursue here.

If we subtract equations (11) and (12) we once again get equation (8), so 'European' firms outside the RJV still achieve less cost reduction than the 'Japanese' firms. We can summarise these results in

Theorem 2   If C1 holds then $z < x < y$; if C2 or C3 hold then $z > x$ and $y > x$

Clearly if C1 holds then no 'European' firm can ever regain the lead through cooperative R & D ventures. The interesting question is whether, if C2 or C3 hold, those in the RJV will ever do more cost reduction than the 'Japanese' firms ($z > y$) and, if they do, whether this will be sufficient to regain the technological lead ($a - z < b - y$).

This is difficult to answer analytically. However, I have the following negative result.

Theorem 3   If $k = n$, and if *either*

(1)   with the cost assumption C3 the following inequality holds

$$\frac{b}{n+m} \le \frac{a}{n^2(m+1)} \tag{14}$$

or

(2)   with the cost assumption C2 the following inequality holds

$$\frac{b}{n+m} \le \frac{a}{n(m+1)} \tag{15}$$

then

$$b - y < a - z$$

Proof: See Appendix.

Thus if the initial cost differences are too great, European firms will not regain the lead, even if all of them join the RJV.

Now I have used the notion of 'catching up' or 'regaining the technological lead' in this Theorem, and elsewhere, in a very literal way. It is, of course, a very difficult condition to verify.

Moreover, as Theorem 3 shows, it is also a very strong condition to require, and under some circumstances may be impossible to achieve. For these reasons, it may be more reasonable to frame the requirement somewhat differently. For example, one might think of 'catching up' in a more natural way as simply increasing the share of 'European' firms in the world market. However even this is not a clearcut requirement since there are now two types of 'European' firms – those inside the RJV and those outside – so is the share we are interested that of the 'European' firms overall, or simply of the leading firms – in my model, those in the RJV?

Given the complexity of the equations involved, I have no analytical results on how market share – however measured – is affected by the formation of RJVs of various sizes. It is, however, a straightforward matter to solve equations (6)–(7) and (10)–(12) numerically and hence see how market shares are affected by the formation of RJVs.

However, once it is accepted that 'catching up' or 'regaining the lead' as formulated in Theorem 3 may not be a very adequate criterion for judging policy, we should recognise that increasing market share may also not be a very desirable policy if this is bought at too high a price in terms of R & D resources. It therefore seems sensible to evaluate the desirability of RJVs in terms of a more direct welfare indicator, and to ask whether market forces will lead to the optimal degree of cooperation.

In thinking about this issue, the final assumption I want to make is that firms in the RJV face *coordination costs*, and that the coordination costs faced by a firm in an RJV of size k are $\varphi.(k-1)$, where $\varphi > 0$ is a coordination cost parameter. It is clearly realistic to assume that firms would face such coordination costs, though the precise form I have assumed is more debatable. In particular, it could be argued that, especially if we are assuming C3, these coordination costs should also depend on the amount of R & D. However, since I am never going to be making direct quantitative comparisons across the three cost cases, this possibility can be allowed for by having the value of γ change across the three cases. We can clearly interpret the creation of an integrated European market as a policy which lowers the real value of φ, while the operation of particular programmes like Esprit can be thought of as a policy of subsidising φ.

The *total profits* of a firm in the RJV are then simply its *overall operating profits* minus its coordination costs. The total profits of every other firm are simply its overall operating profits.

I will take it that the socially optimal value of k is that which maximises the total profits of all the 'European' firms. This ignores consumer surplus issues, but it is not clear that those are at the heart of the discussion of technology policy. The important point about this criterion is that it takes account of the effect of the firms in the RJV on those outside the RJV.

I will take the equilibrium value of k to be that which maximises the profits of an individual member of the RJV. Implicit in this definition is the idea that the RJV will form if firms can make more profits by being in the RJV than by continuing all to act independently but can restrict entry – and will do so if, by including another firm, the profits of existing members would fall. As we will see in section 4, however, there are some problems with this definition of equilibrium when the cost assumption is C1.

I have no analytical results on the comparison of the equilibrium and the optimum values of k, and to make progress on this have had to resort to numerical simulations. These are reported in section 4.

4   Comparing equilibrium and optimal sizes of RJVs

The model developed in section 3 has a large number of parameters. However, two aspects of the model are of particular interest. One is the initial cost difference between 'European' and 'Japanese' firms, and the other is the cost of coordination. So in the simulation results I am going to fix the following parameter values:

$$D = 1000; \quad n = 5; \quad m = 2; \quad b = 100; \quad \gamma = 15$$

and let a and φ vary.

I also want to distinguish the three cost cases introduced in section 3.

4.1   The case where costs satisfy C1

Here, if two firms join an RJV, they no longer compete to try to get an advantage over one another, and so cut back on the amount of R & D (and hence cost-saving) they have been doing to try to gain such an advantage. If there were no other firms around, and if there were no coordination costs, they would certainly be better off from cooperating; these are the basic results of the d'Aspremont and Jacquemin study. However, there are other firms around, both in Europe and in 'Japan', and the reduction in R & D by the firms in the RJV has two effects on them: it increases their profits since they do not face such intense competition from the firms in the RJV, and it leads them to do more R & D because, now they are getting a bigger market share, this increases the profitabiity of R & D. This last reaction in turn has a damaging impact on the profits of the firms in the RJV – though, in all the simulations, not enough to offset the beneficial effects of cooperation. Thus, as long as coordination costs are small, the formation of an RJV can increase everybody's profits. The problem is that in all the cases I have examined, if $k < n$, then the 'European' firms outside the RJV are always better off than those inside the RJV, so it is hard to see how any equilibrium in which $2 \leq k < n$ could be achieved. On the other hand if $k = n$, a firm would always be better off if it left the RJV and the remaining $n - 1$ stayed.

Thus, apart from the case where $n = 2$, if there are no explicit cost advantages to forming an RJV it seems hard to see how market forces alone could lead to their formation, despite the fact that, as long as coordination costs are not too high, it will be socially optimal to have an RJV form. There is a clear market failure, which could be corrected by a policy intervention which involved reversing the advantages of being outside the RJV. This would imply, for example, not merely completely subsidising the coordination costs, but going beyond that to subsidising RJV formation. Alternatively, the policy could involve changing the cost structure to, for example, a C2 cost structure by setting up a central lab to which all partners in the RJV had to contribute. Whether this latter policy would be desirable will depend on how well the market performed in promoting RJVs under a C2 cost structure, and to this I now turn.

4.2   The case where costs satisfy C2

Here the cost advantages to the RJV are such that they engage in more cost-cutting than they would under the non-cooperative outcome, while both the other 'European' firms and the 'Japanese' firms do less than they would have done in the non-cooperative equilibrium. Moreover the larger is the RJV that forms, the further do all firms move from their non-cooperative levels of cost-cutting. This has three implications.

The first is that, *in the absence of coordination costs*, total European profits are typically an increasing and strictly convex function of k. The reason is that if a small RJV forms it will gain a relatively small cost advantage, but any damage it does will be spread over a fairly large number of firms, so the overall gain to Europe is fairly small, whereas the larger the RJV that forms, the greater will be its cost advantage, and while this might inflict a great loss of market share on the remaining 'European' firms outside the RJV, there are fewer of them, so the gains are increasing in k.

The second implication is that, *in the absence of coordination costs*, the profits of an individual firm are typically increasing and concave in k, usually taking a maximum at some $k < n$. The reason is that although, as k increases, this lowers the R & D costs of every firm in the RJV, thus raising their profits, it also means that bringing one more firm into the RJV involves sharing the market with a firm whose market share has fallen further and further behind those in the RJV. So with the 'marginal firm' being so much behind the 'average', the average will tend to fall, giving rise to a powerful counteracting force on average profits, and so the concavity of the individual firm's profit function.

The third implication is that, *in the absence of coordination costs*, the profits of 'European' firms inside the RJV are always higher than those outside, so the equilibrium concept I have been using is perfectly coherent.

Thus, taking the first two implications together, we see that, *in the absence of coordination costs*, there is typically too little cooperation, because members of an RJV take account of neither the gain in total profits from allowing another firm to join their favoured group, nor of the fact that, by admitting another firm, they are spreading any damage they do over fewer outsiders.

If we now allow for coordination costs, then the first thing to point out is that these have no effect on the amount of R & D done by any of the firms. So the 'gross' profits of Europe and of the individual firm within the RJV are precisely the same as in the Zero coordination cost case just discussed. What coordination costs do is to reduce total European profits by the amount $\varphi.k.(k-1)$, but the profits of an individual firm within the RJV by only $\varphi.(k-1)$. The effect of this on total European profits, Π, and on the profits of a representative firm in the RJV, Π^r is illustrated in Figure 8.1.

What we thus see is that, while there is too little cooperation when coordination costs are low, there is too much when they are high. The intuition is straightforward; when thinking about the introduction of another firm into the RJV a representative member of the RJV will contemplate an additional coordination cost of φ, since there is only one other firm to coordinate with. From the point of view of total European profits, however, an additional firm involves φk additional coordination costs as the new firm coordinates with all the existing ones, plus φk additional costs as each existing one coordinates with it. The marginal private coordination cost of the RJV is thus lower than the marginal social coordination cost, and this difference is greater the larger are coordination costs, and the more firms there are in the RJV.

We therefore obtain the striking conclusion that it is advantageous to subsidise coordination costs when they are low, and tax them when they are high.

To illustrate this point, I give a numerical example, where $a = 150$; in Table 8.1, for various values of φ I give the associated values of the optimum number of firms in the RJV, $\hat{k}$, the equilibrium number, k^e, and the percentage loss of European profits from being at the equilibrium rather than the optimum, l.

Within the range over which I varied the initial cost conditions – $a = 120$ and $a = 200$ – there seemed to be very little difference in any of the figures in Table 8.1.

Two further points to note about this case are:

(1) if, in the above example, φ is increased to 400 then both the equilibrium and the optimum involve having no RJV form;
(2) with $a = 200$, and *a fortiori*, with $a = 150$ or 120, condition (15) is not satisfied, yet in no case does the RJV succeed in gaining technological supremacy, even when all 'European' firms are in the RJV.

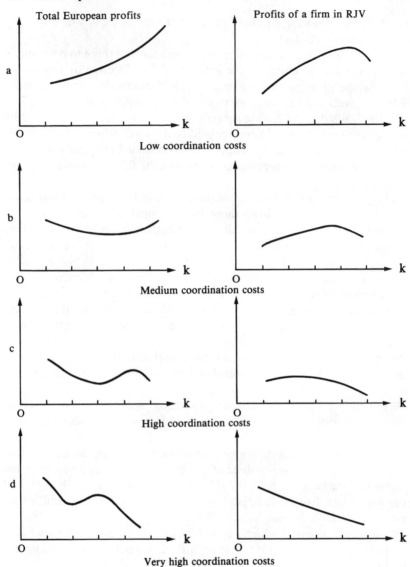

Figure 8.1 Variation in profits with size of RJV

4.3   The case where costs satisfy C3

The broad qualitative features of this case are exactly the same as in the previous one. However, because forming an RJV is so much more profitable in this case, the quantitative features are rather different. Thus for

Table 8.1. *Comparison of equilibrium and optimum sizes of RJV*

φ	5	50	100	150	200
$\hat{k}$	5	5	5	1	1
k^e	4	3	3	3	2
l	2.05	2.57	0.97	0.59	0.63

the range of values of the parameters considered in Table 8.1, it is always the case that $\hat{k} = 5$, and $k^e = 4$. However the loss of European profits, l, ranges from 11.06 for the case where $\varphi = 5$, to 8.87, so the cost of not getting the right size of RJV is very much greater than Table 8.1 indicates.

On the other hand for the higher values for φ of 650, 700 and 750, we get, respectively, $\hat{k} = 5$, $k^e = 4$, $l = 2.30$; $\hat{k} = 1$, $k^e = 4$, $l = 1.43$; and $\hat{k} = 1$, $k^e = 4$, $l = 3.16$. Thus, once again, as φ increases there is a fairly dramatic switch from having too little to having too much cooperation.

Finally, with the parameters considered in the above examples, it turns out that if only four of the firms join an RJV they will regain the technological lead over the 'Japanese'.

5   Conclusions

There are four general conclusions of this study:

(1) discussing technology policy in terms of regaining technological leadership is not a sensible way to proceed;
(2) a more careful examination of potential market failures suggests that while a policy of encouraging RJVs may be desirable, it is not universally so;
(3) in situations where there are potential gains from RJV formation, there is no presumption that market forces will necessarily produce the right amount of cooperation, though they can produce either too much or too little;
(4) the welfare losses from the market's failure to produce the right amount of cooperation are sometimes quite significant.

Taken together, these remarks suggest that at the moment we do not really have a serious technology policy for the completed European market – just a rather general expression of faith in the benefits from cooperation. What, then, should be the direction of future policy discussion?

There is a need to identify more clearly the areas where serious market failure in R & D arise, and to examine whether the formation of RJVs is the right response to these failures. As some of the debate in the literature has highlighted, and as this study has emphasised, crucial to our understanding of the private and social benefits of RJVs is an appreciation of the cost savings that they can bring about, which in turn depends on how the RJV is organised. We need to understand more about this, and to find out what problems might prevent the attainment of the 'full coordination' savings I have discussed in this study.

There are a number of points to consider here. The first is that there could be crucial differences between organising an RJV between firms in the same country, and organising one between firms in different countries, for if the achievement of coordination requires concentrating effort in one lab, this could pose problems if the relevant manpower was not internationally mobile. There is also some evidence that R & D is becoming more internationally footloose, with companies locating their R & D labs where the relevant manpower is located; the implications of this for coordination need to be explored more fully. A start on some of this has been made in Ulph and Winters (1989). A second issue that needs to be explored more fully arises from recognising what I have just assumed – that coordination is potentially beneficial. It could be argued that it is *competition* which is the spur to R & D, and that this would be lost in an RJV: the crucial issue here is whether it is the internal competition within Europe that matters, or the external competition from 'Japan'. There could be a clear role for policy in helping attain full cost savings, and as the results of Esprit and other programmes become available we should evaluate their success in promoting coordination.

Let me turn now to two issues that I think will be of great relevance for policy, but which have been ignored in this study because more work needs to be done on them. The first concerns the formation of RJVs between 'European' and 'Japanese' firms, and whether promoting this would not be a superior strategy to encouraging purely 'European' RJVs. The problem here is to model carefully what takes place in an RJV between initially asymmetric firms. However, this is also a conceptual issue that needs to be addressed if we are fully to understand purely 'European' RJVs, since they will typically take place between asymmetric firms. A related modelling issue that needs to be addressed is to recognise that many RJVs are involved in *product* innovation, whereas the bulk of the theoretical work has focussed on *process* innovation.

The second major issue that is worth focussing on concerns spillovers. A key question is whether, rather than promoting RJVs within Europe, a better strategy might not be simply to free ride on the 'Japanese' R & D.

This is not unrelated to the previous question, since clearly part of the gains from forming RJVs between 'European' and 'Japanese' firms could be to internalise the spillovers. The difficulty with modelling this is that we have very little empirical evidence about the extent of international spillovers on which to base our modelling assumptions. It is still an important issue, on which more theoretical and empirical work needs to be done.

Appendix

(i)   Proof of (2)

Consider a Cournot equilibrium in which $n + m$ firms produce an identical product whose inverse demand is given by

$$p = -D - Q \tag{A1}$$

where

$$Q = \sum_{j=1}^{n+m} q_j$$

and q_j is the output of firm j. $D > 0$ is a constant. Assuming that each firm j has constant unit costs c_j, then in a Cournot equilibrium firm i will take as given the output of all other firms and so will choose q_i to

$$\max \pi_i \equiv q_i \{D - Q_{-i} - q_i - c_i\} \tag{A2}$$

where

$$Q_{-i} = \sum_{\substack{j=1 \\ j \neq i}}^{n+m} q_j$$

Assuming an interior solution, the first order condition for q_i is

$$D - c_i = Q_{-i} + 2q_i = Q + q_i \tag{A3}$$

Notice that it follows immediately from equations (A2) and (A3) that the equilibrium profits of firm i are simply

$$\pi_i = q_i^2 \tag{A4}$$

where q_i is equilibrium output of firm i.

To determine q_1, sum equation (A3) over i to get

$$(n + m)D - \sum_{j=1}^{n+m} c_j = (n + m + 1)Q. \tag{A5}$$

Substitute from equation (A5) into (A3) to get

$$q_i = \frac{\left[D + \sum_{\substack{j=1 \\ j \neq i}}^{n+m} c_j - (n+m)c_i \right]}{(n+m+1)}. \tag{A6}$$

Conditions (A4) and (A6) give equation (2) of the text.   QED

(ii)   Proof of Theorem 3

I will prove the first result – the second follows from an identical line of proof.

To make notation easier let me define

$$\sigma \equiv \frac{\gamma(n+m+1)^2}{n^2(m+1)} \tag{A7}$$

$$\tau \equiv \frac{\gamma(n+m+1)^2}{(n+m)} \tag{A8}$$

Then clearly $\sigma < \tau$.

Now with $n = k$, the solution to the model reduces to equations (10) and (12), where the term in x has vanished from both equations. The equations can therefore be written

$$[\sigma - (m+1)]z + my = D + mb - (m+1)a \tag{A9}$$

$$nz + [\tau - (n+1)]y = D + na - (n+1)b \tag{A10}$$

As before, stability requires both terms in square brackets to be positive. It is easily checked that $\sigma > (m+1)$ implies $\gamma > 1$ which in turn implies

$$\tau > (m+n+1) > (n+1) \tag{A11}$$

Conditions (A9) and (A10) can be rewritten as

$$\sigma a = D + [\tau - (m+1)](a-z) \\ + m(b-y) + (\sigma - \tau)(a-z) \tag{A12}$$

$$\tau b = D + n(a-z) + [\tau - (n+1)](b-y) \tag{A13}$$

Subtract equation (A12) from (A13) to obtain

$$[\tau - (m+n+1)][(b-y) - (a-z)] \\ = (\tau b - \sigma a) + (\sigma - \tau)(a-z) \tag{A14}$$

It is easily seen that condition (14) in the text is equivalent to $\tau b \leq \sigma a$. Since we are obviously interested only in the case where the RJV's costs $(a - z)$ are positive, the RHS of equation (A14) is negative which implies $(b - y) < (a - z)$.   QED

NOTE

The paper was originally presented at the Conference organised jointly by the Centre for Economic Policy Research, the Centro Interuniversitario de Studi Teorici per la Politica Economia, and Confindustria on 'The Impact of 1992 on European Trade and Industry', 15–16 March 1990, Urbino, Italy. I am very grateful to Joanna Poyagou-Theotoky for computing assistance, and to Tony Venables and participants at the conference for helpful comments.

REFERENCES

d'Aspremont, C. and A. Jacquemin (1988) 'Cooperative and Noncooperative R & D in a Duopoly with Spillovers', *American Economic Review*, **78**, pp. 1133–37.
Beath, J.A., Y. Katsoulacos and D. Ulph (1989) 'Strategic R & D Policy', *Economic Journal*, **99** (Conference), pp. 74–83a.
Beath, J.A. and D. Ulph (1989) 'Cooperative and Noncooperative R & D in a Duopoly with Spillovers: A Comment', University of Bristol (mimeo).
Cecchini, P. (1988) *1992, The European Challenge*, Aldershot: Wildwood House.
Dasgupta, P. and E. Maskin (1987) 'The Simple Economics of Research Portfolios', *Economic Journal*, **97**, pp. 70–83.
Dasgupta, P. and J. Stiglitz (1980) 'Industrial Structure and the Nature of Innovative Activity', *Economic Journal*, **90**, pp. 266–93.
Katsoulacos, Y. and D. Ulph (1990) 'Market vs Socially Optimal R & D and the Degree of Market Competitiveness', University of Bristol (mimeo).
Ulph, D. and A. Winters (1989) 'Strategic Manpower Policy and International Trade', University of Bristol (mimeo).

Discussion

ARYE L. HILLMAN

In introducing his theoretical analysis of 'technology policy', David Ulph observes the potential inconsistency between the objectives of a more competitive post-1992 single European market and government-sponsored cooperative ventures aimed at bridging the 'technology gap' between European and foreign producers. Gains are posited from a more competitive market environment, together with prospective gains from cooperation in R & D among the same agents who in their product-market guise are to be competitors. Since resources are bounded, government (or the supranational authorities) may be obliged to 'target' firms for assistance in R & D joint ventures. Against this background, David Ulph asks: Is a policy goal of 'technological leadership' an appropriate welfare objective? And under what circumstances is there a case for government assistance to facilitate cooperation in R & D activities? In turn, if an interventionist role for government can be demonstrated in a particular instance, how can a policy be designed that ensures 'optimal' cooperation among firms?

These questions bring us to the heart of 'technology policy'. In order to seek answers, David Ulph formulates a Cournot–Nash model of an industry wherein firms produce a homogenous product; the industry consists of designated numbers of 'European' and 'Japanese' firms selling in an integrated (non-segmented) international market.[1] Firms are portrayed as independently choosing their profit-maximising outputs, and as making R & D outlays that reduce costs of production. Technological spillovers are absent – that is, firms can be excluded from the benefits of investments that they did not undertake. All firms confront identical R & D technologies, in the sense of opportunities for investments that will with certainty reduce costs of production. 'Japanese' firms, however, have lower initial costs than 'European' firms; so 'European' firms have a gap to bridge in catching up to 'Japanese' firms. In such circumstances, European firms fall further behind if they choose to invest less in R & D than their Japanese counterparts (Theorem 1). The analysis proceeds in the spirit of the presumption that competitive or non-cooperative behaviour in the sale of output is consistent with cooperation in R & D. Firms' independent output decisions are considered in conjunction with prospective joint ventures among 'European' firms in R & D. Outcomes depend upon cost-sharing arrangements in R & D projects and upon cooperation subject to coordination costs.

Depending upon parameter values, joint profit maximisation need not imply that it is ever optimal for the 'European' firms to 'catch up' to their 'Japanese' competitors. A case for outside intervention arises, in that independent behaviour by firms with regard to the number of participants to be admitted to an R & D joint venture in general does not yield the correct number of participants; this reflects the exclusion problem that arises when the objective of participants in a collective endeavour is to maximise average profits rather than total profits.[2] Costs of coordination among participants in the R & D project have a 'congestion' effect that underlies the potential benefits from excluding some firms from a joint project. A joint profit-maximising coalition of firms will consist of a suboptimal number of participants, because the maximisation of the average net benefit of firms in the venture in general will entail exclusion of firms for whom the marginal benefit of participation exceeds the marginal cost imposed via coordination costs of preexisting participants.

Does this make for a case for government monitoring of joint venture R & D projects? David Ulph's analysis shows that while in principle such arguments can be made, the conception of 'technology policy' is complex – more complex than the intuition that R & D gives rise to a public-good input, wasteful duplication of which ought to be avoided by a government's facilitating cooperation and coordination. Further, as Ulph points out, the conception of 'European cooperation' belies the potentially beneficial cooperation that can take place with firms that are not necessarily European.

The manner in which R & D has been portrayed in this study of course makes life less threatening for firms than might be the case. The Cournot–Nash quantity–competition equilibrium permits firms to survive with some positive market share, if they remain technological laggards and have persistently higher costs than competitors. A Schumpeterian focus on quality competition would emphasise continued presence in the market rather than a decision as to whether to increase outlays that reduce production costs but with no threat to survival. The Schumpeterian perspective also brings to the fore the inherent uncertainty associated with R & D ventures. Firms may have the means of reducing costs with certainty by making R & D development outlays; but often it is the case that patents and initial advantage award the gains to the first to achieve the technological advance. David Ulph has, however, demonstrated, without the additional complexities introduced by Schumpeterian competition and risk aversion, the inappropriateness of a government policy that focusses on fostering cooperation among firms with the intent of 'catching up' with foreigners.

Although David Ulph's analysis is motivated by the concerns in western Europe regarding international technological parity, similar concerns that are even more pressing arise in eastern Europe in the socialist economies in transition: do the answers regarding technology policy differ depending on whether the questions are asked in western or eastern Europe? In advice to eastern European governments, one might well be inclined to question whether there is a case for 'technology policy' at all other than fostering the appropriate market environment that sustains the incentive to invest and innovate.

NOTES

1 Hence no firms are disadvantaged or benefit from protectionist policies such as voluntary export restraints or other restrictions on international trade. The implication is that 'Japanese' firms will have free access to the single European market. For an alternative perspective in a model similar to that employed in this study see my paper with Heinrich Ursprung (1988) where we consider how voluntary export restraints and protective tariffs emerge via political competition when, as in the model formulated by David Ulph, an industry transcends international boundaries.
2 The literature that examines this problem is concerned with the 'theory of clubs'. See my paper with Peter Swan (1983).

REFERENCES

Hillman, Arye L. and Peter L. Swan (1983) 'Participation rules for Pareto-optimal clubs', *Journal of Public Economics*, **20**, pp. 55–76.
Hillman, Ayre L. and Heinrich Ursprung (1988) 'Domestic politics, foreign interests and international trade policy', *American Economic Review*, **78**, pp. 729–45.

9   Corporation tax, foreign direct investment and the single market

MICHAEL KEEN

1   Introduction

Corporation tax barely featured in the early discussion of the single market programme, receiving no more than passing mention in the 1985 White Paper on *Completing the Internal Market*.[1] But as a perception grew that the advent of the single market could have significant effects on patterns of investment both within the Community and between the Community and the rest of the world, so too did a perception that something would have to be done about corporation tax. The European Commission has indeed now begun to press its view that 'if Member states want to create a real internal market in which all Community enterprises can compete on an equal footing and which will bring about a more rational allocation of resources, they cannot escape the need to set up a common policy in the field of enterprise taxation'.[2] At the time of writing, three main sets of proposals are under discussion. First, the Commission has revived its 1975 proposal for common adoption of the partial imputation method,[3] the distinguishing feature of which is that part of the tax paid on corporate profits is credited against shareholders' liability to personal taxation on their dividend receipts.[4] In fact, all but five Member States now operate some variant of imputation, though often failing to extend the credit to residents of other Member States in the even-handed way envisaged by the Commission. This proposal also aimed at confining statutory rates of corporation tax to between 45 and 55% (though the Commission has indicated that it would now anticipate something rather lower) and at abolishing withholding taxes on dividend and interest payments within the Community. Second, the Commission is reconsidering a 1988 preliminary proposal for the harmonisation of tax bases,[5] which recommended that depreciation for tax purposes be taken at accounting rates. Third, it has also revived an even more venerable proposal, dating back to 1969, that the home government of a parent company receiving dividends from a subsidiary located in another Member State either exempt such income or allow the parent to credit – more precisely, in the terminology used below, partially to credit – foreign taxes against home liability on that income.[6] In practice, most Member States now apply one or other of these methods on a fairly consistent basis. It seems, however, that the Commission wishes them to converge on the same one.[7]

The purpose of this study is to clarify and address, against the backdrop of 1992, some of the principal issues that arise in evaluating these and other such proposals for the international coordination of corporate taxation.

Three broad sets of issues arise in considering any aspect of international tax policy: efficiency in the allocation of resources; equity in the distribution of tax revenues across jurisdictions; and strategic behaviour by governments. Only the first of these is addressed here.[8] To this end, a central analytical task is the modelling of multinationals' investment behaviour under alternative tax regimes. Previous contributions in this area include Hartman (1985), Sinn (1984, 1987) and – in work most closely related to the present analysis – Alworth (1986, 1988); there seems, however, to be no concise, general and precisely specified treatment to parallel that of King (1974) for the single-jurisdiction firm. It is not hard, of course, to conjure up coordinated tax regimes that would raise strictly positive revenue whilst leaving corporate decisions undistorted: it would be enough to adopt at community level any of the schemes known to be non-distorting in the single-jurisdiction context. The more challenging question – and politically the more relevant in the EC, at least for the present – is that of whether there exist schemes that are not only efficient but are also compatible with some degree of national autonomy in tax policy. In particular, is it possible for a set of countries to coordinate their corporate tax regimes in such a way that the outcome is efficient yet each remains free to set whatever national rate of corporation tax best suits its own revenue and other objectives? This issue, and the bearing upon it of the kind of international integration sought by the single market programme, is a primary concern in what follows.

Section 2 provides a brief account of the main concepts of tax practice and analysis in relation to inter-jurisdiction direct investment, leading to a fairly general parameterisation of the multinational's tax liability. Section 3 embeds this in a simple model of financial and investment behaviour, and Section 4 then characterises the multinational's optimal policy when – as implicitly assumed in previous analyses – the real activities of parent and affiliate are essentially unrelated. Section 5 examines the implications of product market integration, in the spirit of 1992, for the investment decisions of the horizontal multinational. The possibility of designing coordinated tax regimes with attractive neutrality properties is considered in Section 6. Section 7 contains some concluding remarks.

2   The taxation of foreign direct investment

Consider a multinational consisting of a parent company resident in the 'home' country and a wholly-owned affiliate operating in a single foreign 'host' country. It is helpful – though, as will be seen, somewhat restrictive – to think of the global tax liability of such a firm at time t, denoted T_t, as the sum of three components: tax payable to the home country on the domestic profits and equity distributions of the parent T_t^h; tax payable abroad on the profits and distributions of the affiliate, T_t^a; and tax payable at home on the profits and distributions of the affiliate, T_t^{ha}. That is,

$$T_t = T_t^h + T_t^a + T_t^{ha} \tag{1}$$

The first of these components, precisely analogous to the liability of a purely domestic firm, will be taken to be

$$T_t^h = \tau^h \psi_t^h + \sigma^h D_t^h - \gamma^h N_t^h \tag{2}$$

where ψ_t^h denotes taxable profits from the parent's domestic operations – the calculation of which is discussed in Section 3 – τ^h the rate at which they are charged, D_t^h the gross dividend paid, which is taxed at the rate σ^h, and N_t^h net receipts from new equity issued by the parent, which are credited at rate γ^h. All tax rates are assumed to be parametric, a point to which we return shortly.

This formulation encompasses a wide range of possibilities. Analytically the simplest is the 'classical' system of corporation tax, under which $\sigma^h = \gamma^h = 0$ and shareholders are liable for personal income tax on the gross dividend. Only three Member States currently use this system (the Netherlands, Luxemburg and Spain), which is also that employed in the United States. Others systems attempt to alleviate the 'double taxation of dividends' inherent in the classical system. One way of doing this is by allowing dividends as a deduction in computing taxable profits, so that $\sigma^h = -\tau^h$ (while retaining $\gamma^h = 0$); this is the system used in Greece. Another is by charging distributed profits at a lower rate than retentions, as in Portugal. The method used by the other Member States is that of partial imputation. Here liabiilty at the corporate level is effectively deemed to include prepayment of personal income tax on the gross dividend at the rate of imputation s^h, with $s^h < \tau^h$ (hence the 'partial'). The liability at personal level is thus $(m^h - s^h)D_t^h$, where m^h denotes the shareholder's marginal rate of income tax. Formal incidence being irrelevant, such a system is equivalent to one in which gross dividends can be credited against corporation tax at the rate s^h but are then fully taxable at the personal level.[9] It proves convenient to characterise partial imputation in this latter way – that is, by taking $\sigma^h = -s^h$ (and $\gamma^h = 0$). One other possible structure is of particular interest. This is the 'S-base' (or 'net equity') cash flow corporation tax, under which tax is levied only on the difference between dividend payments and receipts from new equity sales. This corresponds to $\tau^h = 0$ and $\sigma^h = \gamma^h > 0$. Such a system is well known to have considerable merits in the single-jurisdiction context; these are discussed in King (1987), and will be brought out below. It will also emerge that the S-base logic has distinctive appeal in the context of the multinational.

The final two terms in equation (1) describe the treatment of direct investments abroad. Here it is useful to begin with two contrasting organising ideas:

(1)   The *residence* (or *world-wide*) *principle*. This requires that the affiliate be untaxed in the host country and taxed in the residence country exactly as a purely domestic firm would be. Thus

$$T_t^a = 0; \quad T_t^{ha} = \tau^h \psi_t^a \tag{3}$$

where ψ_t^a denotes the taxable profits of the affiliate, calculated according to the rules of the residence country (and we have for brevity assumed that intra-company equity flows would in this case be untaxed at home).

(2)   The *source* (or *territorial*) *principle*. Under this, in contrast, the home country exempts the profits and distributions of the affiliate while the host country treats it exactly as it does its own domestic firms. So, by analogy with equation (2),

$$T_t^{ha} = 0; \quad T_t^a = \tau^a \psi_t^a + \sigma^a D_t^a - \gamma^a N_t^a \tag{4}$$

where D_t^a and N_t^a denote respectively the gross dividend paid and new equity issued by the affiliate (in each case to the parent, since this is assumed to be the sole owner), and where ψ_t^a is now computed by the host country's rules.

Note that the home country may still gain (or conceivably lose) revenue from the activities of the affiliate through its taxation of final distributions by the parent.

These two principles of international taxation are closely related to the two central neutrality concepts of tax analysis in this area (the precise definitions of which, however, are somewhat variable). Global application of the resident principle – at both corporate and personal levels – is sufficient (but not necessary) for the achievement of *capital export neutrality* (CEN), in the sense of ensuring that the pre-tax rates of return on the various investments of a multinational resident in any particular jurisdiction are equalised in equilibrium, irrespective of their location. Global application of the source principle is sufficient (but again not necessary) for *capital import neutrality* (CIN) in the sense of ensuring that all firms active in a particular jurisdiction earn the same pre-tax return in equilibrium, irrespective of their parents' residence. Note that CEN and CIN together imply a third kind of neutrality (examined by Sinn, 1984, 1989b): single-jurisdiction firms will also earn the same pre-tax return in equilibrium, irrespective of their locations.

Much of the policy analysis in this area revolves around these criteria of CEN and CIN. Discussion commonly starts with the observation that both could be achieved by full harmonisation of rates and systems of corporation tax (so long as that system did not discriminate between home and foreign investments), dismisses this degree of convergence as chimerical, and then proceeds to consider whether it is CEN or CIN that should in practice be given priority. Though progress has been made on this last issue (see, in particular, Horst, 1980, Dutton 1982 and Giovannini 1989), theory as yet offers no decisive basis for a presumptive superiority of either form of neutrality over the other. But there is in any event a still more fundamental point to emphasise: it may be perfectly possible to achieve *both* CEN and CIN even if both home and host governments charge corporation tax at different rates (perhaps, too, by different methods) and even if they both raise strictly positive revenue on multinationals' operations in the host country. Indeed it may be possible to achieve complete neutrality, with pre-tax returns not merely equalised across jurisdictions but everywhere equal to post-tax returns (and revenue raised from intra-marginal projects); investment decisions would then be entirely undistorted. The point here is simply that the behavioural impact of corporate taxation depends not just on statutory rates of taxation but also on tax bases: full neutrality can be achieved by the adoption of neutral tax structures for domestic firms together with non-distorting arrangements for the home taxation of outward investments. The notion that anything short of full harmonisation requires one to consider some trade-off between CEN and CIN is worth resisting.

Whatever their merits, neither the residence nor the source principle describes the reality of corporate taxation. In practice, governments generally assert both a right to tax foreign-owned firms present in their jurisdictions and a right to tax resident firms' returns from affiliates abroad.

Host countries typically calculate and charge the taxable profits of foreign-owned affiliates just as they would a domestic firm's and, in addition, levy withholding taxes on both dividend and interest payments to parent companies and other non-residents. Rates of withholding tax are subject to bilateral negotiation, and generally differ between dividend and interest income, being lower on the latter. For simplicity, withholding taxes on interest are ignored in what follows. Thus we now take it that

$$T_t^a = \tau^a \psi_t^a + \omega D_t^a - \gamma^a N_t^a \tag{5}$$

where ω can be thought of as an effective rate of withholding tax.

With some exceptions, ω is in practice non-negative. Under the Commission's 1975 proposals, however, ω would be strictly negative. For these envisage that the parent would receive from the host government an imputation credit at the same rate s^a as would a shareholder resident there and, moreover, that no withholding tax would be applied: then $\omega = -s^a$. It should also be noted that the appropriate τ^a in equation (5) may in practice be lower than that applied to the host's own domestic firms. This would be the effect, in particular, of tax holidays on inward investment. Such provisions, by creating time variation in the statutory rate, have subtle behavioural effects (see Mintz, 1989); for brevity, the assumption of non-discriminatory taxation by the host government is maintained throughout the analysis below.

It remains to consider the home country's taxation of investments abroad, T_t^{ha}. Of the many possible arrangements, a few are of particular importance:[10]

(3) *Exemption.* This is the case in which the residence country levies no additional charge on affiliates abroad, so that

$$T_t^{ha} = 0 \tag{6}$$

The situation is then essentially the same as under the pure source principle (with ω replacing σ^h). Exemption is one of the two possibilities envisaged in the Commission's 1969 proposal; it is the current practice in France, the Netherlands and (to a substantial degree) Belgium and Germany.

(4) *Partial credit with deferral.* This is the usual method of taxing subsidiaries (affiliates separately incorporated abroad) which account for the bulk of foreign direct investment. It is the method used, in particular, by all EC countries other than those adopting exemption, and is the second of the possibilities envisaged in the proposal for common taxation of subsidiaries. Tax is payable in the home country only when dividends are recieved by the parent, and is

charged on the income deemed to underlie that distribution; tax deemed to have been paid to the host country on that income is then credited against this liability, subject to the restriction that tax payments at home be no more than extinguished: refunds are not paid. Thus

$$T_t^{ha} = D_t^a \max \left(\frac{\tau^h - \tau}{1 - \tau} - \omega, 0 \right) \tag{7}$$

where τ denotes the rate of underlying tax by which gross dividends are grossed up in order to arrive at deemed profits.

A firm that is unable to offset all foreign taxes in this way is said to have 'excess credits';[11] conversely it has 'deficit credits' if $T_t^{ha} > 0$. Typically, τ is calculated as the ratio of foreign corporate tax payments to the sum of post-tax accounting profits and creditable foreign tax payments. The latter is likely to differ from taxable profits as defined by the host country: accounting profits are liable to diverge from taxable profits; the home country may adopt for this purpose its own definition of taxable profits (as for instance in the United States). Leechor and Mintz (1990) analyse the implications of the endogeneity of τ created by this aspect of US practice. For brevity, it will simply be assumed here that $\tau = \tau^a$.

Two other complications of considerable practical importance should be noted. The first is the existence of provisions to prevent indefinite tax minimisation by the accumulation of undistributed funds in low-tax jurisdictions: the United Kingdom, for instance, issues a 'white list' of countries from which it will not automatically regard distributions to have been made. The second is the possibility of tax sparing clauses in double tax agreements, by which the home country agrees to charge repatriated profits at less than its full domestic rate in order to preserve tax holiday or other incentives offered by the host. These are most commonly found in agreements between developed and less developed countries, but examples do exist in Europe: Ireland, most prominently, has secured a number of agreements under which residence countries deem affiliates located there to have borne tax at a rate higher than the actual Irish rate (for manufacturing, and until 2000) of 10%.

(5) *Full credit with deferral.* Though not observed in practice, one can conceive of there being no limitation on the extent to which foreign taxes are credited against home liability on repatriations, so that where excess credits would have arisen under (4) the home country instead makes a payment to the parent:

$$T_t^{ha} = D_t^a \left(\frac{\tau^h - \tau}{1 - \tau} - \omega \right) \tag{8}$$

(6) *Partial credit without deferral.* This is the most common way of taxing affiliates organised as branches. Liability arises in the home country in each period, not just on repatriation; and tax payments at home are again restricted to be non-negative. Thus, assuming for simplicity that the residence country accepts for these purposes the host's definition of taxable profits,

$$T_t^{ha} = \max\{\tau^h \psi_t^a - T_t^a, 0\} \tag{9}$$

(7) *Full credit without deferral.* With no limitation on the offset of foreign taxes and no deferral

$$T_t^{ha} = \tau^h \psi_t^a - T_t^a \tag{10}$$

Again this is not a system that is observed in practice. But it has its advocates, and will prove important below: from the perspective of the multinational (though not that of the revenue authorities) it is exactly equivalent to application of the residence principle.

(8) *Deduction without deferral.* In this case, foreign taxes are treated as an expense in calculating the parent's liability to tax in respect of the affiliate, which arises each period. So

$$T_t^{ha} = \tau^h(\psi_t^a - T_t^a) \tag{11}$$

where we again assume that the home country accepts the host's definition of taxable profits (and for brevity do not retrict T_t^{ha} to be non-negative).

Deduction has a particular appeal in terms of nationalistic self-interest: for while the national return on domestic investment is given by the return gross of home taxes that on investment abroad is given by the return net of foreign taxes (Feldstein and Hartman, 1979; Musgrave, 1969). The deduction method has indeed been advocated periodically in the United States, though never implemented there. In her imperial heyday, it is interesting to note, Britain applied the deduction method to investments outside the Empire but a form of partial credit with deferral to those within (Davies, 1985, 29–31).

For analytical purposes it is convenient to adopt a general characterisation of the tax treatment of the multinational which, while restrictive, encompasses the possibilities just described and some others of interest. In the analysis that follows it will therefore be presumed that the multinational's global tax liability can be written

$$T_t = \gamma^h \psi_t^h + \sigma^h D_t^h - \gamma^h N_t^h + \tau^* \psi_t^a + \sigma^* D_t^a - \gamma^*(1 + \gamma^a) N_t^a \quad (12)$$

where τ^*, σ^* and γ^* are parametric. Thus τ^* is the total tax rate on retentions in the affiliate, σ^* is the repatriation tax on its distributions and γ^* is the total credit on its (gross of foreign credit) new equity issues.[12]

It will also prove useful to denote by

$$\tau_d^* = \tau^* + \sigma^*(1 - \tau^*) \quad (13)$$

the effective rate at which the affiliate's distributed profits are taxed.

Figure 9.1 gives the values taken by τ^*, σ^* and τ_d^* under each of the regimes (1)–(8) above (found by aggregating the components of T_t and identifying coefficients with equation (12)). Note that all have the feature

$$\sigma^*(\tau^a - \tau^*) = 0 \quad (14)$$

This reflects an assumption that $\omega = 0$ whenever there is no deferral: for then, in the cases examined, $\sigma^* = 0$ in the absence of deferral and (by definition) $\tau^* = \tau^a$ in its presence. Though restrictive, the condition in equation (14) encompasses most cases of interest and implifies the results; it is retained throughout.

This characterisation is highly stylised, and some of its more serious limitations should be emphasised. One is the restriction of the analysis to a two-country world. This precludes a range of tax avoidance strategies (such as the reduction of withholding taxes by judicious rerouteing[13]) and prevents any distinction between the crediting of foreign taxes against home liability on a country-by-country basis (as in the United Kingdom) and in aggregate (as in the United States).[14] A second, and more serious restriction, is the lack of attention to tax asymmetries. The most evident consequence of these in the international context is the practice of starting operations abroad in branch rather than subsidiary form, since early tax losses can then be used to shield domestic profits from home tax. More fundamentally, tax asymmetries effectively endogenise the tax rates facing the firm and so may provide a rationale for interior financial policies. This point is widely recognised in the context of the single-jurisdiction firm (see, for instance, Mayer, 1986). Distinctive consideration of a similar kind may also be important in the international context. Both the United States and the United Kingdom, for instance, tax subsidiaries by partial credit with deferral but allow tax losses at home to absorb deficit credits, so that the effective rate on repatriations increases with taxable profits on

	τ^*	σ^*	τ^*_d
Residence	τ^h	0	τ^h
Source	τ^a	σ^a	$\tau^a + \sigma^a(1 - \tau^a)$
Exemption	τ^a	ω	$\tau^a + \omega(1 - \tau^a)$
Partial credit with deferral:	τ^h	$\max\left\{\dfrac{\tau^h - \tau^a}{1 - \tau^a},\ \omega\right\}$	$\max\{\tau^h,\ \tau^a + \omega(1 - \tau^a)\}$
(i) Excess credit	τ^h	ω	$\tau^a + \omega(1 - \tau^a)$
(ii) Deficit credit	τ^h	$(\tau^h - \tau^a)/(1 - \tau^a)$	τ^h
Full credit with deferral	τ^a	$(\tau^h - \tau^a)/(1 - \tau^a)$	τ^h
Partial credit without deferral[1,2]	$\max\{\tau^h,\ \tau^a\}$	0	$\max\{\tau^h,\ \tau^a\}$
Full credit without deferral[1]	τ^h	0	τ^h
Deduction without deferral[1]	$\tau^a + \tau^h(1 - \tau^a)$	0	$(\tau^a - \tau^h)/(1 - \tau^a)$

Notes:
1 The effective withholding tax ω is assumed to be zero in all regimes without deferral.
2 Assuming $\gamma^a = 0$.

Figure 9.1 Tax parameters

domestic operations. The possibility of ACT prejudice in the United Kingdom (explained in n. 9) also establishes a link between the two, though in this case a negative one. No such features are present in the analysis below. Third, the characterisation rules out some regimes of interest. A particularly serious omission is the unitary system (variants of which are practised by many US states), under which a jurisdiction taxes some proportion of the multinational's global profits, that proportion typically depending (*inter alia*) on the fraction of the firm's total capital stock located within its borders. The unitary method has particular appeal as a response to problems of transfer pricing, and deserves close attention in the context of European integration. But the weighting element again endogenises the effective tax rates facing the firm, and so for brevity – but reluctantly – such a system is not considered here.

3 Taxation and the multinational

Section 3 develops a simple model of the multinational's optimal investment and financial behaviour in the presence of corporate and personal taxes. The model is in the tradition of King's (1974) analysis for the single-jurisdiction firm: as there, the setting is one of partial equilibrium and perfect certainty, and tax rates are parametric.[15]

The multinational is assumed to consist of a parent and a single wholly-owned affiliate, with the parent's equity held only by a single resident of the country in which it is itself resident (these strong ownership restrictions serving to preclude unanimity issues). Capital market equilibrium requires the after-tax return on the parent's equity to equal that on risk-free debt, so that

$$(1 - m^h) r^h V_t = (1 - m^h) D_t^h + (1 - z^h)[V_{t+1} - V_y - N_t^h] \qquad (15)$$

where V_t denotes the market value of the parent's equity, r^h the rate of interest on riskless debt issued in the home country (constant over time) and z^h the shareholder's marginal tax rate on accrued capital gains.

Solving equation (15) subject to a terminal condition precluding indefinite bubbles gives the value of the parent's equity at time zero as

$$V_0 = \sum_{u=0}^{\infty} \{[(1 - m^h)/(1 - z^h)] D_u^h - N_u^h\}(1 + \rho^h)^{-(1+u)} \qquad (16)$$

where

$$\rho^h = (1 - m^h) r^h/(1 - z^h) \qquad (17)$$

The multinational's objective is taken to be the maximisation of shareholder wealth, which requires maximising the equity value in equation (16).

The valuation relation (16) is identical to that for a firm operating only in the home country. The novelty is that distributions to and from the final shareholder now reflect financial flows between parent and affiliate. These are captured in the sources and uses identity of the parent:

$$D_u^h + N_u^a + B_u + T_u^h + T_u^{ha} + (1 + r^h)B_{u-1}^h + qI_u^h$$
$$= (1 - \omega)D_u^a + R^h(K_u^h, K_u^a) + P_u + B_u^h + N_u^h + (1 + \bar{r})B_{u-1}$$

$$(18)$$

where B_u denotes the amount lent by the parent to the affiliate at time u (all debt in the model being one-period) and $\bar{r}$ the interest charged on such intra-company debt, B_u^h the amount borrowed in the home capital market, q the price of the investment good (assumed for simplicity to be the same in both countries), I_u^h the physical investment of the parent, $R^h(K_u^h, K_u^a)$ the net (of non-capital costs) revenue of the parent from its domestic operations (maximised conditionally on the real capital stocks of both parent and affiliate) and P_u a transfer of taxable income from the affiliate, thought of as being achieved through transfer pricing or other paper transactions within the multinational.

Note the the parent is assumed not to borrow in the debt market of the host country; a symmetric restriction will be imposed on the affiliate. Note too that the dividends received by the parent are net of any withholding tax (or inclusive of any tax credit extended by the host country). Similarly, the affiliate's sources and uses are:

$$D_u^a + P_u + (1 + \bar{r})B_{u-1} + T_u^a + (1 + r^a)B_{u-1}^a + qI_u^a$$
$$= R^a(K_u^a, K_u^h) + \omega D_u^a + N_u^a + B_u + B_u^a$$

$$(19)$$

where the notation is analogous to that in equation (18).

Capital is assumed to depreciate exponentially at the same rate δ in each country, so that

$$K_u^i = (1 - \delta)K_{u-1}^i + I_{u-1}^i, \quad (\mu_u^i), \quad i = a, h$$

$$(20)$$

with μ_u^i being the costate variable attached to this equation of motion in the subsequent optimisation.

The tax terms appearing in equations (18) and (19) are as described in section 2, and so depend on the taxable profits of both affiliate and parent. The former are asumed to be of the general form

$$\psi_u^a = R^a(\cdot) - P_u - \alpha^a\{r^a B_{u-1}^a + \bar{r}B_{u-1}\} - \beta^a q I_u^a - \delta^{Ta}K_u^{Ta} \qquad (21)$$

where α^a denotes the proportion of interest payments deductible against tax in the host country, β^a the proportion of investment expenditures allowed immediate expensing ('free depreciation'), δ^{Ta} the exponential rate of depreciation for tax purposes, and K_u^{Ta} the value of the affiliate's capital stock as written down for tax, generated as

$$K_u^{Ta} = (1 - \delta^{Ta})K_{u-1}^{Ta} + (1 - \beta^a)qI_{u-1}^a, \quad (\mu_u^{Ta}) \qquad (22)$$

Similarly

$$\psi_u^h = R^h(\cdot) - P_u - \alpha^h\{r^h B_{u-1}^h + \bar{r}B_{u-1}\} - \beta^h q I_u^h - \delta^{Th}K_u^{Th} \qquad (23)$$

with K_u^{Th} given by the analogue of equation (22).

In practice, interest deductibility is the norm ($\alpha^a = \alpha^h = 1$). Investment incentives, however, vary widely even within the EC: plant and machinery, for instance, are written down at 10% in Germany, Holland and Spain but in Ireland attract 75% expensing and subsequent writing down on the remainder at 25%.[16]

Three features of the model should be noted. The first is the generality of the revenue functions $R^i(\cdot)$ in allowing for the possibility that the extent of the multinational's operations in one jurisdiction may affect the profitability of its operations in the other; sections 4 and 5 below will focus on two polar forms of this potential interdependence. Second, no distinction has been made between real and nominal magnitudes. This would be straightforward to do, but inflation as such is not central to the issues addressed below (though it is of course of great practical importance, affecting the value to the firm of both nominal interest deductibility and historic cost depreciation allowances). Third – a related simplification – exchange rate movements have been assumed away, so eliminating a set of tax issues which whole sections are also sufficiently complex to be best left for later study. Fourth, no restriction is placed on interest rates in home and host country. Extending the model to admit portfolio investment across the two debt markets, the relationship between the two would depend on the way in which such investments were taxed; the implications of this will be touched on briefly below.

In addition to the restrictions of the source and uses relation, the multinational is assumed to face a series of non-negativity constraints on its financial behaviour. Specifically, we impose:

$$\bar{D}^h \geq D_u^h \geq 0(\lambda_{1u}^{Dh}, \lambda_{2u}^{Dh}); \quad \bar{D}^a \geq D_u^a \geq 0(\lambda_{1u}^{Da}, \lambda_{2u}^{Da}) \qquad (24)$$

$$N_u^h \geq 0(\lambda_u^{Nh}); \quad N_u^a \geq 0(\lambda_u^{Na}) \qquad (25)$$

$$B_u^h \geq 0 \, (\lambda_u^{Bh}); \quad B_u^a \geq 0 \, (\lambda_u^{Ba}); \quad B_u \geq 0 \, (\lambda_u^B) \tag{26}$$

the terms in brackets being the Lagrange multipliers associated with each constraint in the optimisation problem.

These retrictions have some basis in normal legal practice, as discussed in the single-jurisdiction context by King (1974, 1977). We are simply assuming, for instance, that share repurchases by the affiliate would be treated for tax purposes as equivalent to the payment of a dividend, while the upper bounds on dividends, $\bar{D}^i$ (i = a, h), can be thought of as a crudely approximating provisions intended to prevent dividend payments other than from accumulated operating income. Note too that the analysis would be unaffected if dividends were instead to be bounded strictly above zero (perhaps to capture a signalling function or to prevent the exercise of anti-avoidance provisions of the kind referred to in section 2). Perhaps least convincing as a description of reality are the restrictions on debt issues in equation (26). The legal argument rests on the view that substantial lending could be deemed *ultra vires* for non-financial firms of the kind with which we are concerned; but the restrictions serve, in any event, as a useful analytical device (that on intra-company borrowing having no other justification).

The multinational's problem, then, is to maximise its equity value (16) subject to: the sources and uses conditions (18) and (19); the tax rules (5), (12), (21) and (23); the equations of motion in (20), (22) and the home analogue of the latter; and the financial constraints (24)–(26). The first-order conditions for this problem, which form the basis of the subsequent analysis, are reported in Appendix A.

4   Costs of capital under independent profitability

Here we consider the case in which the revenue functions of parent and affiliate take the simple form $R^i(K_u^i)$ (and each is strictly concave), so that the profitability of the multinational's operations at home and abroad are entirely independent of one another. This is the case on which, implicitly, the previous literature has focussed. There are two ways in which such an independence assumption might be rationalised. The first is by supposing parent and affiliate to sell the same product in a single competitive market (with the production of each subject to decreasing returns to scale). The second is by supposing that although both parent and affiliate have some power in the goods markets they serve, those markets are entirely segmented from one another; this in turn might reflect either dissimilarity of products or impossibility of arbitrage across goods markets. For the

Source of finance at $t - 1$	Cost of capital
Retentions	$(\rho^h + \delta)\left(\dfrac{q^{*h}}{1 - \tau^h}\right)$
New equity	$(\rho^h + \delta)\left(\dfrac{q^{*h}}{1 - \tau^h}\right) + \left(\dfrac{1 - \theta}{\theta} - \gamma^h\right)\Delta^h$
Debt	$(\rho^h + \delta)\left(\dfrac{q^{*h}}{1 - \tau^h}\right) + \{(1 - \alpha^h\,\tau^h)r^h - \rho^h\}\Delta^h_1$

Notes:
1 Equilibrium value of $R^h_K(K^h_t)$, assuming $\lambda^{Dh}_{it} = 0$, $i = 1, 2$.
2 Where: $\Delta^h = (1 - \beta^h\,\tau^h)(1 + \rho^h)q/(1 - \tau^h)(1 + \gamma^h)$
$\quad\quad\quad\Delta^h_1 = \Delta^h(1 + \gamma^h)/(1 + \rho^h)$.

Figure 9.2 Costs of capital for domestic investment

present, the precise explanation offered for independent profitability is unimportant. The immediate purpose is to identify the ways in which, conditional on such independence, taxation affects the multinational's incentives to invest at home and abroad. Analytically, the task is to derive the costs of capital for such investments at some date t – the quantities, that is, to which value maximisation requires that the marginal revenue products of capital in each location be equated.

It is useful to begin with the multinational's optimal policy in respect of investment at home. In the presence of taxation, the cost of capital will in general depend on both the way in which funds are raised for the project at $t - 1$ and the use that is made at t of the funds that it generates. For simplicity, the number of financial regimes to consider will be limited by supposing throughout that the parent pays at t and in all subsequent periods a dividend that is strictly positive but beneath the upper bound; hence

$$\lambda^{Dh}_{1u} = \lambda^{Dh}_{2u} = 0, \qquad \forall u \geq t \tag{27}$$

Even this leaves a wide range of possibilities. We address here only the three that would remain open to a single-jurisdiction firm:[17] financing by retaining profits, issuing new equity or borrowing in the home market. Each of these regimes corresponds to a restriction on the Lagrange multipliers in equations (24)–(26): retention finance corresponds to $\lambda^{Ph}_{1,t-1} = \lambda^{Ph}_{2,t-1} = 0$, and the others to $\lambda^{Nh}_{t-1} = 0$ and $\lambda^{Bh}_{t-1} = 0$ respectively.[18] Using these restrictions, and defining

$$\theta = (1 - m^h)/(1 - z^h)(1 + \sigma^h) \tag{28}$$

it is straightforward to derive from the first-order conditions the costs of capital reported in Figure 9.2; details are in Appendix B. These formulae involve the concept of the *effective price* that the firm faces for the investment good in the home country; defined as

$$q^{*h} = [1 - \beta^h \tau^h - (1 - \beta^h) \tau^h \delta^{Th}(\rho^h + \delta^{Th})^{-1}]q \tag{29}$$

this is just the price q net of the present value (at the shareholder's discount rate ρ^h) of the associated tax breaks.

These costs of capital are similar to those of King and Fullerton (1984), and so need little further comment; indeed the two coincide exactly under free depreciation and interest deductibility, though more generally the present explicit inclusion of tax depreciation in the optimisation exercise gives somewhat different expressions. There are, though, two points that it will prove useful to emphasise. First, new equity is penalised relative to retentions whenever $(1 + \gamma^h) \theta < 1$. This will be the case, for instance, under a classical corporation tax so long as dividends are taxed more heavily than accrued capital gains ($\sigma^h = \gamma^h = 0$, $m^h > z^h$). Such a situation gives rise to the 'trapped equity' view of dividend taxes: they are non-distorting when retentions are the marginal source (since θ does not then enter the cost of capital) but discourage investment financed by new equity issues.[19] The reason is straightforward: funds already within the firm cannot escape taxation on distribution, so that the dividend tax becomes effectively lump sum; equity injections, in contrast, initially lie outside this trap. Under an imputation system ($\sigma^h = -s^h$, $\gamma^h = 0$) the comparison between new equity and retention finance ceases to be clear-cut: tax-exempt institutions ($m^h = z^h = 0$), for instance, will prefer new equity. Note, though, that the cost of capital will continue to differ across these two sources unless it so happens that $(1 - m^h)/(1 - z^h) = (1 - s^h)$.

This leads to the second point. Adoption of the S-base cash flow tax ($\gamma^h = \sigma^h$, $\tau^h = 0$), combined with either an expenditure or comprehensive income tax at personal level ($m^h = z^h$), achieves full neutrality in the sense that – whatever the marginal source of finance – the cost of capital is $(r^h + \delta)q$; investment and financing decisions are undistorted. This neutrality is easily explained. In the absence of taxation, the firm would simply seek to maximise the present value of its net distributions $D_u^h - N_u^h$; a tax on those distributions (at an unchanging rate) is thus in effect lump sum. Decisions are not distorted at the margin, but revenue is raised from intra-marginal investments.

Turning to the cost of capital for investment abroad, the affiliate will be assumed to distribute in all periods from t onwards, a dividend that is strictly positive but beneath the lower bound; thus

$$\lambda_{1u}^{Da} = \lambda_{2u}^{Da} = 0, \qquad \forall u \geq t \tag{30}$$

This is the direct analogue of equation (27) for the parent. In general, however, it will still be the case that the affiliate's cost of capital depends not only on its own financial policy but also on that of the parent. For brevity, and to focus attention on the financing of the affiliate itself, the range of possibilities will therefore be retricted still further by now supposing the parent's marginal source of finance at $t - 1$ to be retained profits; the assumption that

$$\lambda_{1,t-1}^{Dh} = \lambda_{2,t-1}^{Dh} = 0 \tag{31}$$

is thus added to equation (27). The derivation of the cost of capital for the affiliate now proceeds along the same lines as that for the parent, details being given in Appendix C. The results are shown in Figure 9.3, where

$$q^{*a} = [1 - \beta^a \tau^* - (1 - \beta^a) \tau^* \delta^{Ta}(\rho^a + \delta^{Th})^{-1}]q \tag{32}$$

denotes the effective price of investment faced by by affiliate.

Comparing Figure 9.3 with Figure 9.2 (and supposing, as in practice, that $\gamma^* = \gamma^h = 0$), the cost of capital for the affiliate under each of the first three regimes is seen to differ from the corresponding expression for the parent only in two simple respects: the rate of tax on retentions in the affiliate replaces that on retentions in the parent (with the investment incentive rules of the host country naturally replacing those of the home country in calculating the effective price); and the repatriation tax σ^* replaces the dividend tax term $(1 - \theta)/\theta$. The first of these reflects the simplifying assumptions made on the future distribution policies of parent and affiliate: if, for example, the affiliate were to issue new equity at some future date then the repatriation tax would generally enter into the effective price. The second implies a powerful conceptual symmetry: conditional on retention finance in all future periods (a restriction that can be dispensed with under free depreciation) the significance of taxation on repatriation for foreign direct investment is precisely analogous to the more familiar significance of dividend taxation in the single-jurisdiction context. The trapped equity argument, in particular, is directly applicable to the taxation of foreign affiliates: funds within the affiliate cannot escape the tax liability on repatriations. This observation was first developed, in settings somewhat less general than the present, by Hartman (1985) and Sinn (1984). It has striking implications.

To see these most clearly, suppose that the home country defers its taxation of profits retained abroad ($\tau^* = \tau^a$), and leave intra-company borrowing for separate consideration later. The first conclusion that follows might be called the Hartman–Sinn neutrality proposition: under

Affiliate's source of finance at t − 1	Cost of capital
Retentions	$(\rho^h + \delta)\left(\dfrac{q^{*a}}{1 - \tau^*}\right)$
New equity	$(\rho^h + \delta)\left(\dfrac{q^{*a}}{1 - \tau^*}\right) + (\sigma^* - \gamma^*)\Delta^a$
Host debt	$(\rho^h + \delta)\left(\dfrac{q^{*a}}{1 - \tau^*}\right) + \{(1 - \alpha^a\tau^*)r^a - \rho^h\}\Delta^a_1$
Borrowing from parent	$(\rho^h + \delta)\left(\dfrac{q^{*a}}{1 - \tau^*}\right) + \{\sigma^*\rho^h - [\sigma^* + \alpha^a(1 - \sigma^*)\tau^* - \alpha^h\tau^h]\bar{r}\}\Delta^a_2$

Notes:
1 Equilibrium value of $R^a_K(K^a_t)$, assuming $\lambda^{Di}_{jt} = 0$, for i = a, h and j = 1, 2.
2 Where: $\Delta^a = (1 - \beta^a\tau^a)(1 + \rho^h)q/(1 - \tau^a_d)$
   $\Delta^a_1 = \Delta^a(1 - \sigma^*)/(1 + \rho^h)$
   $\Delta^a_2 = \Delta^a/(1 + \rho^h)$.

Figure 9.3 Costs of capital for investment abroad

deferral, the investment decisions of a 'mature' affiliate – one, that is, which is retention-financed in every period – are entirely unaffected by both the rate of corporation tax in the home country and the form of double tax relief available at repatriation (and this is so, most remarkably, even if partial credit with deferral is in operation and the parent will have deficit credits on repatriation). For a 'young' affiliate reliant on new equity, in contrast, both will matter. The second is that affiliates should prefer retention finance to new issues[20] whenever $\sigma^* > 0$: indeed it is easily shown that with $\sigma^* \in (0, 1)$ they should never simultaneously pay dividends and issue new equity,[21] a direct analogue of the familiar dividend puzzle for single-jurisdiction firms. The welfare implications are equally strong. Since the cost of capital for a firm resident and operating only in the host country follows by analogy from the results in Figure 9.2, it follows that – assuming ρ^a (the foreign shareholder's discount rate, defined in the manner of equation (17)) to coincide with ρ^h – the cost of capital for the foreign investment of a mature multinational is the same as that for a retention-financed foreign firm: to that extent, CIN is achieved. Unless, however, both countries give free depreciation and disallow interest deductions, CEN will not be achieved (except by fluke) so long as their rates of corporation tax differ.

Comparing Figures 9.2 and 9.3 in this way points to three principal tax distortions bearing distinctively on foreign direct investment. One is the discrimination against new equity finance implied, as just mentioned, by taxes on repatriation. The welfare effects of these exactly parallel those of dividend taxes, analysed in Sinn (1989a). In the long run, when funds generated by the affiliate are more than sufficient to exhaust investment opportunities earning at least the shareholder's discount rate, there is no distortion; repatriation taxes are lump sum. It is during the growth to maturity that the taxation of repatriation generates welfare losses: the affiliate must then use more expensive means of finance, leaving its capital stock too low. The second distortionary feature is the inter-jurisdiction variation in effective tax rates on retained profits that arises whenever statutory rates differ and taxation is deferred ($\tau^* = \tau^a$). Such variation has complex effects, impinging not only on the returns from investment but also on the costs of debt finance and the effective prices of investment in different locations; it tends towards the violation of CEN and the distortion of competition between single-jurisdiction firms. Similar effects are to be expected from the third distortion, which is the diversity across countries in the generosity of investment incentives.

It remains to consider intra-company borrowing. Here there are two points to emphasise. The first and more familiar is the incentive to use such loans as a vehicle for transfer pricing. Assuming interest to be deductible in both countries, it is clear from Figure 9.3 (on recalling equation (13) and noting that $\Delta_2^a > 0$) that the multinational will wish, for instance, to set an infinitely high interest rate on loans to the affiliate iff

$$\tau_d^* > \tau^h \tag{33}$$

so that the effective tax rate on profits distributed by the affiliate to the parent exceeds that on the undistributed profits of the latter. And this is simply the general condition for transfers of taxable income towards the parent to be privately desirable.[22] These avoidance possibilities are widely recognised, and reflected in the existence of thin capitalisation rules enabling interest payments from affiliates to be treated as distributions. The second and less obvious point is that borrowing from the parent strictly dominates new equity finance of affiliates whenever $\sigma^* > 0$: this emerges on comparing the two costs of capital in Figure 9.3 when $\bar{r} = 0$ (and noting from the definitions that $\rho^h \Delta_2^a < \Delta^a$). The reason for this is that an interest-free loan to the affiliate is equivalent to an equity purchase except that the principal is returned tax-free in the former case but not (except perhaps in the event of liquidation) in the latter.[23] The possibility of borrowing from the parent does not eliminate the distorting effects of current deferral procedures: even at a zero interest rate retentions remain a cheaper source of finance (since $\Delta_2^a > 0$). It may, however, serve a useful role in cushioning the consequent welfare loss.

5   The consequences of market integration

Though conventional, the assumption of independent profitability underlying the results of section 4 is not an appealing one. Even with segmentation of goods markets, it carries an unattractive presumption that local sales can come only from local production. Integration of goods markets, in contrast, establishes a direct link between the profits of a parent and affiliate producing the same good, since the common price at which they sell that good will reflect the production of both. Links of this kind doubtless already exist within horizontal multinationals operating in the EC. The single market programme, moreover, is naturally characterised as in large part precisely an attempt to integrate segmented European markets (Smith and Venables, 1988) so that these interdependencies seem set to become increasingly important. The purpose in this section is to consider their implications for the analysis of tax effects on foreign direct investment.

Suppose, then, that parent and affiliate produce for a single market, in which they exercise a collective market power. Revenues are then

$$R^i = p(Y^h + Y^a)Y^i, \qquad i = a, h \tag{34}$$

where $p(\cdot)$ is the inverse demand function and $Y^i = F(K^i)$ denotes output in location i.

Denoting by e (>0) the elasticity of inverse demand, by $\kappa^j = Y^i/(Y^h + Y^a)$ the proportion of the multinational's output produced in country i, and defining

$$\xi = (\tau_d^* - \tau^h)/(1 - \tau_d^*) \tag{35}$$

one now finds (along lines described in Appendix D) that the optimal capital stock of the affiliate is characterised by

$$pF_K^a(K_t^a) = [1 - e - \xi e \kappa^h]^{-1} c_a \tag{36}$$

where c_a denotes the cost of capital in Figure 9.3, and that of the parent by

$$pF_K^h(K_t^h) = [1 - e + (\xi e \kappa^a/(1 + \xi))]^{-1} c_h \tag{37}$$

where c_h is the cost of capital in Figure 9.2.

The implication is clear. When goods markets are integrated and direct investment flows unrestricted, any difference between the effective tax rates on the distributed profits of the affiliate and the undistributed profits of the parent is inherently distortionary: assuming each $F^i(\cdot)$ to be strictly concave, the integration of previously separated markets can be expected to discourage outward and encourage inward investment whenever $\tau_d^* > \tau^h$ (though the pattern of output price changes could be such as to offset this). The reason is equally clear: market integration gives the multinational some latitude in choosing, through its location decisions, the jurisdiction in which to take its profits. Indeed location becomes, in part, akin to a transfer pricing device: recalling equation (33), the condition under which integration tends to discourage outward investment, $\xi > 0$, is exactly that under which there is an incentive to set intra-company prices so as to shift taxable income to the parent.

The point is a simple one, but has profound consequences for the analysis of tax effects on foreign direct investment. Under independent profitability, distortions arise only from cross-country variation in *marginal* rates of effective taxation: if the source principle applies and each country uses a cash flow tax, for instance, full neutrality would be achieved irrespective of any difference in statutory rates. With integrated markets, however, *average* tax rates also matter: in the example just given, investment in low tax jurisdictions would be favoured. Two consequences of this deserve emphasis. First, simple analogues of the single-jurisdiction marginal effective rates in the tradition of King and Fullerton (1984) will generally misrepresent the distortions at work in the international setting.[24] Moreover, the presence of the elasticity e in equations (36) and (37) suggests that even the direction of misallocation may depend not only on tax parameters and the like but also, and more troublesomely, on aspects of market structure and strategic conduct. Second, the Hartman–Sinn neutrality proposition fails. Under a system of partial credit with deferral, for instance, $\xi = (\tau^a - \tau^h)/(1 - \tau^a)$ whenever $\tau^a > \tau^h$ (ignoring withholding taxes): a sufficiently large fall in the rate of corporation tax at home will always reduce the attractions of retention-financed investment by the mature affiliate. By the same token, changes in the form of double tax relief will also, under integration, affect the mature multinational's investment behaviour: movement to deduction without deferral, for instance, would ensure $\tau_d^* > \tau^h$ and consequently encourage investment at home while discouraging it abroad.

The intuition behind the breakdown of the Hartman–Sinn proposition is straightforward, but in view of its prominence in the tax literature, worth elaborating. Suppose that the only taxes are those on the income of the parent, at τ^h, and on the distributions of the affiliate, at τ_d^*. Suppose, too, that the only investment opportunity facing the multinational is a lumpy project that costs unity, yields a single-period return with present value (at the shareholder's discount rate) of A (> 1) and can be undertaken only by retaining profits either at home or abroad. Finally, suppose that the current post-tax income of the parent and earnings of the affiliate are both exactly unity. The multinational then has two options to compare. The first is to undertake the project in the parent, distributing the income of the affiliate to shareholders: after tax, this yields the shareholder $(1 - \tau^h)A + (1 - \tau_d^*)$. The other is to undertake the project abroad and distribute the earnings of the parent: this yields $(1 - \tau_d^*)A + (1 - \tau^h)$. Clearly the choice turns on $\tau_d^* - \tau^h$. If for instance $\tau_d^* > \tau^h$ then it is worth suffering the tax penalty on distributions from the affiliate now in order to enjoy in the future the relatively favourable tax treatment of income earned directly by the parent.

Market integration thus restores the natural presumption that double tax arrangements and cross-country variation in statutory tax rates are liable to distort corporate decision-making. In the limiting case – identical constant returns technologies in the two countries – production will be entirely concentrated wherever the effective average tax rate is lowest. Transport costs and the presence of country-specific fixed factors provide some basis for production to continue in distinct jurisdictions despite different effective tax rates; but here too the aims of the single market programme – of, for instance, liberalising transport services and facilitating labour mobility – come into play. They must clearly be expected to increase still further the potential impact of taxation on corporate location decisions.

6 Achieving neutrality

The results of sections 4 and 5 enable one to address with some precision the issues of efficiency raised in the introduction. What kinds of tax arrangements raise revenue without distorting financial and investment decisions? Is it possible to achieve neutrality whilst allowing statutory tax rates to vary across jurisdictions and at the same time having both home and host governments receive positive revenue from investments in the latter? These are the issues taken up here, though the discussion will be far from exhaustive. Attention is focussed entirely on the achievement of full neutrality, by which is meant a situation in which not only are CEN and CIN ensured but, moreover, the common value of the cost of capital is precisely as it would be in the absence of taxation: corporate decisions must in that sense be entirely undistorted. Weaker neutrality properties are not considered, and nor are the merits of schemes that fall short of this high standard. To avoid excessive taxonomy, it will be assumed throughout this section that arrangements are in force which ensure that borrowing rates in the two countries coincide:

$$r^h = r^a = r \tag{38}$$

This would be the no-arbitrage condition under residence-basis taxation of portfolio income.[25]

Consider first the system proposed by the Commission, described at the outset. From the results in Figure 9.2 and the definition of ρ^h in equation (17), indifference between retention and debt finance for home investment (given, as apparently envisaged, the continuation of interest deductibiilty $(\alpha^h = 1)$) requires that

$$(1 - m^h)/(1 - z^h) = 1 - \tau^h \tag{39}$$

This could be ensured by deliberate policy in tax setting: exempting capital gains and imposing a common flat tax on corporate and personal dividend income (in effect, taxing capital gains at source). Or, in a richer model, it might emerge as an equilibrium condition implied by indifference of the marginal shareholder between these two sources (Miller, 1977). Given equation (39), the achievement of indifference between retentions/debt and new equity under the imputation method ($\sigma^h = -s^h$, $\gamma^h = 0$) imposes the further restriction that

$$\tau^h = s^h \tag{40}$$

so that imputation must be full rather than partial. Full neutrality requires not merely the indifference implied by equations (39) and (40) but, moreover, that the common cost of capital be exactly $(r + \delta)q$.

Recalling the definition of q^{*h} in equation (29) and using equation (39), this can be guaranteed by setting

$$\delta^{Th} = \delta; \quad \beta^h = 0, \tag{41}$$

which describes a system of true economic depreciation. The Commission's proposals on investment incentives might, at some risk of over-rationalisation, be interpreted as attempting to approximation equation (41). Turning to investment abroad, and for the moment assuming independent profitability, equality across parent and affiliate in the cost of capital for retention finance can be seen (comparing Figures 9.2 and 9.3) to require, given equation (41) together with its foreign analogue and the anticipated continuance of deferral ($\tau^* = \tau^a$), that

$$\tau^h = \tau^a \tag{42}$$

Rates of corporation tax (and hence also, from equation (40), of imputation) must thus be completely aligned; and this is so, it should be noted, even in the absence of the integration effects examined in section 5. Supposing such harmony to have been achieved, the requirement that the cost of capital for new equity financing of the affiliate also reduce to $(r + \delta)q$ imposes the further condition that

$$\sigma^* = 0 \tag{43}$$

so that the effective tax rate on repatriations must be zero. Note too that, recalling equation (13) and since $\tau^* = \tau^a$, equations (42) and (43) imply

$$\tau_d^* = \tau^h$$

so that the critical parameter ξ in the analysis of integration vanishes. It is straightforward to check that the costs of capital for local and intra-company borrowing by the affiliate also reduce to $(r + \delta)q$. Conditions (38)–(43) are thus jointly sufficient for full neutrality to be achieved under the imputation method.

The further restrictions which this discussion indicates need to be added to the Commission's proposals in order to ensure full neutrality are for the most part conceptually minor, though they may have considerable behavioural and welfare implications. One point worth emphasis, however, is the implication of equation (43) that the host government not pass on the imputation credit with dividend payments by the affiliate; or, if it does, that the home government tax the credit away. This is not merely a matter of ensuring that credit is taken only once: attaching a credit to repatriations would encourage new equity rather than retention finance of affiliates in precisely the same way that the imputation system was noted earlier to cause tax-exempt institutions to prefer new equity in the single-jurisdiction context. To avoid this distortion in the financing of affiliates, the imputation credit must come into play only with the payment of dividends by the parent to final shareholders.

A disadvantage of the scheme just described is that it requires full convergences of statutory tax rates. There are (at least) two alternative strategies enabling full neutrality to be achieved without imposing this restriction.

To develop the first of these, recall that one of the major sources of distortion identified in section 4 was the practice of deferral. An obvious direction for reform is thus to begin with its abolition, instead taxing affiliates concurrently at the home country rate:

$$\tau^* = \tau^h \tag{44}$$

The ending of deferral has indeed been a constant theme in the discussion of international double taxation, a forceful advocate being Alworth (1988). Given $\gamma^* = 0$, comparison of the costs of new equity and retention finance of the affiliate imposes the requirement that there then be no taxation on repatriation: $\sigma^* = 0$. Recalling Figure 9.1, the required system is thus one of full credit without deferral. It is straightforward to check that full neutrality will then be achieved in either of two sets of circumstances. One is that in which $\alpha^h = \alpha^a = 1$ and conditions (39)–(41) are satisfied: a scheme, that is, involving full imputation, interest deductibility and true economic depreciation. The other is a classical tax regime ($s^i = 0$, i = a, h) with no interest deductibility ($\alpha^i = 0$),[26] free depreciation ($\beta^i = 0$) and

$$m^i = z^i, \quad i = a, h \tag{45}$$

so that (as under a comprehensive income or personal expenditure tax) there is no discrimination in the personal tax treatment of interest income and capital gains.[27] Full credit with deferral directly implies $\xi = 0$, so that market integration imposes no additional conditions for neutrality.

This strategy has two sets of disadvantages. First there are the difficulties associated with full crediting. Countries with low tax rates will find that they are subsidising resident corporations' investments abroad. Such inter-governmental transfers naturally raise equity concerns and may induce collectively harmful strategic behaviour (Bond and Samuelson, 1989). Though revenue-sharing arrangements equivalent to full crediting but assuring positive revenue to both jurisdictions could clearly be devised, these seem likely to prove administratively cumbersome. The second set of problems concerns the abolition of deferral. For it is the conventional wisdom of practitioners that concurrent taxation would raise a battery of legal, accounting and other horrors: 'Abolishing deferral would be a technical nightmare'.[28]

It is thus of some importance to note that all the efficiency properties possessed by these schemes of full credit without deferral can be achieved by an alternative strategy that retains the administrative merits of deferral. That strategy is to apply in the international context the logic of the S-base cash flow tax. It was seen earlier that such a tax, combined with an appropriate personal tax regime, is fully neutral in the single-jurisdiction context. The same logic that underlies that result has a further, distinct appeal in the international setting. Recall that one of the concerns in this area is the discrimination against new equity financing of affiliates consequent upon the taxation of repatriated dividends ($\sigma^* > 0$). The strategy of abolishing deferral removes this by taxing concurrent profits rather than dividends. But the same effect can be achieved by instead taxing affiliates on an S-basis – continuing, that is, to tax dividends coming out of the affiliate but combining this with a credit, at the same rate, on injections of new equity going in.

Specifically, the costs of capital in Figures 9.2 and 9.3 all – with one exception, which for the moment we put aside – reduce to $(r + \delta)q$ if equation (45) holds and

$$\tau^i = \tau^* = 0, \quad i = a, h \tag{46}$$

$$\sigma^h = \gamma^h; \quad \sigma^* = \gamma^* \tag{47}$$

Under independent profitability, full neutrality can thus be assured by taxing both parent and affiliate on an S-basis. Moreover there is in this case no need for any crediting arrangement between home and host governments: the only restriction is that the total burden on net distributions by the affiliate be less than 100%. Thus the difficulties associated with full crediting need not arise. The reason (hinted at in King, 1987, 394) is simple: if the multinational is unable to shift pure profits between jurisdictions then no distortion arises from taxing pure profits arising in different jurisdictions at different rates.

The exception is intra-company borrowing. In this case the cost of capital reduces, given equations (46) and (47), to $(r + \delta)q + \sigma^*(r - \bar{r})$, so that if $\sigma^* > 0$ there is an incentive to return income to the parent as interest rather than dividends. Thin capitalisation rules would be needed to ensure positive revenue from the taxation of net distributions by the affiliate. This in turn is but an instance of a more general potential problem of transfer pricing: with $\sigma^* > 0$, equations (46)–(47) imply $\tau_d^* > \tau^h$, so that the multinational would always wish to transfer taxable income to the parent company.

Putting this last observation together with the close connection between the incentive to transfer price and the effects of market integration noted in section 5, it is no surprise to find that the irrelevance of double tax arrangements under the S-base strategy breaks down when markets are integrated. Using equations (46) and (13) and in equation (35), one has $\xi = 0$ iff $\sigma^* = 0$. Once again, full neutrality requires full crediting.

7 Conclusions

Both the distorting consequences of corporate taxation and the answer to the question raised at the outset – whether full neutrality in corporate taxation is compatible with cross-jurisdiction variation in statutory tax rates – have been shown to depend on the extent to which a multi-national's activities in one jurisdiction affect the profitability of its operations in others: to depend, in that sense, on the extent of integration between the economies concerned. It is conceptually straightforward to reconcile neutrality with national fiscal autonomy when – as is implicit in much of the tax literature in this area – the pre-tax return on investing in an affiliate abroad is independent of the parent company's investment at home. One way involves ending the standard practice of deferral (by which the home country taxes the earnings of subsidiaries abroad only when repatriated to the parent) and adopting procedures equivalent to the granting by the home country of a full credit (including the possibility of refunds) for tax paid abroad. Another, which has been less widely noted, is by taxing both parent and affiliate on an S-base (net equity) cash flow basis. The latter strategy has particular appeal. It has the considerable merit of retaining the administrative convenience of deferral (the tax on repatriations being balanced by a credit on new equity injections). And it does not require full crediting; indeed it dictates no particular form – or even the existence – of double tax relief. There is, though, a potential transfer pricing problem with the S-base option: in the absence of full crediting, multinationals will have an incentive to avoid taxes on the net distributions of their affiliates through non-equity financial transactions (such as high interest loans) that transfer taxable income directly to the parent. Prospects become dimmer still when – as one would expect to be the case in a single European market – returns on investments in different locations are interdependent. In this case full crediting is needed under the S-base option in order to avoid distorting location decisions. For firms can then choose where to take their pure profits, so that neutrality requires that the effective rate at which these are taxed be unaffected by that choice: otherwise the same considerations as give rise to the transfer pricing problem will give rise to distortions in real investment behaviour, an area in which the potential collective welfare losses are presumably far larger. Short of full crediting, the achievement of full neutrality in international corporate taxation within the environment of the single market requires, it seems, a substantive loss of national autonomy in tax setting.

Appendix A

After some remarkably tedious manipulations (details of which are available from the author), the necessary conditions for the problem described at the end of section 3 can be written:

$$K_u^h: (\theta + \lambda_u^{Dh})(1 - \tau^h)(R_h^h(K_u^h, K_u^a)$$
$$+ [(\theta + \lambda_u^{Dh})(1 - \tau_d^*) + \lambda_u^{Da}(1 - \tau^a)]R_h^a(K_u^h, K_u^a)$$
$$+ \mu_{u+1}^h(1 - \delta)(1 + \rho^h)^{-1} - \mu_u^h = 0 \tag{A1}$$

$$K_u^a: (\theta + \lambda_u^{Dh})(1 - \tau^h)(R_a^h(K_u^h, K_u^a)$$
$$+ [(\theta + \lambda_u^{Dh})(1 - \tau_d^*) + \lambda_u^{Da}(1 - \tau^a)]R_a^a(K_u^h, K_u^a)$$
$$+ \mu_{u+1}^a(1 - \delta)(1 + \rho^h)^{-1} - \mu_u^a = 0 \tag{A2}$$

$$I_u^h: -[(\theta + \lambda_u^{Dh})(1 - \beta^h \tau^h) - \mu_{u+1}^{Th}(1 - \beta^h)(1 + \rho^h)^{-1}]q$$
$$+ \mu_{u+1}^h(1 + \rho^h)^{-1} = 0 \tag{A3}$$

$$I_u^a: -[(\theta + \lambda_u^{Dh})(1 - \sigma^*)(1 - \beta^a \tau^*)$$
$$- \mu_{u+1}^{Ta}(1 - \beta^a)(1 + \rho^h)^{-1} + \lambda_u^{Da}(1 - \beta^a \tau^a)]q$$
$$+ \mu_{u+1}^a(1 + \rho^h)^{-1} = 0 \tag{A4}$$

$$B_u^h: \theta + \lambda_u^{Dh} + \lambda_u^{Bh}$$
$$- (\theta + \lambda_{u+1}^{Dh})\{1 + (1 - \alpha^h \tau^h)r^h\}(1 + \rho^h)^{-1} = 0 \tag{A5}$$

$$B_u^a: -[(\theta + \lambda_{u+1}^{Dh})(1 - \sigma^*)\{1 + (1 - \alpha^a \tau^*)r^a\}$$
$$+ \lambda_{u+1}^{Da}\{1 + (1 - \alpha^a \tau^a)r^a\}](1 + \rho^h)^{-1}$$
$$+ \lambda_u^{Da} + \lambda_u^{Ba} + (1 - \sigma^*)(\theta + \lambda_u^{Dh}) = 0 \tag{A6}$$

$$N_u^h: (\theta + \lambda_u^{Dh})(1 + \gamma^h) + \lambda_u^{Nh} - 1 = 0 \tag{A7}$$

$$N_u^a: \lambda_u^{Da} - \sigma^*(\theta + \lambda_u^{Dh}) + \lambda_u^{Na} + \gamma^*(\theta + \lambda_u^{Dh}) = 0 \tag{A8}$$

$$K_u^{Th}: (\theta + \lambda_u^{Dh})\tau^h \delta^{Th} - \mu_u^{Th} + \mu_{u+1}^{Th}(1 - \delta^{Th})(1 + \rho^h)^{-1} = 0 \tag{A9}$$

$$K_u^{Ta}: [(\theta + \lambda_u^{Dh})(1 - \sigma^*)\tau^* + \lambda_u^{Da}\tau^a]\delta^{Ta}$$
$$- \mu_u^{Ta} + \mu_{u+1}^{Ta}(1 - \delta^{Ta})(1 + \rho^h)^{-1} = 0 \tag{A10}$$

$$B_u: [(\theta + \lambda_{u+1}^{Dh})\{(1 - \sigma^*)\alpha^a \tau^* + \sigma^* - \alpha^h \tau^h\}$$
$$- \lambda_{u+1}^{Da}(1 - \alpha^a \tau^a)]\bar{r}(1 + \rho^h)^{-1} + [\sigma^*(\theta + \lambda_{u+1}^{Dh})$$
$$- \lambda_{u+1}^{Da}](1 + \rho^h)^{-1} + \lambda_u^{Da} + \lambda_u^B - \sigma^*(\theta + \lambda_u^{Dh}) = 0 \tag{A11}$$

$$P_u: [\delta L/\delta P_u)(1 + \rho^h)^{1+u} = (\theta + \lambda_u^{Dh})(\tau_d^* - \tau^h)$$
$$- \lambda_u^{Da}(1 - \tau^a) = 0 \tag{A12}$$

together with the complementary slackness conditions corresponding to equations (24)–(26), where R_j^i denotes $\delta R^i/\delta K_j$, L the Lagrangean and $\lambda^{Di} = \lambda_2^{Di} - \lambda_1^{Pi}$ (i = a, h); the multipliers λ_u^{Dh} and λ_u^{Na} here are the originals of equations (24) and (25) divided by $1 + \sigma^h$ and $1 + \gamma^a$ respectively.

Appendix B

To derive the costs of capital in Figure 9.2, first solve equation (A9), using equation (27), to give the shadow value of the depreciation allowances attached to an additional unit of home investment at u − 1 as

$$\mu_u^{Th} = \theta \tau^h \delta^{Th}(1 + \rho^h)(\rho^h + \delta^{Th})^{-1}, \quad \forall u \geq t \tag{B1}$$

Then equation (29) becomes

$$q^{*h} = [1 - \beta^h \tau^h - (1 - \beta^h)\mu_u^{Th}\{\theta(1 + \rho^h)\}^{-1}]q, \quad \forall u \geq t \tag{B2}$$

Using equations (27), (B1) and (B2) in (A3) gives the shadow values of real capital in place at t and t + 1 as

$$\mu_t^h(1 + \rho^h)^{-1} = \theta q^{*h} + \lambda_{t-1}^{Dh}(1 - \beta^h \tau^h)q$$

$$\mu_{t+1}^h(1 + \rho)^{-1} = \theta q^{*h}$$

which, used together with equation (27) and $R_h^a = 0$ in equation (A1), gives the cost of capital for home investment as

$$R_K^h(K_u^h) = (\rho^h + \delta)(q^{*h}/(1 - \tau^h)) + \lambda_{t-1}^{Dh}\Delta^h(1 + \gamma^h)/\theta \tag{B3}$$

where

$$\Delta^h = (1 - \beta^h \tau^h)(1 + \rho^h)q/(1 - \tau^h)(1 + \gamma^h) \tag{B4}$$

The value of the multiplier λ_{t-1}^{Dh} in equation (B3) depends on the means by which the firm finances the investment at t − 1 that determines the capital stock at t: the use of retention finance at the margin directly implies that $\lambda_{t-1}^{Dh} = 0$; new equity finance ($\lambda_{t-1}^{Nh} = 0$) implies, from equation (A7), that $\lambda_{t-1}^{Dh} = (1 + \gamma^h)^{-1} - \theta$; and when the marginal source is borrowing in the home country ($\lambda_{t-1}^{Bh} = 0$) λ_{t-1}^{Dh} is obtained from equation (A5). Substituting in this way for the second term in equation (B3) give the results shown in Figure 9.2.

Appendix C

The derivation of the results in Figure 9.3 parallels that of those in Figure 9.2. Solving equation (A.10) gives, by virtue of equation (30),

$$\mu_u^{Ta} = \theta(1 - \sigma^*)\tau^* \delta^{Ta}(1 + \rho^h)(\rho^h + \delta^{Ta})^{-1}, \quad \forall u \geq t \tag{C1}$$

so that, from equation (32),

$$q^{*a} = [1 - \beta^a \tau^* - (1 - \beta^a)\mu_u^{Ta}\{\theta(1 - \sigma^*)(1 + \rho^h)\}^{-1}]q, \quad \forall u \geq t$$

$$(C2)$$

Using equations (C2), (30) and (31) in (A4) one finds

$$\mu_t^a(1 + \rho^h) = \theta(1 - \sigma^*)q^{*a} + \lambda_{t-1}^{Da}(1 - \beta^a \tau^a)q$$

$$\mu_{t+1}^a(1 + \rho^h)^{-1} = \theta(1 - \sigma^*)q^{*a}$$

which produce, on substituting into equation (A2), setting $R_a^h = 0$ and recalling (13),

$$R_K^a(K_t^a) = (\rho^h + \delta)q^{*a}/(1 - \tau^*) + \lambda_{t-1}^{Da}(\Delta^a/\theta)$$

where

$$\Delta^a = (1 - \beta^a \tau^a)(1 + \rho^h)q/(1 - \tau_d^*)$$

The derivation is then completed, as before, by specifying the affiliate's marginal source of finance and using the restrictions in the text to solve for λ_{t-1}^{Da} from the appropriate necessary condition.

Appendix D

Equations (36) and (37) follow on noting that, given equation (34) and maintaining assumptions (27) and (30), the first-order conditions (A1) and (A2) become

$$\theta(1 - \tau^h)[1 - e + \{(\xi e \kappa^a/(1 + \xi)\}]pF_K^h(K_t^h)$$
$$- \mu_t^h + \mu_{t+1}^h(1 - \delta)(1 + \rho^h)^{-1} = 0$$

$$\theta(1 - \tau_d^*)[1 - e - \xi e \kappa^h]pF_K^a(K_t^a)$$
$$- \mu_t^a + \mu_{t+1}^a(1 - \delta)(1 + \rho^h)^{-1} = 0$$

These expressions are of the same general form as arise under independent profitability, with simple transforms of the marginal physical products of capital F_K^i replacing marginal revenue products. Since all other first-order conditions are unchanged, the equilibrium values of the former under each financial regime follow directly from the analyses underlying Figures 9.2 and 9.3.

NOTES

I am grateful to conference participants, Julian Alworth, Mike Devereux, Mervyn King, Mark Pearson, Hans-Werner Sinn, Tony Venables and Ian Wooton for comments and advice, though the views and errors are mine alone. The hospitality of CORE, where part of this work was completed, is acknowledged with thanks.

1 Commission of the European Communities (1985).
2 Fitchew (1989, p. 19).
3 Commission of the European Communities (1975).
4 [Added in the press] The Commission has subsequently withdrawn their proposal.
5 Commission of the European Communities (1988).
6 Commission of the European Communities (1969).
7 Fitchew (1989, p. 13).
8 Sørensen (1989) surveys inter-nation equity and strategic considerations in corporate taxation.
9 There is an important caveat to this description. To the extent that a firm's gross dividend payment exceeds its taxable profits, it is denied the ability to credit tax payments in respect of the former (known in the United Kingdom as Advanced Corporation Tax (ACT)) against its liability on the latter; part of the ACT thus remains 'unrecovered'. Corporation tax liability is thus of the general form (ignoring carrying provisions)

$$\tau^h \psi_t^h + s^h D_t^h - s^h . \min\{D_t^h, \psi_t^h\} + T_t^{ha}$$

Note too that the dividend limitation here is only to the extent of *domestic* taxable profits, ψ_t^h. This is indeed the practice in the United Kingdom. Its consequence is that firms whose earnings are principally from abroad are in particular jeopardy of incurring unrecovered ACT: this is the 'prejudice problem', which has for several years been one of the principal tax concerns of UK multinationals (see for instance Chown, 1989).
10 The account that follows draws heavily on Alworth (1988, Chapter 4).
11 Provisions differ as to whether excess credits may (as in the United States) or may not (as in the United Kingdom) be carried to other years; it is assumed here that they cannot.
12 The parameter τ^* is exactly as in Alworth (1988); σ^* is related to Alworth's θ^*, the difference being that the latter presumes that the parent immediately distributes dividends received from the affiliate.
13 See Giovannini (1989).
14 The implications are discussed in Alworth (1988, pp. 85–7).
15 Unlike King (1974), tax rates are here assumed to be unchanging over time; this removes a potential source of distortion that could arise even with cash flow taxation of the kind discussed later (Sandmo, 1979).
16 Table 2.4 of Devereux and Pearson (1989) provides a useful summary description of depreciation allowances in the Member States.
17 An additional option for the multinational, for instance, would be to finance investment at home by repatriating profits from abroad.
18 A fourth possibility is that the parent may pay no dividend and issue neither new equity nor debt, so that retentions are the marginal source in a sense rather different from that of the text. This regime, analysed in Sinn (1989a), is not examined here.
19 This needs some qualification: dividend taxes continue to be non-distorting if new equity is issued in adjacent periods (Edwards and Keen, 1984). A similar point applies to the discussion of repatriation taxes below.
20 Hines and Hubbard (1990) report evidence that US affiliates do indeed find

retention attractive; in 1984 nearly 70% of a large sample of controlled foreign corporations paid a dividend of zero.
21 With $\lambda_u^{Na} = \gamma^* = 0$ and $\sigma^* \in (0, 1)$ equation (A8) gives

$$\lambda_u^{Da} = \sigma^* \theta/(1 - \sigma^*) > 0 \tag{N1}$$

But (recalling the definition in Appendix A) $D_u^a > 0$ implies $\lambda_u^{Da} = -\lambda_{1u}^{Da} \leq 0$, contradicting (N1).
22 See equation (A12) in Appendix A.
23 It almost goes without saying that this point too is noted by Hartman (1985, n. 15).
24 This is recognised in the empirical work of Devereux and Pearson (1989).
25 Though formally the norm, the residence principle for portfolio income is in practice often undermined by tax evasion. This lends particular interest to the alternative assumption of source-basis taxation, modelled by the no-arbitrage condition $(1 - m^h)r^h = (1 - m^a)r^a$; this would lead to neutrality conditions different from those that follow in the text.
26 Equivalently, interest deductibility might be retained but loans and repayments brought into tax.
27 Sinn (1989b) argues that, conditional on residence-basis taxation of portfolio income, equality of costs of capital between single-jurisdiction firms in different locations requires the true economic depreciation. Yet it is clear from the scheme just described that the same effect can be achieved by a strategy that instead involves free depreciation. The source of these differing results is the assumption in Sinn's analysis that personal tax parameters satisfy not condition (45) but condition (39) and its analogue abroad.
28 Mutén (1983, p. 331).

REFERENCES

Alworth, J.S. (1986) 'A cost of capital approach to the taxation of foreign direct investment', in J.S.S. Edwards, J. Franks, C. Mayer and S. Schaefer (eds), *Recent Developments in Corporate Finance*, Cambridge: Cambridge University Press.
   (1988) *The Finance, Investment and Taxation Decisions of Multinationals*, Oxford: Basil Blackwell.
Bond, E.W. and L. Samuelson (1989) 'Strategic behaviour and the rules for international taxation of capital', *Economic Journal*, **99**, pp. 1099–1111.
Chown, J. (1989) 'Tax harmonisation in Europe', in M. Gammie and B. Robinson (eds), *Beyond 1992: A European Tax System*, London: Institute for Fiscal Studies.
Commission of the European Communities (1969) 'Draft directive concerning the common system of taxation applicable in the case of parent corporations and subsidiaries of different member states', **COM(69) 6** final.
   (1975) 'Proposal for a council directive concerning the harmonisation of systems of company taxation and of withholding taxes on dividends', *Official Journal*, **C253**.
   (1985) *Completing the Internal Market*, **COM(85)** p. 310.
   (1988) 'Preliminary draft proposal for a directive on the harmonisation of rules concerning the taxable profits of undertakings', **XV/27/88**.
Davies, D.R. (1985) *Principles of Double Tax Relief*, London: Sweet & Maxwell.

Devereux, M. and M. Pearson (1989) *Corporate Tax Harmonisation and Economic Efficiency*, Institute for Fiscal Studies Report Series, **35**, London: Institute for Fiscal Studies.

Dutton, J. (1982) 'The optimal taxation of international investment income: A note', *Quarterly Journal of Economics*, **97**, pp. 373–80.

Edwards, J.S.S. and M.J. Keen (1984) 'Wealth maximisation and the cost of capital: A comment', *Quarterly Journal of Economics*, **99**, pp. 211–14.

Feldstein, M.S. and D.G. Hartman (1979) 'The optimal taxation of foreign source income', *Quarterly Journal of Economics*, **94**, pp. 613–29.

Fitchew, G. (1989) 'The single European market and tax harmonisation', in M. Gammie and B. Robinson (eds), *Beyond 1992: A European Tax System*, London: Institute for Fiscal Studies.

Giovannini, A. (1989) 'National tax systems versus the European capital market', *Economic Policy* **9**, pp. 346–71; 381–6.

Hartman, D.G. (1985) 'Tax policy and foreign direct investment', *Journal of Public Economics*, **26**, pp. 107–21.

Hines, J.R. Jr. and R. Glenn Hubbard (1990) 'Coming home to America: Dividend repatriations by US multinationals', in A. Razin and J. Slemrod (eds), *Taxation in the Global Economy*, Chicago: University of Chicago Press.

Horst, T. (1980) 'A note on the optimal taxation of international investment income', *Quarterly Journal of Economics*, **95**, pp. 793–8.

King, M.A. (1974) 'Taxation, investment and the cost of capital', *Review of Economic Studies*, **41**, pp. 21–35.

(1977) *Public Policy and the Corporation*, London: Chapman and Hall.

(1987) 'The cash flow corporate income tax', in M.S. Feldstein (ed), *The Effects of Taxation on Capital Accumulation*, Chicago: Chicago University Press.

King, M.A. and D. Fullerton (eds) (1984) *The Taxation of Income from Capital: A Comparative Study of the US, UK, Sweden and West Germany*, Chicago: Chicago University Press.

Leechor, C. and J.A. Mintz (1990) 'On the taxation of multinational corporate investment when the deferral method is used by the capital exporting country', University of Toronto (mimeo).

Mayer, C.P. (1986) 'Corporation tax, finance and the cost of capital', *Review of Economic Studies*, **53**, pp. 93–112.

Miller, M. H. (1977) 'Debt and taxes', *Journal of Finance*, **32**, pp. 261–75.

Mintz, J.A. (1989) 'Tax holidays and investment', World Bank PPR working paper, **WPS178**.

Musgrave, P.B. (1969) *United States Taxation of Foreign Investment Income: Issues and Arguments*, Cambridge, MA: Harvard Law School.

Mutén, L. (1983) 'Some topical issues concerning international double taxation', in S. Cnossen (ed), *Comparative Tax Studies: Essays in Honor of Richard Goode*, Amsterdam: North-Holland.

Sandmo, A. (1979) 'A note on the neutrality of the cash flow corporation tax', *Economics Letters*, **4**, pp. 173–6.

Sinn, H.-W. (1984) 'Die Bedeutung des Accelerated Cost Recovery System für den internationalen Kapitalverkehr', *Kyklos*, **37**, pp. 542–76.

(1987) *Capital Income Taxation and Resource Allocation*, Amsterdam: North-Holland.

(1989a) 'The vanishing Harberger triangle', University of Munich discussion paper, **88–05**.

(1989b) 'Tax harmonisation in Europe', University of Munich (mimeo).

Smith, A. and A.J. Venables (1988) 'Completing the internal market in the European Community: Some Industry Simulations', *European Economic Review*, **32**, pp. 1501–25.

Sørensen, P. (1989) 'Issues in the theory of tax coordination', University of Copenhagen (mimeo).

Discussion

IAN WOOTON

This is a very comprehensive study on the forms of corporate taxation that might be adopted by nations, and their consequences for the investment and financial behaviour of multinational enterprises. Of especial interest to me is the analysis of the potential consequences of 1992. This is assumed to take the form of integration of previously segmented national markets, with the result that both the parent and the affiliate of the multinational end up supplying goods to the same market. Such an event has a dramatic outcome. In a segmented market regime, countries have a degree of independence in their choices of statutory tax rates; within an integrated market, differences in these rates are liable to distort investment decisions with the result that 'production will be entirely concentrated wherever the effective average tax rate is lowest'.

The focus of the study is the multinational firm that has both parent and affiliate located within a customs union (such as the EC). In the absence of a harmonisation of national corporate tax schedules, market integration will thus result in the eventual concentration of production in the location that has the most favourable tax climate for the firm (which might even be a third country within the EC). I am particularly interested in how this result relates to the predictions made from international trade theory as to the effects of market integration.

In the presence of increasing returns to scale in manufacturing, it is clear that it is more efficient for a firm to produce all of its output in a single location. It may be argued that the choice to operate as a multinational is due, in some degree, to the prohibitive costs of jumping barriers to international trade. A goal of 1992 is the elimination of such obstacles, increasing the benefits to a firm of concentrating its production in one large-scale plant. Harmonisation of corporate taxes across the community might thus not be enough to ensure the continued existence of all of the production locations. But it would ensure that, should a firm decide to concentrate its activities, its choice of country would not be distorted by differences in the tax regimes.

Related to this is the question of the likely impact of 1992 on firms based outside the EC. Consider, for example, that prior to 1992 a foreign firm exports its products into each of the segmented markets of the EC. The removal of internal trade barriers would increase the relative benefit of producing at a plant within the EC (as the relative cost of exporting to the EC would have risen). Harmonisation of tax rates within the EC will again ensure that an efficient locational decision is made, but now in addition the levels of rates matter, as the EC as a whole is in competition with the home country of the firm to extract tax revenues from it.

10 Japanese direct manufacturing investment in Europe

STEFANO MICOSSI and GIANFRANCO
VIESTI

1 The basic facts

Japanese direct investment in advanced countries is a relatively recent phenomenon,[1] but an impressive acceleration has taken place since 1985. Investment in western Europe expanded gradually during the second half of the 1970s and the early 1980s and picked up sharply after 1986 (Figure 10.1). Investment has been mostly in finance (banking and insurance), services, and real estate, with industrial investment representing less than 10% of yearly flows in the 1970s, rising to 12–13% in the early 1980s and to some 20% towards the end of that decade.

The growing Japanese presence in manufacturing has attracted much attention and has been a source of debate and controversy within the EC: a quick look at the data in Table 10.1 can help focus the nature of the problem.[2]

The Japanese presence in Europe is still quite small. It is small as a share of total Japanese investment abroad: Europe represents only about 16% of the total, running well behind North America (40% of the total), Asia (23%) and Latin America (19%). Even smaller, comparatively, is the share of manufacturing: only 10% of total investment in Europe, compared with 48% of the total going to manufacturing in North America, 38% in Asia and 24% in Latin America (Watanabe, 1988).

It is small, too, if compared with other foreign presences in European countries. For instance, according to some estimates by EUROSTAT, intra-EC direct investment amounted in 1980–6 to about 35 billion dollars, and US investment in Europe was 46 billion dollars in 1982–7 (out of which over 60% was in manufacturing). According to Julius and Thomsen (1988), the shares of foreign-owned firms in sales, manufacturing employment, and assets in France, Germany and the United Kingdom vary between 15 and 25%; the Japanese component, however, is very small.

200

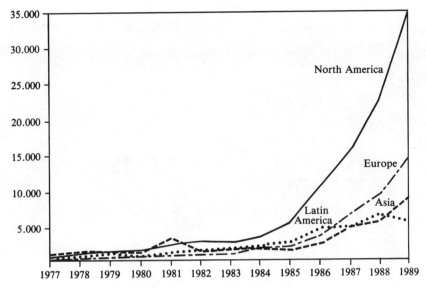

Figure 10.1 Japanese direct investment abroad by main areas (yearly flows, million dollars)

Based on the 1989 DATAR survey, the total assets of Japanese-controlled manufacturing companies in western Europe are in the order of 5 billion dollars (Table 10.2); their total employment still remains below 120,000 employees (although the numbers could rise rapidly with the start of operation of new automobile plants under construction). Stopford (1989) compares the US and Japanese presence in the United Kingdom and finds that the latter accounted in 1986 for only about 0.5% of manufacturing output and total capital invested in the United Kingdom; at that time the corresponding shares for the United States were between 12 and 15%. Dunning and Cantwell (1989) provides a measure of total Japanese involvement in EC manufacturing, obtained by adding up exports, local production and production by non-affiliate firms under licencing, and come up with an estimate of 45 billion dollars in 1986; this compares with a total US presence that is almost six times larger (256 billion dollars). Local production represents 79% of total sales for US firms but only 16% for Japanese ones.

Rather than in aggregate size, the reason for European concerns about Japanese penetration in their markets is to be found in the rapid growth and sectoral concentration of this presence in recent years; the flows of the years 1988–9 account for over 40% of total cumulative flows in 1951–89. Moreover, the acceleration of investment in the late 1980s has followed a

Table 10.1. *Japanese overseas direct investment, million US dollars*

	World	North America	Western Europe	United Kingdom	Federal Republic of Germany	France	Nether-lands	Luxem-burg	Spain	Italy
			Total flows 1951 to 31 March 1989							
Grand Total[1]	186,356	75,091	30,164	10,544	2,364	1,764	5,525	4,729	1,045	370
Non-manufacturing	131,999	49,949	24,098	9,258	1,508	949	4,582	4,725	119	131
– Banking and insurance	41,876	12,370	14,853	5,732	292	228	2,494	4,574	2	12
– Services, commerce and transportation	45,112	16,791	5,626	1,104	1,138	587	1,691	26	96	114
– Agricultural, fisheries and mining	15,635	2,157	1,117	844	—	60	—	3	1	—
– Real estate, construction and others	29,376	18,631	2,051	1,578	78	75	398	122	20	5
– Branch expansion and other real estate	4,514	1,198	1,209	189	388	271	5	—	126	77
Manufacturing	49,843	23,944	4,857	1,107	468	544	938	4	800	162
– Transport machinery	6,956	3,030	913	188	9	29	51	—	547	45
– Electrical machinery	10,196	5,952	1,261	431	165	79	375	4	81	19
– Other machinery	4,716	2,610	626	172	98	116	135	—	12	30
– Chemicals	6,540	2,311	594	43	105	31	252	—	77	23
– Others	21,435	10,041	1,463	273	91	289	125	—	83	45
Nr. of Plants/Enterprises in Manufacturing[2]	15,173	3,906	411	92	67	85	27	—	41	24
– Transport machinery	833	275	27	7	1	3	1	1	10	1

Table 10.1 (*Cont.*)

	World	North America	Western Europe	United Kingdom	Federal Republic of Germany	France	Netherlands	Luxemburg	Spain	Italy
– Electrical machinery	2,622	761	120	39	26	22	3	—	9	6
– Other machinery	1,943	630	68	14	19	11	8	—	6	3
– Chemicals	1,690	372	85	10	10	16	7	—	8	8
– Others	8,085	1,868	111	22	11	33	8	—	8	6
			Flows in FYs 1987–8 (to March 1989)							
Grand Total[1]	80,356	37,685	15,693	6,429	812	794	3,188	2,421	444	167
Non-manufacturing	57,714	23,571	12,710	5,673	482	413	2,448	2,421	56	61
– Banking and insurance	23,777	6,119	8,876	4,343	218	202	1,078	2,393	—	12
– Services, commerce and transportation	16,502	6,635	2,364	544	264	158	1,051	23	36	49
– Agriculture, fisheries and mining	1,922	513	224	27	—	5	—	3	—	—
– Real estate, construction	15,513	10,304	1,245	759	1	49	320	1	20	—
– Branch expansion and other real estate	1,005	75	586	133	139	154	1	—	50	44
Manufacturing	21,637	14,039	2,397	623	191	227	739	—	338	62
– Transport machinery	2,754	1,524	415	91	—	23	50	—	246	3
– Electrical machinery	5,462	3,220	735	253	39	27	345	—	23	13
– Other machinery	2,119	1,375	348	82	29	68	113	—	5	23
– Chemicals	2,203	1,348	367	37	84	13	184	—	33	11
– Others	9,099	6,572	532	160	39	96	47	—	31	12

Sources: Japan's Ministry of Finance, on notification basis; Jetro (1988).
Notes:
1 Grand total includes investments in manufacturing, non-manufacturing sector, branch establishment and expansion and other real estate.
2 Number of plants for World and North America (Ministry of Finance, total up to 31 March 1989); number of enterprises for Western Europe and individual European countries (Jetro, 1988, total up to 31 January 1989). The total number of plants for Europe is 1,481 (transport machinery 56; electrical machinery 220; other machinery 240; chemicals 144; others 821).

Table 10.2. *Japanese manufacturing firms in western Europe: capital and employment*

	Capital[1]	Employment[2]
Countries		
Austria	87.9	748
Belgium	231.6	6,284
Denmark	1.0	70
Finland	0.3	40
France	462.7	18,923
Germany	413.3	16,331
Greece	0.9	1,128
Ireland	136.4	2,904
Italy	115.6	5,284
Luxemburg	58.9	415
The Netherlands	179.4	2,791
Norway	3.3	70
Portugal	49.7	4,909
Spain	744.2	23,826
Sweden	3.2	366
Switzerland	20.3	320
United Kingdom	2,101.9	31,690
Sectors[3]		
Transport machinery	2,091.5	26,408
Electric machinery	1,166.8	35,656
Other machinery	219.7	6,885
Chemicals	626.1	29.253
Others	506.9	17,897
Total Europe	4,611.3	116,099

Source: DATAR (1989).
Notes:
1 Million US dollars.
2 Units.
3 DATAR does not supply sectorally aggregated data; the allocation of individual firms to the five sectors is ours, and is open to considerable margin of error.

period of growing penetration in Europe by Japanese exports that has led to a sizeable aggregate trade imbalance (over 20 billion dollars) between the two areas. Japan's exports of manufactured goods to Europe more than doubled between 1980 and 1987 (Table 10.3), with extremely rapid increases for office and telecommunication productions (280%), cars (150%), electronics (80%); as a consequence the market shares of Japanese products in open markets in Europe have also grown rapidly, leading

Table 10.3. *Japan: export growth and export shares in main world markets[1]*

		Manufacturing		Automobile		Office and telecom. machines		Other electronic goods and transport equipment		Household type electrical goods	
		1980	1987	1980	1987	1980	1987	1980	1987	1980	1987
World[1]	a	11.2	13.0	21.8	24.4	13.4	21.5	10.7	11.7	29.9	30.3
	b	80.2		104.8		308.0		62.4		72.9	
North America	a	20.4	23.5	36.0	35.4	21.9	35.1	15.8	19.5	44.7	46.6
	b	167.7		164.3		457.5		153.4		148.6	
Europe	a	4.5	6.4	11.2	13.5	8.4	14.2	4.6	5.3	20.1	23.2
	b	118.0		153.4		280.9		80.8		73.6	
Germany[2]	a	7.4	9.0	19.9	24.5	16.1	19.7	5.0	6.4	37.4	35.1
France[2]	a	4.5	5.2	6.0	6.4	10.0	14.2	3.9	4.3	24.4	21.3
United Kingdom[2]	a	7.1	7.8	14.4	12.9	11.0	15.0	5.1	7.2	29.6	24.9
Italy[2]	a	3.3	3.6	2.5	1.4	9.0	9.0	3.9	4.2	14.6	13.3
Others[3]	a	15.3	15.7	25.0	26.5	15.6	22.9	14.0	13.5	33.0	34.1
	b	27.6		10.5		209.8		31.2		21.5	

Source: our estimates based on GATT data.
Notes:
1 For each area or country the Japanese export share is given by the percentage ratio imports from Japan/total imports.
2 The first column for each sector refers to 1984.
3 'Others' include Asia, Latin America, Africa, Australia and New Zealand.
a Export shares in reference years.
b Increase in exports, %, 1980–7.

Table 10.4. *Japanese parent company participation in European manufacturing firms, no. of companies*

	Share of capital				
	100%	50–99%	10–49%	Unclass.	Total
Total	206	91	42	52	391
By country					
United Kingdom	66	9	2	15	92
Federal Republic of Germany	39	16	4	8	67
France	38	28	10	9	85
Spain	15	13	10	3	41
Italy	6	6	8	4	24
Others	42	19	8	13	82
By sector					
Transportation machinery	17	9	8	4	38
Electric machinery	72	30	7	15	124
Other machinery	26	120	6	7	49
Chemicals	37	23	8	16	84
Others	54	19	13	10	96
By stage of production					
Assembly	82	40	15	16	153
Components	61	17	10	13	101
Unclassified	63	34	17	23	137

Source: Jetro (1989a).

to trade frictions and consideration of restrictive measures by the EC Commission and/or individual countries.

As to the sectoral composition of Japanese establishments in Europe, over 50% of total investment in recent years has concentrated in electronics and transport machinery – that is, in mass-market consumer durables and office equipment where the Japanese producers have gained a significant competitive edge; this is also reflected in the high share of 'downstream' or 'assembly' plants (Table 10.4). Component procurement in Europe remains low, notably for assembly-type industries, but is increasing, more rapidly where specific requirements are imposed by the EC or national authorities.

Another feature of Japanese investment in manufacturing that should be noted is its geographical pattern, since this highlights the particular locational advantages being sought. The United Kingdom, Germany and Spain clearly emerge as preferred locations, owing to varying combinations of government policies and incentives,[3] good infrastructures, quality and cost of labour. The large share of investment in the Netherlands (and also Luxemburg, where most of the money goes to non-manufacturing sectors), on the other hand, reflects the legal and tax advantages of establishing holding or parent companies, as clearly emerges from comparing investment flows with the number of plants or enterprises (Table 10.1). A sectoral concentration in particular countries is also apparent, with electric–electronic equipment and machinery mostly concentrated in the United Kingdom, Germany, and more recently France, transportation machinery in the United Kingdom and Spain and food and textiles in France and Ireland.

As regards the average size of Japanese firms in Europe, most of them belong to the small-to-medium size group (Figure 10.2). Labour-intensive firms are concentrated in Spain;[4] large firms (over 1,000 employees) are most common in assembly-type activities in electronics, transport machinery, and in rubber and metal products.

In over half of cases reported by Jetro (1989a) parent company participation in European subsidiaries is equal to 100% of capital, and in another quarter of surveyed companies to at least 50% of capital. Joint ventures, in most cases (70%) with no less than 50% of capital, are more common in textiles, pharmaceuticals, ceramics, and in consumer electronics, where they have played an important role in opening European markets to Japanese products in the presence of physical or technical barriers to entry (Cawson, 1989); capital participation in pre-existing companies is more often observed in transport machinery.

Geographically, joint venture or capital participation are more frequent (60% of cases) in southern European countries (notably Spain), partly because of restrictions on inward investment imposed by the authorities, and partly because of greater difficulty in meeting local legislation or labour management requirements. Wholly-owned subsidiaries, on the other hand are found more often (some 60% of cases) in the United Kingdom, the Netherlands, Germany and Belgium–Luxemburg, where the policy on inward investment is liberal or aggressively supportive.

It is interesting to note that most companies present in Europe report more positive profit performances for firms that have been there for longer and inferior results, often with losses, for newcomers. There is also evidence that average returns of Japanese firms in Europe tend to be lower than corresponding sectors' returns in Japan (but they appear higher than in the United States),[5] possibly reflecting efforts to establish their presence in new markets. An alternative explanation present in the answers to the Jetro surveys, and mentioned by Watanabe (1988), could be the market structure in Europe, characterised by a high degree of

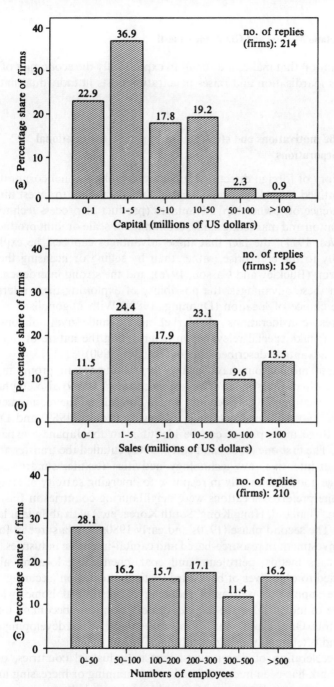

Figure 10.2 Japanese manufacturing firms in Europe by capital, sales and employment, January 1989

Source: Jetro (1989a)

segmentation that makes it difficult to exploit fully the economies of scale from standardisation and raises penetration costs in individual national markets.

2   The motivations and strategies of Japanese multinational corporations

The theory of foreign direct investment and multinational corporations[6] has identified three key components in the motivation to invest abroad: the existence of 'ownership' advantages (product or process technology, organisation and marketing skills, economies of scale or joint production, see Caves, 1971); the fact that these advantages can best be exploited internally to the enterprise, rather than by selling or licensing them to other firms (Buckley and Casson, 1976); and the strong interdependence between these advantages, the possibility of exploiting them internally, and the choice of location (Dunning, 1988). With oligopolistic market structures, considerations of market access and 'rival' oligopolistic behaviour take special relevance in determining the nature of the three types of advantage described above (Graham, 1990).

All these motivations have had a clear influence in promoting the Japanese direct investment drive abroad; Ozawa (1989) also emphasises the close relationship between investment abroad and the requirements of domestic industrial restructuring. Following Ozawa (1989) and Dicken (1988), three main phases can be identified in the Japanese expansion abroad. The first one (1960s and early 1970s) entailed the transfer abroad of labour-intensive, low-technology activities (textile, sundries, other low-wage goods), basically in response to emerging scarcity of labour at home; the preferred locations were neighbouring countries in East Asia (Taiwan, Thailand, Hong Kong, South Korea, etc.) with abundant labour supply. The second phase (1970s and early 1980s) saw a surge in foreign direct investment in resource-based and capital-intensive industries (steel, non-ferrous metals, petroleum and coal, chemicals); locating abroad responded to objectives of backward vertical integration (securing stable resource supply) as well as of reducing congestion at home, where a shortage of industrial space and heavy pollution were becoming binding constraints. Once again, most of this investment was in developing countries, and often involved joint ventures.

The acceleration of direct investment in industrial countries, on the other hand, has been mainly related to maintaining or increasing market shares in mass-market consumer durables (cars and electronic products) where Japanese producers had gained substantial competitive advantages. The appreciation of the yen during the second half of the 1980s added to the pressure to locate production abroad, but the main determinant seems to have been the emerging trade frictions, following rapid growth of exports and export penetration in Western countries.

Watanabe's (1988) detailed description of developments in the automobile and consumer electronics (VCRs, paper copiers, microwave ovens) highlights the direct relationships between rapid export penetration, trade frictions and the establishments of local production facilities.[7] The Jetro survey (1989a) confirms that avoidance of trade frictions ranks first in the decision to set up local assembly units in general, electronic and transport machinery. In this regard, the European internal market programme has clearly been perceived as a major change that has induced a reasssessment of Japanese corporate strategies in Europe, both for 'defensive' (fear of being locked out) and 'offensive' (access to expanding markets) reasons. The Jetro surveys (1989a–1989c) make this aspect very clear; they also show that production location in European countries is always targeted at the European unified market rather than at single national markets.

Circumventing trade barriers has been a main trigger of Japanese foreign direct investment in advanced countries, but it is not the only one. A significant presence in other sectors (chemicals, pharmaceuticals, textiles, ceramics, pulp and paper, non-ferrous metal) is related to other objectives such as gaining access to technology, raw materials, design or other special skills. When this is the motive, the joint venture or other form of collaborative association with western investor is more frequent. It should be stressed, however, that the main reason underlying the dramatic increase in Japanese direct investment is Japan's organisational–technological lead in particular industries.

The Japanese advantage has become especially pronounced in a range of 'scale-intensive' industries, from steel to motorcycles and cars, to consumer electronics products. These are the sectors of great export success, as well as those where direct investment has concentrated (Ozawa, 1989; Dunning and Cantwell, 1989). The ingredients of Japanese superiority in manufacturing, extensively analysed in the literature,[8] include several factors: more extensive, flexible and integrated (system design) use of automation, shorter product cycles, just-in-time methods, tight quality control, ability to change production flexibility to meet demand, great simplification of product design (fewer components), a pyramidal system of subcontracting that is very important in ensuring tightly centralised decision-making; superior productivity and quality control are complemented by greater product differentiation and aggressive marketing and after-sales tactics (Dunning, 1986).

It should be emphasised that no single factor, among those mentioned above, can be taken as the principal or exclusive source of competitive advantage; rather it is their combination in a 'work organization that balances and integrates the people or social system with the technical system' (Rehder, 1988). Impressive evidence, in this regard, is supplied by Osterman (1989): he shows that heavy 'inflexible' automation combined with the traditional ('Ford–Sloan') assembly methods has been ineffective, in a GM plant, in reducing the productivity and quality gap with Japanese producers. On the other hand, in the Nummi plant, jointly owned by Toyota and GM in the United States, organisational–managerial changes à la Japanese with little automation managed to bring about striking improvements in productivity and product quality. Similar results are reported by Lewis (1982) for a Motorola colour TV factory in Illinois taken over by Matsushita (with 30% productivity increases and defects falling to a tiny fraction of former levels).

The peculiar mix of technology, industrial organisation and consensus – that has been referred to as their 'humanware' (Shimada and MacDuffie, 1986) – makes the strategies and behaviour of Japanese corporations in advanced countries quite similar across the different sectors and industries. The following eight aspects, in particular, should be stressed.

2.1   'Greenfield' ventures

There is a clear preference for setting up new factories rather than taking over existing units. In this Japanese firms differ from western multinationals, that resorted instead to acquisitions. In Europe, only 44 out of 216 Japanese subsidiaries surveyed by Jetro in 1989 were organised through capital participation in European industries or merger with them. Out of the seven Japanese-owned large factories operating in the United States only one is operating in a pre-existing establishment (the Nummi joint venture mentioned above).

2.2   Full control of subsidiaries

This aspect is closely related to the previous one. Joint ventures with foreign firms in advanced countries appear rarer than in the earlier phases and areas of Japanese expansion abroad (Asia, LDCs). In Europe, at the end of FY 1988, out of 339 cases for which information was available 206 were 100%-owned. Tight control of subsidiaries by their parent companies also entails low managerial autonomy and few horizontal interrelationships among subsidiaries. As was mentioned above, the exceptions are mostly found in 'difficult' markets, where local partners may play an important role in helping commercial penetration, or where the Japanese investment is designed to acquire local assets (technology, design, raw materials, etc.).

2.3   Location

Consistent with this picture, notably with the importance attached by Japanese companies to the attitude and motivation of labour, a distinct preference is observed for locations without a long-established industrial presence in the particular sector in which they are investing. Accordingly, car factories in the United States were built in Ohio and Tennessee, electronic factories in the United Kingdom in Wales. This strategy was often favoured by incentives made available such as subsidies to invest in less-developed, high-unemployment areas in such countries as the United Kingdom, Ireland, Spain, and Germany (regional governments' subsidies).[9]

2.4   Careful selection and training of workforce

The policy has been to choose employees from a large pool, to hire younger workers, and to invest heavily in their training.[10] Among Japanese subsidiaries in Europe 60% have trained their workforce in Europe and 70% have had programmes involving workers being sent to Japan (Jetro, 1989a). Labour relations policies are seen by 63% of a sample of Japanese managers operating in Europe as the key to their success (Booz, Allen and Hamilton, 1989).

2.5   Sourcing

The close relationships between producers and users of industrial components, based on mutual long-term commitment and tightly observed productive requirements (on specification, delivery, etc.), is a main source of flexibility, quality control and effective just-in-time management. The preferred course for Japanese firms has always been to rely on their traditional suppliers in Japan and import from them parts and components. Over time, this attitude has given rise to complaints in the host countries and has led to the imposition of 'local content' requirements. In assembly-type industries, the Jetro (1989a) survey reports 57% of components coming from Japan at the start of operations; this estimate would be raised if distribution costs and profits were included in locally-produced value-added. MITI information also shows that a high share of the total value of equipment investment is satisfied with direct imports from Japan (42% in 1986: Sumitomo, 1989).

2.6   'Bandwagon' direct investment by part and component suppliers

When direct sourcing from Japan was no longer practicable for political reasons, or became too expensive due to the rising yen, Japanese 'assemblers' encouraged their suppliers in Japan to follow them abroad. In the United States the phenomenon has already reached a remarkable scale: in August 1987 there were 102 Japanese car components suppliers, 47 of which had opened their factories after 1984 (GAO, 1988); their number is reported to have almost trebled by June 1989 (*Financial Times*, 8 June 1989). In the Japanese controlled electronic firms in Europe, that have been there longer, there are already 65 plants of component suppliers (*Electronic Europe 1992*, 1989). When requested to state the main reasons for investing in Europe 19 out of 71 electronic subsidiaries in Europe explicitly mentioned 'acquiring orders from existing Japanese European Industry' (Jetro, 1989a).

2.7   Oligopolistic competition

Another key feature of the Japanese model that has been exported abroad is intense competition among firms in the same industry. In this respect Japanese corporations behaved precisely as described by scholars of multinational corporations (Knickerbocker, 1973; Flowers, 1976; Graham, 1990): in industries with a limited number of non-collusive oligopolists, when one of them decides to invest abroad, its competitors immediately followed suit. The evidence in this respect is quite strong.[11]

2.8   'Patient' money

Each company's main goal is the conquest of the largest possible market share: in order to achieve this goal, Japanese multinationals are ready to accept lower returns for prolonged periods. It is worth recalling that less than half of Japanese corporations surveyed by Jetro in Europe reported profits in the early years of operations (Jetro, 1989a).

When Japanese investments in industrial countries picked up a few years ago, observers wondered whether they could really succeed. As was said earlier, many thought that it would not be possible for Japanese corporations to maintain their competitive edge while producing abroad. Since the phenomenon is relatively recent, it would be premature to come to definite conclusions. The evidence that is available, however, is striking.

In the US car industry Japanese-owned plants are not only more efficient than those of US companies, but almost as efficient as those located in Japan (Krafcik, 1988; Osterman, 1989). Detailed data on productivity and product quality (see among others Krafcik, 1988; Womack, 1989; Jones, 1988a and 1988b; GAO, 1988) as well as information regarding labour relationships (Shimada and MacDuffie, 1986), all point towards such a conclusion. Some studies are also becoming available on the UK experience that tend to confirm the success not only of Japanese firms, but also of the Japanese 'formula' in European companies (Oliver and Wilkinson, 1988). The Japanese producers abroad tend to agree with this assessment: 146 out of 211 respondents to the 1989 Jetro survey reported their experience in Europe as a success, 56 said that it was yet not known; only one said that the venture was a failure (Jetro, 1989a). A somewhat longer list of failures is reported in Watanabe (1988).

3   The effects of Japanese investment in the EC

Section 3 is devoted to a review of the evidence available on the effects of Japanese direct investment in Europe. Following much of the literature on this subject,[12] we discuss separately, in a partial equilibrium framework, possible effects on the labour markets; external trade; various supply-side effects on such things as production capacity, competition, R & D and innovation diffusion; and possible resulting asymmetries within the EC.

3.1   Activity and employment

The employment effects of foreign direct investment are the net result of direct employment creation, on one hand, and possible displacements on the other,[13] as a result of local competitors closing down or reducing their workforce. The first component – job creation – is usually larger for Japanese than for other foreign investment due to the larger share of 'greenfield' ventures; it is safe to conclude that a large share of Japanese firms' jobs in Europe are new jobs.

The measure of any (impact) displacement effect will vary across industries; a lower adverse impact can be expected the 'younger' the industry and the faster the growth of demand. Accordingly, one would expect less displacement in the electronics industry, where new products have been introduced (VCRs, faxes, camcorders, etc.). Another issue that must be considered in this context is: what is displaced by local Japanese production? To the extent that sales of local Japanese subsidiaries are a substitute for Japanese exports, the displacement effect will be reduced. Some calculations made by GAO (1988) for the US car industry can help make the point: other things being equal, if 85% of Japanese production displaced US firms' sales, they estimated that 45,000 US jobs would be lost; but if Japanese production substituted exports from Japan, 112,000 new jobs would be created.

European observers (Dunning and Cantwell, 1989; Stopford, 1989) tend to view production generated by direct investment more as an addition to

Japanese exports than as a substitute; the Japanese opinion, not surprisingly, is quite the opposite (Dillow, 1989; Sumitomo, 1989). In some cases, such as VCRs, there is evidence that Japanese exports to Europe declined after the establishment of local production facilities.

A more general point is made by Graham and Krugman (1989); in summing up the discussion about the employment effects in the United States, they argue that if one looks at Japanese investments in a general equilibrium framework, total employment effects will be negligible since employment levels are determined by the supply of labour rather than by demand; in other words, there is little reason to believe that Japanese investment will greatly change the NAIRU (unless, of course, union or government policies regard employment adjustment between firms, industries or areas).

A different, also quite common, critique raised against Japanese firms is that they tend to create 'lower-quality' jobs, these being mainly for assembly operations that require lower skill. One way of measuring this effect that has been used is to compare average compensation per worker. In this respect US data show no difference between Japanese and non-Japanese factories.[14] In Europe, data are available for the United Kingdom: they show yearly wages for manual workers of £6,773 in Japanese firms, £7,787 for British companies and £8,566 for other EC countries' companies. One suggested interpretation for this difference is that, consistent with Japanese recruiting behaviour, their workers tend to be younger than the industry average (Dillow, 1989).

Jobs created by Japanese investment are different in one important respect: duties of production workers tend to be less differentiated than in western-owned companies. According to GAO (1988) there are 82–95 job classifications in the three US major car producers but only 2–4 in Japanese subsidiaries. It is also apparent that labour unions, both in the United States and in Europe, typically play a smaller role in Japanese-owned firms. Out of 212 Japanese firms operating in Europe for which data is available, only 96 have unions in their factories, and very seldom more than one representative organisation; even in these cases, 75 of 96 firms experienced no strikes in 1988 (Jetro, 1989a).

What remains to be seen is whether similar results will be obtained by Japanese firms operating in countries where union power is more entrenched, such as Germany, France and Italy. Actually, the choice of locating many companies in the United Kingdom seems to be explained, inter alia, by the climate of industrial relations, which is very favourable to the introduction of its system.

3.2   External trade effects

MITI officials explicitly state that they are advising firms to invest in the EC precisely to reduce trade imbalances and trade frictions; and Japanese-sponsored analyses tend to support the conclusion that this is indeed the result of direct investment.[15] In practice, the effects of direct investment on trade flows will depend on Japanese subsidiaries' direct imports, the extent to which exports from Japan will be substituted by local producton, and the extent to which host-country exports will be generated by direct investment.

As for direct imports (from Japan), we have noted already that Japanese subsidiaries tend to import more per unit of output. There is no agreement, however, on the reasons for this behaviour: it is not clear, in particular, to what extent this is due to their being Japanese rather than to their being more recently established subsidiaries. In fact, there is evidence showing that over time the import-from-Japan ratio of Japanese subsidiaries tends to decline.[16] The issue, however, is far from settled. First of all there is no agreement on the method for measuring the 'local content' of production. The question is technically quite complex: suffice to recall that the local content of Nissan's Bluebird car was placed at 60% by British authorities but at 21% by Fiat (Viesti and Zanzottera, 1989).

Leaving aside methodological issues, existing studies lead to an impression that Japan is indeed in the process of recreating abroad its entire production system: this will involve both integrating investment in assembly-type operations with investment by component suppliers and increasing recourse to local suppliers (Jetro, 1989b). Nevertheless, the process will take time and will require substantial restructuring of the local supplier industry. Almost 70% of Japanese firms operating in Europe have declared that they are not satisfied with their local suppliers (Jetro, 1989a). No information is available to determine whether this is due to lower quality of European suppliers, or simply to a preference for their traditional suppliers. In some instances it is difficult to believe such statements as 'we cannot get steel of the quality we need in Europe' (statement by a Japanese manager operating in the United Kingdom, cited in Ishikawa, 1990). It also seems quite clear from past experience that the speed of integration of Japanese producers in the European economy and their willingness to buy components from European suppliers can be accelerated by political pressure by the host countries; to the extent that appropriate supply is not available locally, this may retard or make more costly the Japanese expansion in local markets.

As for export-substitution effects of Japanese investment, the evidence is not conclusive, and the situation seems different in different industries.

Sumitomo (1989) reaches the conclusion that, as a whole, Japanese investment-generated sales will substitute $67.4 billion of Japanese exports to the EC by 1993 (based on estimates of a substitution rate of 15% in 1988, rising gradually to 25% in 1993).

Finally, as for European exports generated by Japanese investment, few positive effects can be expected since these investments are aimed at the European market. On the basis of information provided by MITI (1990), it can be estimated that re-exports to Japan from European subsidiaries represent today about 3% of their total sales. The evidence of large production capacity in Japan in the industries where direct investment has concentrated provides further support for this conclusion (barring, of course, dramatic exchange rate changes in favour of European exports).

3.3   Supply-side effects

The effects of Japanese direct investment on the structure of European industry will be the outcome of a complex process, and one can only speculate about some possible forces at work. The increase in competition that this investment is already generating all over Europe can be seen in general as positive; it can be expected to produce precisely the type of gains that were sought with the launch of the internal market programme.

Fears of adverse effects of Japanese producers competing directly in Europe cannot be dismissed lightly. Especially in electronics, Japanese producers' laser-like strategies can create intense competitive pressure on European firms, as a result of a real technological lead as much as of aggressive ('unfair') competitive practices. The possibility is also very strong that Japanese investment may lead to overcapacity, notably in the car industry. In the United States overcapacity in the car industry has already become substantial as a result of Japanese investment (Jones, 1988b): GM and Chrysler have had as a consequence to close some of their plants. The same outcome is likely in Europe where Japanese car makers are announcing investments that will raise their capacity to perhaps 1.5 million unions by the mid-1990s; overcapacity is also foreseen for impact printers, faxes, CTVs and VCRs (*Electronics Europe 1992*, 1989).

On the positive side, the lesson from post-Second World War economic history is clear: the United States enjoyed technological superiority across the board and US direct investment in Europe contributed to the diffusion of American technology and stimulated imitation and rapid catching-up by European industry (Dunning and Cantwell, 1989). This is often referred to as the 'demonstration effect' of foreign direct investment: 'the greatest single source of benefit probably stems not from the performance of the Japanese-owned assets themselves, but from the stimulus to improve competitiveness their presence has given to British competitors' (Stopford, 1989).

'Le défi japonais' (to paraphrase the title of a famous 30-year-old book written from the United States' standpoint) will mainly lie in the European capacity to distinguish superior Japanese technologies and techniques and eventually imitate them, taking the best from Japanese success. Oliver and Wilkinson (1988) and Stopford (1989) discuss some cases where this is already happening in the United Kingdom, especially as regards management techniques, just-in-time procedures and quality control. A positive contribution to the efficiency of European industry may also derive from assembler–supplier relationships, to the extent that Japanese subsidiaries rely more on local suppliers and, more generally, that local suppliers are forced by Japanese competition to meet the quality standards imposed by Japanese subsidiaries.

The changes in technology and organisation involved in such relationships may become substantial in the medium term. However, so far, any direct contribution of the Japanese presence to the European technological base appears limited. R & D by Japanese firms in Europe is very small, and mainly addressed to product development for adaptation to local markets (Jetro 1989a; Stopford 1989); it is impossible at this stage to determine whether this is due to a peculiar Japanese strategy or again is mainly linked to the 'young age' of Japanese investment.

An important aspect with respect to all effects of Japanese investment that have been discussed so far is the existence of possible asymmetries in the impact on different countries and regions, owing to its skewed geographical pattern. Positive effects on competitiveness and industrial efficiency, employment and exports are likely to concentrate in the countries of location of Japanese subsidiaries, while any adverse displacement or competition effect may be stronger on the other European partners. In the car industry, for instance, it can be expected that the share of European markets taken up by UK-based Japanese producers will increase substantially, thus contributing to redress the UK external trade deficit. For the other European countries, however, larger exports from the United Kingdom will mean larger imports and fiercer competition in the domestic and third-country car markets.

In sum, the issue of the impact of Japanese investment in Europe is far from settled, both in theory and in practice. Much of the outcome, of course, will depend on the timing of the effects of the various forces at work, notably on the speed with which the positive effects of increased competition and changing technology and organisation can offset initial adverse effects of progressive market strategies, oligopolistic 'rival' behaviour, and possible overcapacity in European industry.

4　European policies *vis-à-vis* the Japanese presence in Europe

A legitimate question to be discussed at the outset is: why do we worry so much about Japanese investment in Europe?[17] No such concern arises, for instance, with regard to other intra-OECD direct investment: to the extent that FDI takes place because foreign firms have firm-specific assets that give them a competitive advantage in management and technology, welfare and efficiency will increase in the host country and in the total outcome. No special policy is usually advocated: both the EC Commission and the US government, in TRIM discussions at GATT, have argued that international investments should not be limited or constrained by special rules (e.g., local content, performance requirements, etc.).

Why should it be different for Japan? One line of reasoning is that in some way Japan is an 'unfair' competitor and that, while the EC can limit and control their exports, when they come to manufacture in Europe there is no effective policy instruments to check their invasion. A related argument is that the rules of free trade (and free movement of capital) cannot be applied to Japan because of lack of reciprocity in access to Japanese markets.

Industrial policy considerations have also been prominent in this debate. First, it is a fairly well established result that the optimal trade policy for oligopolistic industries is not necessarily *laissez-faire* (Dixit, 1984). Second, the cumulative nature of innovation (economies of scale) and the existence of externalities in the generation and diffusion of technical progress (Pavitt, 1984) can justify government intervention to upgrade 'national' technological levels and protect domestic industry in the meantime. Aggressive market strategies coupled with a significant technological lead seem to make these arguments especially relevant when dealing with Japan.

In practice, the argument boils down to the notion that the EC cannot afford to see some of its ('strategic') industries simply disappear (as happened to the US and UK colour TV industries and is happening now to the British motor industry), notably in high-technology sectors where dynamic economies of scale are important. Adverse effects on employment are also feared in 'scale-intensive' industries (such as auto industries) where overcapacity is likely to emerge. Needless to say, others simply reject all these arguments and maintain that markets are the best judges, that the entire 1992 project in Europe is based on opening markets to all, and that Japanese producers are market players equal to the others.

The history of trade relations between Japan and the EC is one of frictions, controversies and selective bilateral agreements always on the border of infringement of GATT rules.[18] It is also, within the EC, a record of contradictory action by the different countries and the EC Commission that has probably raised the costs, and sometimes frustrated the goals, of individual countries. The EC Commission has tried to bring about greater uniformity by encouraging or requesting the elimination of country-specific restrictions and, where feasible and desirable, by replacing them with Community-wide measures.[19] The EC's hand in these matters has been strengthened by the approval (in 1985) of the internal market programme; sectoral concentration and integration in industry have also increasingly shifted sectoral issues to the supranational level, adding to the tendency for the Commission to take a greater role in these matters.

The Commission has tried to expound broad policy principles in its relations with Japan, centred around the need to redress payments imbalance and, more broadly, to bring about an 'acceptable balance of benefits' from mutual economic relationships; strong emphasis has been accordingly placed on a requirement of 'reciprocity' of concessions in various areas (export access to national markets, conditions for inward investments, technical standards, and so on). Needless to say, the application in practice of these principles, and their very legitimacy as a basis for regulating trade relations between advanced countries, has been an endless source of controversy.

The acceleration of inward investment by Japanese companies has complicated matters for various reasons. Once again, the EC member countries have adopted widely divergent policies on such investment, with some countries (United Kingdom, Ireland, to an extent Germany) actively encouraging it in various ways, including generous incentives, others (Denmark and the Benelux countries) maintaining a liberal but fairly neutral policy and others again (France, Spain) adopting an approach of selective government-controlled access. A few countries (Italy, Portugal, Greece) have explicitly or *de facto* kept Japanese investors' presence very low. The result has been in practice that Japanese producers could often select the best conditions and locations for their 'greenfield' plants.[20] Over time, when production in these plants started, rows between individual EC countries have developed over the conditions of access of transplants' products to 'closed' markets in the EC.[21]

The Commission does not dispose of specific instruments to deal with direct investment, although it is entitled to question subsidies and incentives on grounds of competition policy. Its main instrument to restrain Japanese exports to the Community had been the anti-dumping rules: in 1987 these rules were strengthened with the approval of the so-called 'screwdriver' regulation, which introduced 'local content' requirements designed to avoid non-EC manufacturers circumventing anti-dumping duties by setting up assembly plants in the Community that use 'dumped' parts and components.[22] The anti-dumping apparatus has thus remained as the backbone of defensive policies, with European producers filing anti-dumping suits (in respects of finished products, components and parts) and the Commission imposing provisional duties and then reaching agreements based on commitments on local content by Japanese transplants in Europe.

These policies and approaches within the Community are, however, showing various weaknesses. The first one is that broad use of anti-dumping, rules of origin, and local content requirements is increasingly being challenged as protectionist not only by Japanese producers, but also by western governments – including the United States and some EC countries – that have developed a vested interest in the success of Japanese transplants that they consider 'American' or 'British'.[23]

Second, it has become evident that the different attitudes of EC member states, or their national producers, can determine the failure of national policies or protection.[24] In some cases, conflicts of interest directly opposed companies within the same industry: restrictions and minimum price agreements on imports of semiconductors have been supported by the producers of these goods but opposed by their users as an intermediate product, damaged not only by higher costs, but also by having to employ lower-technology integrated circuits.

Third, at a more basic level, the question of just what an effective EC policy to meet the Japanese challenge should do is not yet resolved. Restrictions on trade and anti-dumping suits have managed to contain competitive pressures in the short term, but have also worked to accelerate Japanese productive settlements in Europe. Moreover, over time it has become evident that protection has not helped to develop efficient industries in Europe: indeed, the gap with Japanese competitors has widened. One reason is that protection from outsiders has not gone hand in hand with policies to maintain sufficient competitive stimuli within the protected industries. In addition, VERs and other restrictions have granted Japanese producers rent profits (that were used to accelerate investment and the introduction of new technologies), ample room to upgrade the quality of their products and enter new market segments, and comfortable market niches in which to consolidate their superiority (Feenstra, 1988; Curzon and Curzon, 1987; Jones, 1988a; Cawson, 1989).

Clearly, there is a need to go beyond purely 'defensive' policies and to strive to close the gap between Japanese and European producers, if these are to survive in the long term. It is also important to recognise that electronics and information technology are really changing fundamentally not only industrial processes, but also consumption (and, more broadly, behavioural patterns) of developed societies. Failure to gain command of these technologies can have far-reaching effects on the global ability of industries and countries to compete.

Two major questions are involved here. The first, running throughout the growing literature on Japanese foreign investment, is how much one can count on the Japanese themselves – or at least on the spurring effect of their presence – to promote an upgrading of competitiveness of local industry. This issue has already been discussed extensively in section 3: as we have seen, the final judgement still is suspended. The second question is what the role of public policies in fostering and assisting the restructuring of industries threatened by Japanese superiority should be. Two main lessons from the Japanese experience are worth noting. First, to the extent that barriers are raised to restrict external competition, they should at least go hand in hand with intense competition within the protected area to generate a strong stimulus to innovate and adjust. Second, the public sector can play a fundamental role in identifying priorities and channelling (public and private) resources to research on 'next generation' technologies. The Commission has recognised this as an urgent need, and is stepping up its efforts in various directions (joint research programmes), but this is clearly an area where, compared with the Japanese system, there is still a large gap. It is not easy to coordinate EC and national governments' efforts, and coordination and competition within industry are difficult to reconcile. At the same time, market pressures are already pushing many European groups to set up joint ventures and conclude agreements with Japanese corporations.

A very complex final issue is that of determining the appropriate mix of public pressure and private initiatives in dealing with Japanese corporations. In this regard, the image of Japanese corporations as a solid, single-purposed bloc is misleading. The race for world markets has had losers and winners among Japanese corporations, as shown today by the difficulties of smaller Japanese car producers, and by many other cases in the electronics industry in the past (Cawson, 1989). On the other hand, large Japanese corporations can indeed move very aggressively as a result of tight integration of decisions; economies of scope (resulting, in the large conglomerates, from such factors as the joint availability of finance, trading networks, research, world-wide networks of subcontractors and sourcing); and a longer time horizon for corporate decisions. The case for a negotiated approach designed to put pressure on these corporations as regards market practices, access to technology, sourcing, and other matters, cannot be dismissed lightly. The particular trade-offs between the various interests at play in each case are difficult to assess: the risk is always high that 'defensive' considerations may tilt the balance of negotiations against the long-term interests of efficiency and competitiveness.

Obviously there is no simple response to all these questions; pragmatic solutions will have to be found case by case. There is little doubt, however, that there is no alternative to learning to live with an increasing presence of Japanese firms in Europe. The countries and areas more effective in integrating them in local industry, and in learning the lessons of their success, will come out ahead in the global market that is emerging in Europe.

5   Conclusions and prospects

Our main conclusions can be briefly summarised as follows. Japanese direct investment in Europe in manufacturing is still a relatively small, but rapidly growing, phenomenon that has very profound implications for the European economy and economic policies. Japanese investment in manufacturing has been a consequence, basically, of an organisational and technological superiority of Japanese producers in particular sectors (notably in scale-intensive, mass-production, assembly industries) and technologies (electronics). The Japanese penetration in European markets is therefore likely to increase, and to be accompanied by growing investment by components and parts suppliers, with competitive pressures spreading from 'downstream' to 'upstream' segments of the markets.

Clearly, in the long term, there is no alternative for European countries other than to confront Japanese competition and to work to fill the gap that has developed in technology, productivity, organisational and managerial methods. Direct investment in Europe by Japanese producers will inevitably increase competitive pressures on European industry; it will also provide a better chance to understand and imitate the factors of Japanese success, to integrate them in the European industry, and in the process, to generate important welfare and efficiency gains that will benefit European producers and consumers alike.

A crucial issue, in this context, is the pace of Japanese penetration in European markets, and the corresponding pace of adjustment of European industry. The requests by European producers for transitional periods extending beyond 1992 cannot be dismissed lightly; it is apparent that there are benefits to be gained from a managed, negotiated access of Japanese firms to European markets. It is essential, however, that any such agreement or decision coexist with increased efforts to close the existing competitive gaps. We should be aware, in this regard, that the present fragmentation and lack of coordination of national policies may represent a serious impediment to reaching agreement on Community-wide policies. There is a definite risk that the pace of adjustment will be dictated largely, or exclusively, by the decisions of those countries (such as the United Kingdom) that have decided to rely on expanded Japanese presence to restructure their ailing industry.

Difficult questions arise, finally, from the very skewed geographical pattern of Japanese investment. The risk here is that the balances of costs and benefits of the Japanese presence in Europe may vary a great deal between the EC countries. With the creation in the next few years of an integrated, unified market in Europe, there is little question that Japanese producers will emerge as major Europe-wide competitors, and that no country will be able to keep their products out. The European countries that have encouraged Japanese investment on their soil may thus find themselves in a more advantageous position, and latecomers to the game may have to bear greater adjustment costs later.

NOTES

This study was originally prepared as a paper for the conference on 'The impact of 1992 on European Trade and Industry', organised by CEPR, Centro Studi Confindustria and STEP (Urbino, 15–16 March 1990). The authors are grateful to A. Venables, H. Yamawaki and participants in the Urbino conference for useful comments, and to G. Alesii for excellent research assistance; they retain sole responsibility for the opinions expressed.

1 In 1985 Japan could still be considered a 'minor' international investor, especially relative to its economic strength. At that time the stock of outward FDI represented about 3% of GDP for Japan, 6% for the United States, 8% for Germany and 26% for the United Kingdom. Since then, investment growth has been exponential, with annual rates of increase of yearly flows of 70–80%.

2 Direct investment in principle is ownership of assets carrying with it control (Graham and Krugman, 1989; Hager, 1989); in practice this definition is quite difficult to apply. The data presented here are Ministry of Finance data on a *notification* basis; they do not include reinvested profits and no attempt is made to revalue past investment on the basis of market prices, which is likely to entail some underestimate of actual stocks. As customary in the literature, cumulative flows (since 1951) are taken as a measure of current stocks.

3 Policies are discussed at greater length in section 4 below.

4 One-third of the Japanese firms in Spain that answered the 1989 Jetro survey have more than 500 employees, and their average workforce is 850 (as against 350–400 in the United Kingdom, Germany and France).

5 See MITI (1989).

6 A quick but complete survey of key concepts and contributions is in Graham and Krugman (1989, Chapter 2 and Appendix B).

7 Watanabe's discussion of developments for semiconductors and machine tools, where local production facilities have been slower to come despite rapidly growing market shares and trade frictions, underlines the importance of a broad market and of firms' size in making it possible direct investment.

8 For a comparison of Japanese manufacturing techniques with Western techniques see Oliver and Wilkinson (1988), Cawson (1989) for consumer electronics, and Womack (1989) and Osterman (1989) for cars. Jaikumar (1989)

analyses in detail the properties and advantages of flexible manufacturing systems.

9 Stopford (1989) has calculated that in some cases the total benefits obtained by Japanese start-ups in the United Kingdom have been as high as £5,000 per worker employed. A total contribution equivalent to one-third of reinvested capital is not infrequent.

10 Evidence for the United Kingdom is reported by Dillow (1989) and Oliver and Wilkinson (1988).

11 In the United States in the colour television (CTV) industry, after the first subsidiary established by Sony, six competitors followed between 1974 and 1979 (Burton and Saelens, 1987); in the car industry, within four years from the announcement by Honda of its investment (1980) all other Japanese producers had followed (GAO, 1988). In Europe 'a rush of plant start-ups' has been reported in electronics (*Electronics Europe 1992*, 1989). In the VCR industry, where Sony had been present since 1973, between April 1981 and March 1984 subsidiaries were established by Sharp, Victor (United Kingdom and Federal Republic of Germany), Sanyo (United Kingdom and Federal Republic of Germany), Toshiba, Matsushita, Hitachi and Akai; NEC, Orion and Funai entered between 1986 and 1987 (Watanabe, 1988 and Jetro, 1989a); in the photocopier industry, the pioneer was Canon (1972); between August 1983 and December 1986, Canon opened two more factories, soon imitated by Minolta, Matsushita, Konica, Toshiba and Ricoh (Watanabe, 1988); in microwave ovens, after Toshiba started operations (1985), in 1987 production was commenced by Matsushita, Hitachi, Sharp, Brother and by another Toshiba plant (Watanabe, 1988). The process of 'imitative' investment is also extending in the car industry.

12 As general references, see Caves (1982) and Graham and Krugman (1989).

13 Some of the anti-foreign investment literature produced in the United States has emphasised this effect (Glickman and Woodward, 1989); Graham and Krugman (1989) argue, more convincingly, in favour of the opposite view.

14 In the car industry, hourly wages for starting workers for Japanese corporations from $10.49 (Toyota) to $11.95 (Nummi); they compare with the $10.90 paid by GM, Ford and Chrysler (GAO, 1988). In US manufacturing as a whole, Japanese affiliates have been found to pay higher wages than non-Japanese foreign affiliates; in 1986 yearly compensation was $34,990 for the former and $32,890 for the latter (Graham and Krugman, 1989).

15 Fuji (1989) has estimated that local motor vehicle production is going to reduce Japanese car exports to the United States by 750,000 units in the 1988–92 period. Dillow (1989) has similarly estimated that direct Japanese investment in the United Kingdom will improve the British trade balance by over £13 billion by the year 2000. Sumitomo (1989) has estimated that the surplus reduction effect of all Japanese investments abroad will increase from 19.6 billion dollars in 1990 to 58.3 in 1993. In particular, sales of Japanese subsidiaries will substitute $67.4 billion of Japanese exports to the EC by 1993: this estimate depends crucially upon the assumption that the substitution rate will rise to 25% in 1993.

16 In the US car industry the ratio of local sourcing of Honda was 30% when its factory was established, 60% in 1987, and is forecast to reach 75% in the early 1990s. Corresponding figures for Nissan are 47%, 63%, 75–80%; Mazda shows a similar behaviour (GAO, 1988 and Graham and Krugman, 1989).

The Jetro survey in Europe also shows increasing local sourcing: in assembly-type operations imports from Japan accounted for 57% of procurement at the start of operations but on average 44% in 1988 (Jetro, 1989a).

17 That Japanese direct investment is stirring concern is obvious. Several books recently published in the United States have argued that 'foreign money is changing the face of our nation' (Tolchin and Tolchin, 1988; Glickman and Woodward, 1989). Some of them specifically identify Japanese investment as a serious danger for the United States: 'the threat to America' (Burstein, 1988) is mounting because 'we allowed the Japanese to take the lead' (Prestowitz, 1988) and 'we are letting Japan buy our land, our industries, our financial institutions and our future' (Frantz and Collins, 1989). In Europe similar arguments are less frequent but nonetheless present 'The figures [i.e., the consequences] for Japanese investments are appreciably less favourable for host countries than equivalent investments by Sweden, Switzerland, the United States and Canada. The difference is attributable to the civic sense of the Japanese and their [professonal] attachment to their fellow citizens, which are much stronger than in Western countries'; and 'the Japanese are prepared to consider their foreign employees as hostages enabling them to put pressure on the governments of sovereign states' (EGIS, 1989).

18 A description of European policies on trade with Japan and Japanese investment is in Ishikawa (1990). Commission of the EC (1989) and (1990) describe respectively the policies for the electronics and motor vehicle industries. A highly critical assessment of European policies on Japanese penetration is in Curzon and Curzon (1987).

19 The Commission's jurisdiction over commercial policy is mandated by Art. 3 and 110–116 of the Treaty. Art. 113 states, in particular, that 'the common commercial policy shall be based on uniform principles' . . . in regard to . . . tariff rates, . . . tariff and trade agreements, the achievement of uniformity in measures of liberalization, export policy and measures to protect trade such as those . . . in case of dumping or subsidies'. Since the EC Commission had not managed to establish exclusive authority in external trade relations, up until the early 1980s trade regimes with Japan were mostly a national matter, leading to an extreme variety of selective quotas, technical barriers, and bilateral arrangements to limit exports (VERs) and setting minimum prices for specific products. These agreements have emerged as a frequent solution to trade frictions and have been applied over time to a broad range of products. In some cases VER agreements were negotiated with no formal government involvement (industry-to-industry). With only minor exceptions, tariffs are imposed at Community level; on occasion Community-wide minimum prices have been imposed for certain Japanese products.

20 Dunning and Cantwell (1989) argue that the 'visibility' of assembly-type large investments, and the resulting need to appease the local public opinion, still in many cases makes locational decisions suboptimal. The same constraint is not present for smaller (often 'upstream') production units, that can therefore enjoy the full advantages of setting up 'greenfield' ventures.

21 The best known cases are those of the Triumph Acclaim and the Bluebird cars produced in the United Kingdom respectively under licence by Honda and directly by Nissan, that were eventually accepted as 'European' products by France and Italy.

22 The Community's anti-dumping rules are now consolidated in Regulation

2423/88 that sets a local content requirement of over 40% of all parts and materials used in producing goods whose exports into the Community are subject to an anti-dumping duty. In July 1987 a specific requirement was introduced of 45% of value-added and parts on radio receivers, TV sets and tape recorders. More recently the Community has been trying to define 'rules of origin' on a range of 'sensitive' products, including integrated circuits, various consumer electronics and office equipment products, petroleum products; see Ishikawa (1990). The recent tendency in this area has been that of identifying certain phases in the production process that qualify, or do not qualify, a product as coming from a given country.

23 Being charged within GATT not only by Japan and Hong Kong, but also by the United States, of using rules of origin as an instrument of trade policy to protect domestic industry, the Commission had recently to agree that these rules should be 'non-discriminatory, neutral, transparent, predictable and consistent', and that they should be challengeable before a judicial authority in the importing country (*Financial Times*, 15 February, 1990).

24 The attempt to protect the Phillips VCR format and to halt JVC products penetration in European markets was doomed by the open policy on Japanese transplants of the UK and Germany, and the decision of Thorn and Telefunken to form a joint venture in Europe to sell the JVC products under European brand names (Cawson, 1989). By the same token, Japanese cars and motorcycles could establish a solid presence and gain shares in European markets, undermining in the long term the policies of tight restriction maintained by France, Italy and Spain.

REFERENCES

Booz Allen & Hamilton, *Wall Street Journal* (1989) 'Japan in Europe. A survey of European Chief Executives and Japanese Executives based in Europe' (mimeo).

Buckley, P.J. and M.C. Casson (1976) *The Future of Multinational Enterprise*, London: Macmillan.

Burstein, D. (1988) *Yen: Japan's New Financial Empire and its Threat to America*, New York: Simon and Schuster.

Burton, F.N. and F.H. Saelens (1987) 'Trade barriers and Japanese Foreign Direct Investment in the Colour Television Industry', *Managerial Decisions Economics*, **8** (4).

Caves, R. (1971) 'International Corporations: The Industrial Economics of Foreign Investment', *Economica*, **141**, pp. 1–27.

(1982) *Multinational Enterprise and Economic Analysis*, Cambridge: Cambridge University Press.

Cawson, A. (1989) 'Sectoral Governance in Consumer Electronics in Britain and France', paper prepared for the conference on *Comparing capitalist economies: variation in the governance of sectors*, Bellagio, 29 May–2 June.

Commission of the EC (1989) 'The EC Policies for Semi-conductors' (July).

(1990) 'A Single Community Motor-Vehicle Market', Communication to the Council of Ministers (January).

Curzon, G. and V. Curzon (1987) 'Follies in European Trade Relations with Japan', *The World Economy* (June).

Cusumano, M.A. (1985) *The Japanese automobile industry. Technology and management at Nissan and Toyota*, Cambridge, Mass.: Harvard University Press.

DATAR (1989) 'Les Investissements de Production Japonais dans 17 Pays d'Europe' (April–May).

De Melo, J. and P.A. Messerlin (1988) 'Price, quality and welfare effects of European VERs on autos', *European Economic Review*, **32** (7) (September).

Dicken, P. (1988) 'The changing geography of Japanese foreign direct investment in manufacturing industry: a global perspective', *Environment and Planning A*, **20**.

Dillow, C. (1989) 'A return to a trade surplus? The impact of Japanese investment in the UK', Nomura Research Institute (August).

Dixit, A.K. (1984) 'International trade policy for oligopolistic industries', *Economic Journal* Supplement, **94**, pp. 1–16.

Dunning, J.H. (1986) *Japanese participation in British Industry*, Beckenham: Croom Helm.

    (1988) 'The Electric Paradigm of International Production: A Restatement and Some Possible Extensions', *Journal of International Business Studies*, **1**, 1–31.

Dunning, J.H. and J.A. Cantwell (1989) 'Japanese Manufacturing Direct Investment in the EEC, post 1992: Some Alternative Scenarios', discussion papers in International Investment and Business Studies, University of Reading, Department of Economics, Series B, **II** (1989–90) (September).

EGIS (1989) 'Evaluating Japanese Investments in Europe' (June).

Electronics Europe 1992 (1989) 'Special Report, **1.2** (July); **3** (August).

Feenstra, R.C. (1988) 'Quality change under trade restraints in Japanese autos', *Quarterly Journal of Economics* (February).

Flowers, E.B. (1976) 'Oligopolistic Reactions in European and Canadian Direct Investment in the United States', *Journal of International Business Studies*, **7** (3).

Frantz, D. and C. Collins (1989) *Selling out. How we are letting Japan buy our land, our industries, our financial institutions and our future*, Chicago: Contemporary Books.

Fuji Research Institute Corporation (1989) 'Coping with the strong yen: progress in Corporate Countermeasures' and 'Japan's Surging Foreign Direct Investment', *Fuji Economic Review* (July–August).

General Accounting Office of the United States (GAO) (1988) 'Foreign Investment. Growing Japanese Presence in the U.S. Auto Industry', Report to Congressional Requesters (March).

Glickman, N.J. and D.P. Woodward (1989) *The new competitors. How foreign investors are changing the U.S. Economy*, New York: Basic Books.

Graham, E.M. (1990) 'Strategic interaction among multinational firms and International Direct Investment', in C.N. Pitelis and R. Sudgen (eds), *The Nature of the Transnational Firm*, London: Routledge.

Graham, E.M. and P.R. Krugman (1989) *Foreign Direct Investment in the United States*, Washington, D.C.: Institute for International Economics.

Hager, W. (1989) 'Japanese Inward Investment in Europe' (Fall) (mimeo).

Ishikawa, K. (1990) *Japan and the Challenge of Europe 1992*, London: The Royal Institute of International Affairs.

Jaikumar, R. (1989) 'Japanese Flexible Manufacturing Systems: Impact on the United States', *Japan and the World Economy*, vol. 1, Amsterdam: Elsevier, pp. 113–43.

Jetro (1988) *Japan's changing overseas direct investment* (July).

(1989a) *Current management situation of Japanese manufacturing enterprises in Europe: 5th Survey Report* (Tokyo) (March).

(1989b) '1989 Jetro White Paper on world direct investments. New phase in Foreign Direct Investments and Strategic Alliances' (Tokyo) (March).

Jones, D.T. (1988a) 'Measuring Technological Advantage in the Motor Vehicle Industry', paper prepared for the International Motor Vehicle Program International Policy Forum (May).

(1988b) 'Corporate Strategies for a Truly European Car Industry', paper prepared for the Prince Bertil Symposium on Corporate and Industry Strategies for Europe (Stockolm, 9–11 November 1988) (mimeo).

Julius, D. and S. Thomsen (1988) 'Foreign-owned Firms, Trade and Economic Integration', Tokyo Club papers **2**, London: Royal Institute of International Affairs.

Knickerbocker, F.T. (1973) 'Oliogopolistic reactions and multinational enterprise', Division of Research, Graduate School of Business Administration, Boston: Harvard University.

Krafcik, J.F. (1988) 'Triumph of the Lean Production System', *Sloan Management Review* (Fall).

Kreinin, M. (1988) 'How closed is Japan's market? Additional evidence', *The World Economy*, **2**.

Lewis, J.D. (1982) 'Technology, Enterprise and American Economic Growth', *Science*, **215**, 1204–11.

Mann, C. (1989) 'Determinants of Japanese direct investment in US manufacturing industry', International Finance discussion papers, Board of Governors of the Federal Reserve System, **362** (September).

MITI (1989) 'The 18th Survey on Japanese Business Activity Abroad' (Tokyo) (April).

MITI (1990) 'The 19th Survey on Japanese Business Abroad' (Tokyo) (April).

Oliver, N. and B. Wilkinson (1988) *The Japanization of British Industry*, Oxford: Basil Blackwell.

Osterman, P. (1989) 'New Technology and Work Organization', paper prepared for the Stockolm Conference on Technology and Investment (November) (mimeo).

Ozawa, T. (1989) 'Europe 1992 and Japanese Multinationals: Transplanting a Subcontracting System in the Expended Market', paper presented at the Round-Table on Multinational Firms and European Integration at the University of Geneva (12–13 May, 1989).

Pavitt, K. (1984) 'Patterns of technological change: towards a taxonomy and a theory', *Research Policy*, **6**.

Prestowitz, C. (1988) *Trading places. How we allowed the Japanese to take the lead*, New York: Basic Books.

Rehder, R.R. (1988) 'Japanese Transplants: A New Model for Detroit', *Business Horizons* (January–February).

Shimada, H. and J.P. MacDuffie (1986) 'Industrial relations and humanware', Alfred P. Sloan School of Management, Massachusetts Institute of Technology, working paper, no. 1855–87.

Stopford, J.M. (1989) 'Japanese Investment in Europe: The British Experience' (mimeo).

Sumitomo Life Research Institute (1989) 'Development of Overseas direct investment of Japan and its impact on trade balance' (Tokyo) (November).

Tolchin, M. and S. Tolchin (1988) *Buying into America. How foreign money is changing the face of our nation*, New York: Times Books.

Viesti, G. and L. Zanzottera (1989) 'Japanese Multinationals and the EEC: The Case of a Car Industry', CESPRI (Università Bocconi), working papers, **30** (November).

Watanabe, S. (1988) 'Trends of Japan's Direct Investment in Europe. Mainly Investment in Manufacturing into EC', *Exim Review*, **9** (1), The Export–Import Bank of Japan (October).

Womack, J.P. (1989) 'The automobile industry', in M.L. Dertouzos, R.K. Lester, M.R. Solow and the MIT Commission on Industrial Productivity, *Made in America. Regaining the productivity edge*, Cambridge, Mass.: MIT Press.

Discussion

HIDEKI YAMAWAKI

This study provides a well-balanced survey on the recent development of Japanese direct investment in Europe. It is specially useful in that the authors address many important questions concerning the motivation and strategy of Japanese direct investment in Europe, and its effects on European industries, and attempt to answer these questions with available evidence.

One of the interesting questions that the authors raised in the study, but to which they could not provide any clear-cut answer, is that of who benefits most from Japanese direct investment. Is it the member state that hosts Japanese investment, or the EC as a whole? This question is particularly important when one discusses the policy implications of Japanese direct investment: should we consider the Japanese investment problem from the perspective of each member state, or from the EC-wide perspective? Some examples will serve to illustrate this point. The UK government has been quite keen to invite Japanese automobile manufacturers to the depressed regions with the expectation that Japanese investment will revitalise the regional economy. While such policy is formulated from the perspective of the UK government, it has important economic consequences for the other member states when exports from the UK subsidiaries of Japanese automobile manufacturers reach their markets and compete with their products. On the other hand, Japanese investment in Spain may speed up the adjustment process that is necessary for the completion of a single EC market if it contributes to reducing the economic gap that exists between Spain and the other member states. In this case, regional policy towards Japanese investment may benefit the EC as well. Providing a framework in which to analyse the question of whether the issues on Japanese investment should be treated on a regional or an EC-wide basis is thus a crucial step towards formulating relevant economic policies.

To deepen our understanding on this issue, we need more information on the inter-industry and inter-country pattern of Japanese investment in EC manufacturing. The study examines the host country's tax and subsidy policies as the determinant of the locational choice of Japanese multinational corporations. Another finding that complements the hypothesis is that Japanese direct investment in a particular industry tends to go to the country where its industry has a comparative advantage. According to the data on 232 majority-owned manufacturing subsidiaries of Japanese firms, which operated in 15 European countries in 1988, the geographic pattern of Japanese investment varied across industry. For example, while manufacturers of electrical equipment tended to go to the United Kingdom, manufacturers of machinery and precision instruments preferred West Germany. Japanese firms in automobiles and chemicals were more likely to invest in Spain, but those in glass, stone, and clay products invested in Belgium. It is thus quite important both to recognise and to analyse the inter-industry and inter-country pattern of Japanese direct investment in the EC before formulating any discussions of a common tax policy toward foreign direct investment in the EC.

Another interesting question that Micossi and Viesti address is that of whether direct investment is or is not complementary to trade. The previous empirical literature on this issue tended to show, at least for US multinationals, that net sales of foreign affiliates were complementary to exports (e.g., Bergsten, Horst, and Moran 1978; Lipsey and Weiss, 1984). This question of complementarity between direct investment and exports is particularly relevant for the case of Japan because Japanese manufacturing firms invest heavily in distributional as well as manufacturing activities in the United States and the EC. Japanese direct investments in wholesale trade are aimed at establishing distributional channels and service facilities, and providing customer services in the local markets. These distributional activities of foreign affiliates tends to promote exports of goods produced in Japan (Yamawaki, 1990). We thus need to examine direct investment not only of manufacturing but also in wholesale trade and other non-manufacturing activities to address the question of complementarity between direct investment and exports.

Finally, while Micossi and Viesti present several useful examples of the success of Japanese management practices abroad, it might be also useful to remind ourselves that Japanese firms abroad are not always successful. In particular, there exist several cases where foreign subsidiaries of Japanese firms started to stumble when they matured and became more and more localised in foreign markets: it seems that one of the key aspects determining if a Japanese firm will be successful as a local entity is whether the firm is able to maintain its Japanese-style employment policy, particularly on hiring and promoting workers and managers and negotiating with unions. Another important aspect for the Japanese manufacturer may be whether it can establish a steady relationship with suppliers of parts and other components in the local market. When the Japanese manufacturer fails to manage these labour and sourcing problems well, the initial success of Japanese investment in Europe may not necessarily last.

REFERENCES

Bergsten, Fred C., Thoas Horst and Theodore H. Moran (1978) *American Multinationals and American Interests*, Washington, D.C.: Brookings Institution.

Lipsey, Robert E., and Merle Yahr Weiss (1984) 'Foreign Production and Exports of Individual Firms', *Review of Economics and Statistics*, **66** (May) pp. 304–6.

Yamawaki, Hideki (1990) 'Exports and Foreign Distributional Activities: Evidence on Japanese Firms in the United States', *Review of Economics and Statistics* (forthcoming).

Index